Memories of the Arct
The memoirs of Father Robert Le ___, OMI
from his days in the 'Great North'

"Memories of the Arctic" depicts the man as I have known him. I am certain that all those who will read this book will be left with the portrait of a man completely dedicated to his mission, to the people he called his own. How I wish that more priests like him would come to the North to show what love is all about and what service means. He indeed lived to the full the belief that "there is no greater proof of love than to give your life for those you love".

Bishop (retired) Denis Croteau, OMI
Diocese of Mackenzie-Fort Smith

"Father Le Meur had a strong belief that with the changing times, the rich Inuvialuit knowledge and language must be recorded and documented in their own words, and not left only to memory. He dedicated himself to that task. It was a privilege to team up with him and share what we were doing to record stories and legends at radio station CHAK in Inuvik, and through the Committee for Original People's Entitlement programs. Father Le Meur was an inspiration to work with. He had such love for the people, and respected their achievements."

Nellie J. Cournoyea, former Chair and CEO
Inuvialuit Regional Corporation

Dedication

This memoir is dedicated to all the people who shared their lives and stories with Father Robert Le Meur.

Memories of the Arctic
The memoirs of Father Robert Le Meur, OMI, from his days in the "Great North"

Father Robert Le Meur, OMI
Edited posthumously by Inuvialuit Regional Corporation, Inuvik, Northwest Territories

© Inuvialuit Regional Corporation, 2017
In respect and recognition of the intellectual and cultural property rights of all Inuvialuit whose stories are presented in this book.

National Library of Canada Cataloguing in Publication Data

ISBN 978-0-9813944-2-8

1. Inuvialuit – Culture and History 2. Father Robert Le Meur 3. Roman Catholic Church Missionaries

Editor: Charles D. Arnold
Copy Editor and Design: Peggy Jay, Inuvialuit Regional Corporation
Cover Design: Zoe Ho

Photo Credits:
Front Cover: Father Robert Le Meur, Tuktoyaktuk, 1981. (©Harry Palmer); Father Le Meur on arrival at Tuktoyaktuk, 1946. (Le Meur Family Collection)
Back Cover: Father Robert Le Meur returning from the Hornaday River near Paulatuk, circa 1946. (Le Meur Family Collection); Father Le Meur standing in front of a map of Tuktoyaktuk outside the Hamlet Office, date unknown. (Photo courtesy of Dennis Lowing)

All copyright to photographs resides with the creators.
Printed by CreateSpace

Contact:
Inuvialuit Regional Corporation
Bag Service 21, Inuvik, NT X0E 0T0
info@inuvialuit.com

Inuvialuit Regional Corporation

Table of Contents

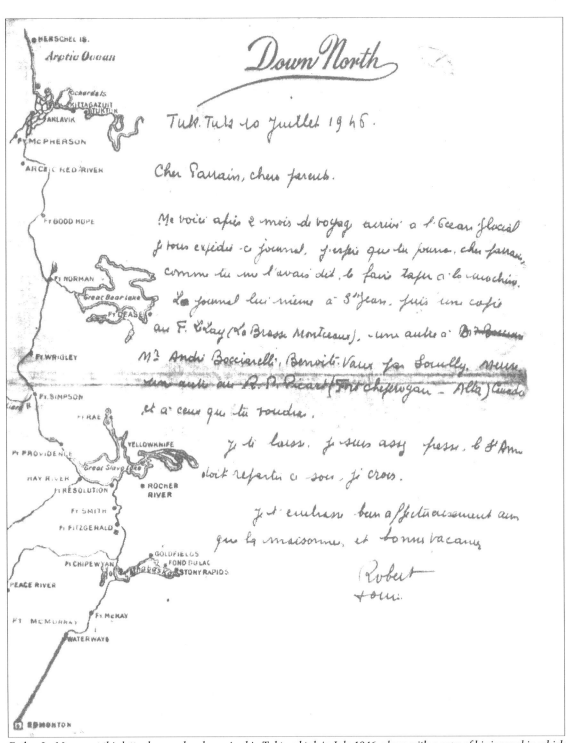

Father Le Meur sent this letter home when he arrived in Tuktoyaktuk in July 1946, along with a copy of his journal in which he tells about his preparations for life in Arctic Canada and his trip along the way.

Foreword

Robert Le Meur was born on November 18, 1920 at Saint Jean du Doigt in northwestern France. In his later years he recalled that it was his ambition from an early age to become a missionary. He was ordained as a priest in the Roman Catholic religious order Missionary Oblates of Mary Immaculate (OMI) in 1943, but since France at that time was under German occupation it wasn't until 1946 that he had an opportunity to be assigned to a foreign mission. He was first invited by the church to go to Africa. He accepted, but in his reply he stated that his preference was to go to northern Canada, which he had heard about from Bishop Pierre Fallaize, the bishop who had ordained him and who had served in the church's Mackenzie Region in the northwestern part of Canada from 1931 until the outbreak of the Second World War. The Church agreed to his request, and in 1946, at age 26, Father Le Meur was sent to the Mackenzie Region. During his time in the North he served at the Roman Catholic Church missions at Paulatuk (1946-1950), Holman Island (1950-1951), Tuktoyaktuk (1951-1953), Stanton (1953-1955), and again at Tuktoyaktuk (1955-1985), except for two years, 1974 to 1976, when he worked at Grandin College in Forth Smith.

Father Le Meur had a storied career in the Arctic. He learned the local language, now called Inuvialuktun, and how to live off the land. He travelled by sleds pulled by dogs that he bred, raised and trained. When local political systems were being developed in the north he was active in establishing the Settlement Council for Tuktoyaktuk, and for two years sat as a Councilor. He met the Queen, Pope Paul VI and Heads of State from countries around the world. He gave lectures across the North and at universities in Canada and France. In 1982 he was awarded the Order of Canada. His investiture document states that he had "devoted himself unstintingly to the Inuit population as educator, advisor and friend. Radio Station CFCT of Tuktoyaktuk, which he founded and for which he is the main on-air personality, is at the heart of his efforts to preserve and promote this Aboriginal culture".

CFCT ('Radio Tuktoyaktuk') came about because the signal from the nearest radio station, in Inuvik, was weak and power lines in the community created interference. Father Le Meur was able to obtain financial and logistical assistance from a radio station, CHUM, in Toronto, and with their assistance CFCT went on the air in January, 1970 providing local news, weather, children's programs, and programs for adults, and a 'request show' that could be heard as far away as Old Crow, Sachs Harbour and Paulatuk. In addition, there were four hours a day with Father Le Meur as host. His focus was on Inuvialuit history and culture, and for his show he recorded oral histories, drum songs and interviews with Inuvialuit and replayed them with commentary in Inuvialuktun and English translations. In a French language interview with Radio Canada in 1972 Father Le Meur commented on his extensive notes, letters, taped recordings and historical and ethnological research materials from his 25 years in the North, saying "there's a whole life in there". Fortunately, after his death in 1985 his treasured archive was gathered by the Roman Catholic Church, and currently is in the Grandin Archives Collection at the Provincial Archives of Alberta.

Father Le Meur was highly respected by Inuvialuit "for his commitment and dedication to the North, for the strong leadership role he played in Tuktoyaktuk, for his lifelong experiences and his love of people" (excerpt from Funeral Service for Father Le Meur). At the request of the citizens of Tuktoyaktuk, he was buried in Tuktoyaktuk, and more than 30 years after his death he is still fondly remembered by Inuvialuit.

However, memories fade. With the aim of keeping knowledge of Father Le Meur alive, and perpetuating awareness of the stories and local knowledge of Inuvialuit culture and history that he documented, the Inuvialuit Regional Corporation is pleased to make available a memoir that Father Le Meur wrote but which was unpublished at the time of his death in 1985. 'Memories of the Arctic' is more than just an autobiography. It is also an adventure story – Father Le Meur's, and that of the people he came to know and admire – and a glimpse into a time of rapid change in the Canadian Western Arctic.

Father Robert Le Meur, OMI, receiving his Order of Canada medal from Governor-General Ed Schreyer and congratulations from Lily Schreyer, 1982. (Provincial Archives of Alberta/OB 7639)

Editors Comments

Father Robert Le Meur wrote his memoir, *Souvenirs de l'Arctique*, in French. The original typescript is in the Grandin Archives Collection at the Provincial Archives of Alberta. Editing an English version consisted of removing repetitions and redundancies, correcting grammar and phrasing (English was not Father Le Meur's first language), and updating Inuvialuktun spellings of the names of people, places, animals and other terms. Father Le Meur used the word 'Eskimo' in his memoir. The term has fallen out of favour in Arctic Canada, and the term 'Inuit', meaning 'people', is used when speaking generally about the original peoples of the Canadian Arctic. More specifically, Inuit in the western Canadian Arctic refer to themselves as 'Inuvialuit', meaning 'real people', and the memoir has been updated with these changes. Some of the text has been rearranged to break up long paragraphs and to improve the flow of the narrative, and in some cases longer sections of the manuscript were divided into smaller chapters.

Most of the chapter titles were created by the editors. Father Le Meur included in his memoir several stories from an unpublished compilation that he titled 'True Experiences: Men of the North', and from notes in his draft memoir it is evident that he had planned to add others from that compilation. The editors have taken the liberty of adding two of those stories. Information from lecture notes and other documents written by Father Le Meur has also been added to fill in some gaps and provide additional information about some of the topics he wrote about. Photographs from various sources, most importantly from family members in France, have been added to help readers visualize the people, places and events that are brought to life in *Memories of the Arctic*.

We hope that Father Le Meur would have approved the posthumous changes to his memoir. As much as possible, his voice and narrative style have been preserved. They reflect the attitudes of his time, as well as his own opinions and observations.

Charles Arnold
Coordinator
'Memories of the Arctic' Editorial Team

Acknowledgements

The following individuals and organizations contributed to the preparation of this edition of Father Robert Le Meur's memoir, 'Memories of the Arctic':

Inuvialuit Regional Corporation
Inuvialuit Cultural Resource Centre
Government of the Northwest Territories
Grandin Archives at the Provincial Archives of Alberta
OMI Lacombe Canada
Sister Fay Trombley
Bishop (retired) Denis Croteau, OMI
Isabel Milne
Catherine Cockney
Beverly Amos
Nellie Cournoyea
Charles Arnold
Jean-Yves Deuff, Hervé Bodeur and other members of Father Le Meur's family
Bob Simpson
Peggy Jay
Zoe Ho
Michael O'Rourke

Places Mentioned in this Book

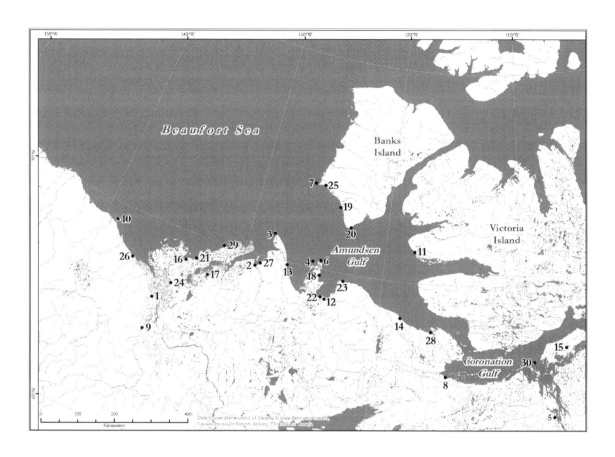

Prelude to the Great North

Saint Jean du Doigt, in France's Brittany District, where Robert Le Meur was born on November 18, 1920. The house with the white wall to the right of the church spire is the Le Meur family home, date unknown.

I am writing down a few thoughts on my experiences during the war, and on my first years as a missionary in the Great North among the Inuvialuit.

Thinking back, if memory serves me well it seems to me I always wanted to be a missionary, and in a harsh land, perhaps the harshest. The Oblates of Mary Immaculate are in charge of all the Roman Catholic Church missions in the Canadian North and that's why I chose that congregation, which is devoted to the poor and the most disadvantaged all over the world. I will quickly review the early years in France – my novitiate in Île de Berder, and my philosophy and theology studies at La Brosse Montceaux, a small village in Seine et Marne, well known since the Second World War due to atrocities committed by the Gestapo in our seminary. We were all conscientious objectors, but many of the Oblates were volunteers helping the *Forces françaises de l'Intérieur,* and some were even officers in the movement. In a raid on the seminary in 1944, five were shot and others taken to a concentration camp.[1]

During those years we were trained for the hard life that awaited us in the missions: character was honed, and manual labour was compulsory and frequent. Every day, we worked in the garden, cleared land, and carried out many other tasks. Because of the war conditions and restrictions we were accustomed to hardship and hunger. At the same time, however, we were learning to be resourceful, to find solutions to our problems. We cut up car tires for shoes and added straps to make sandals. As a conscientious objector, I also had to go into hiding for a few months and, like many others in the resistance, make false identification cards.

Left: *Robert Le Meur as 'Saint John the Baptist' with his mother Jeanne-Marie ('Mimi') during the annual Saint Jean du Doigt religious festival, circa 1925. The woman at the right in the photograph may be his godmother. (Le Meur Family Collection)* **Right:** *Newly ordained priest Father Robert Le Meur on a visit to his home in Saint Jean du Doigt before his assignment to the 'Great North', circa 1943. He is standing with his father, Jean-Louis Le Meur, and his grandmother. Father Le Meur's mother, Jeanne-Marie, died when he was a child. (Le Meur Family Collection)*

Since the situation with the war was becoming dangerous and visits from the Gestapo were more frequent, our Superior decided to advance the date for us to receive Holy Orders, making it sooner than usual for a very valid reason: if we were taken prisoner by the Germans, we could at least render greater service as priests.[2] I was ordained on May 12, 1943 by Monseigneur Pierre Fallaize, a bishop who had spent most of his life in the Great North as a missionary to the Inuit on the Arctic coast in the Mackenzie River region. After our ordination, as was then the custom we wrote to the Superior General in Rome to tell him of the field in which we wanted to work. I

Father Le Meur in his French Army uniform, France, 1945. (Photo courtesy of Jean Gruben)

explained my reasons for choosing the Oblates. I gathered my courage and said that I didn't feel it was my vocation to remain in France, and was interested only in mission countries. Also, because of my health I needed the sea air and lots of space. As the war wasn't over yet, I was asked to go to eastern France, to Notre Dame de Sion, where I got my first experience in parish service, missionary preaching and parish retreats. I also gave the local priests a hand, even replacing them when needed. From Sion, I was asked to go to Benoîte Vaux in la Meuse on a pilgrimage and to do parish work. In 1945 I then spent a few months as a volunteer chaplain for the French army in Nancy and in Germany.

The year 1945 brought me, if not everything I wanted, at least the certainty and assurance that I would soon be leaving for the foreign missions. A letter came from the Vice-Superior General asking if I would go to Natal in South Africa. The request was urgent and I was to reply immediately. Meanwhile, we had heard that the Arctic was now closed to us French. Where that rumour came from I don't know, but it was, in fact, false. In any case, I answered the Superior General that I agreed to go to Africa, but added that my preferences were and remained in the Great North – in order of choice, the Mackenzie, Hudson Bay or Yukon Districts. If I was to go to Africa, I would be more interested in Basutoland. Finally, as I knew that the French Expeditionary Force was preparing to leave for Indochina and that we had missions in Laos, and since many of my friends and relatives were there during the war, I asked permission to join them. That done, I continued my work in Germany. I remember some good times with the troops, and some unusual experiences. One fine day the mail clerk delivered a letter from Rome. What did they want from me now, I wondered. It was a fairly long letter, in which the authorities told me they appreciated my answer very much, congratulated me on my enthusiasm, and recommended patience. As for thinking about Indochina, no, that wasn't in the plan at all, and there was no point thinking about South Africa. However, to console me and to reassure me, the Superior General gave me my obedience for the Mackenzie.

My hopes and wishes were about to be realized. I went home to France on leave at Christmas. When I got there I was told I was on the demobilization list. Six of us would be heading to the Mackenzie. That news took me completely by surprise. I had planned to have a small operation, to have my appendix removed in hospital before leaving France – because, having done my research and learning a lot from the visits of former missionaries, I knew doctors were rare in the North and distances enormous – but that news made it impossible to go into hospital. I still have my appendix, I think.

After a quick visit home to Saint Jean du Doigt I took care of getting my papers and passport. The process didn't take long and the necessary postwar investigation – a security measure – was quickly done, thanks to our record of underground involvement during the war and our activities as rebels and conscientious objectors.

Now there was only one thing left to do – the most difficult thing: find transportation to America. There was no question of travelling by air, so it would have to be by boat. One of our priests was in charge of all the arrangements and, one fine spring day, he asked me to be in Paris by the end of April or early May. I travelled to Paris, and the next day I visited the United States embassy and got a visa. I left the same evening for Saint Jean for a few days holiday and to say my goodbyes. I had barely arrived, had something to eat and slept a bit when my sister woke me and told me a telegram had just arrived, and I had to return to Paris. Everything was ready and we were to leave in a couple of days. There was just enough time to go back to visit La Brosse, where we had done all our studies, and to say goodbye to friends and to tease those who should already have been in South Africa but unfortunately had trouble getting an entry visa.

We left from Le Havre on a cargo ship, the *Oregon*, each with just one suitcase, all that we were allowed. We were at sea for thirteen days and there were occasional alerts, because there were still mines drifting about. The time didn't seem long to us. The crew was very pleasant, and most of the sailors were Bretons. We got together every evening for a drink. I can still remember a few of the passengers. One was a film tycoon from Lebanon, a stout man, nearly two metres tall. His boy was with him, and we called the boy his slave. We got a lot of laughs out of watching

*Father Robert Le Meur (**fifth from left**) and his Oblate companions Gilbert Levesque, Jean Mouchet, Joseph Lusson, Max Ruyant, Cyprien Haramburu and Aloyse Brettar on the cargo ship Oregon en route to New York, 1946. (Le Meur Family Collection).*

their nutcracking operation, the boy cracking nuts and delicately putting them in his boss' hand. What a production, and what a sight! We also got to know a number of other passengers, one an intelligence officer in the American army, a nice fellow, really helpful and good to us. Since we were sleeping in the hold on bunks, these gentlemen no doubt found the accommodations, the meal sittings and other arrangements unsatisfactory. But we had seen worse during the war, and to us, it was a luxury, especially the food.

As soon as we disembarked in New York we found a friend in the person of Monseigneur Arsene Turquetil, the first bishop of the Hudson Bay Prefecture, a legend of the North. He welcomed us on the dock and placed us, some with the Congregation of the Blessed Sacrament, others with the Oblates at Palisade Park. Despite the distance that separated us, we got together every day. The railways were on strike for a few days, and so we took the opportunity to tour the city and visit the stores. Coming from France, it was hard to realize that here we could find practically anything, clothes and shoes in particular. But we were short of money, so we contented ourselves with looking in the windows.

Most of us were wearing the so-called *costume Pétain*, a navy blue suit, with a beret and rough boots. It was what the army had given us when we were demobilized.[3] While definitely lacking in class, it earned us a lot of salutes from GIs we met everywhere on the streets and in stores. We were also asked a lot of questions – *Where are you from? I was in France, too, at such-and-such a place, do you know such-and-such a village or town?* And on it went. Those infamous suits we were wearing also earned us some adventures in Canada, particularly in Ottawa and Hull. A well-publicized article appeared in the newspapers, in which a reporter recounted our journey like an epic, saying that we had come from France by our own resources and were working along the way. The Oblate community in Ottawa wasn't very pleased with the article. I think they felt almost humiliated by it. Maybe we were thought to be beggars. In any case, we had the opportunity to visit quite a few Oblate

4

charities in Montreal and the surrounding area, as well as in Ottawa and Winnipeg. Were they showing off to the cousins from France? In Hull, we were asked to participate in a High Mass, and I was designated to act as sub-deacon. What an experience! I had succeeded in getting a good pair of shoes when I left the army but they had nails in the soles, which wasn't ideal for moving around on a marble chancel floor. I could feel myself start to slip several times. I think I must have been as red as a tomato when I had to move from one place to another to do the reading. In the great silence of the church, full of people, I could hear my own steps – *clack, clack, clack* – and I was taking small steps to avoid falling. What a session after Mass! I swore I would never again accept an invitation to any such ceremonies in the future.

And so we arrived in Edmonton, the gateway to the North. You have to go through Edmonton to get to the North, and you get all supplies there. We stayed there about a week. We covered a lot of miles on foot after unsuccessful attempts to take the bus – we took the wrong one every time. Our berets were a hit in the city. To attract less attention, we took possession of some fedoras that belonged to the priests at St. Joachim's, the French church. Unfortunately, one day as we were coming back in the Provincial, a priest was at the door waiting for us. With a smile on his face, he looked all three of us over and asked, "Which one of you took my hat by mistake?" Well, again, I was the guilty one.

We would have good memories of Edmonton, and of our welcome there. We were invited to one of the city's colleges, Collège Saint Jean, run by the Oblates. The Superior treated us royally, serving us a French-style dinner and even wine with the meal, one of the last times we had that luxury for a long time. From Edmonton the next stage of the journey was by train, a real rattletrap, very slow, one of those small trains like the ones we used to have around Saint Jean before cars appeared on the scene. There were stops here and there along the route, and a lengthy stop at Lac La Biche, where everyone got off the train for a meal at the "hotel" – I don't know if this was the proper name or a pejorative term, but in any case it had no stars, not even one. Brother Sarreault, who had come to meet us in Edmonton, taught us something, a new Canadian etiquette that might not apply to everyone, but did to us members of the clergy. When we were ordering our meal we had noticed a few people drinking beer. Like any good Frenchmen, we were going to order either wine or beer, too. Fortunately the Brother noticed, and he told us that this was not at all recommended for clerical etiquette, in public at least. We had trouble understanding that etiquette. Later, in 1955, I happened to travel from Edmonton to Montreal by train, and in some provinces, you couldn't drink on the train once it entered those provinces. Fortunately, that has changed now. I must admit that I'm not a man to be ruled by convention. People have to take me as I am, that's all.

This stage of the journey ended at Fort McMurray, at that time a small town, where the Church had the hospital and a boarding school. We arrived in the morning. As soon as we got out of the car we went to the chapel for devotions, prayers and Mass. Then came lunch, and our introduction to canned and dried milk. Seeing our surprise and amusement, the good Brother Sarreault couldn't resist telling us that it would now be a part of our diet. I couldn't resist commenting that the milk was pretty watered down. "Well, powdered milk and water..." he said. Then came the solemn moment when we met with the authority, the only authority in fact for us in the North, the Bishop – and, I might add, almost the Pope where we were concerned – Monseigneur Joseph-Marie Trocellier,

OMI, a former missionary on the Arctic coast. At that point a minor incident put us on guard. After the usual greetings, we surrounded the venerable Superior, answering his questions about the situation in France. All of us had been part of Free France and the *Forces françaises de l'intérieur*, so we launched into more or less flattering comments about de Gaulle. Oh, that was dangerous territory! The Bishop had fought in the last war, in 1914-1918, and Pétain was his idol.[4] We backtracked and, since I was in one of the back rows, I retreated and left unnoticed to go outside.

Not for long, though. The mosquitoes didn't allow you to stay long outside, unless you had a good dose of repellent on your face and hands, or a net over your head. We would become well acquainted with those insects! The next day the weather was fairly warm, so two companions and I decided to go bathing in the river. Everything went well on the way there, but as soon as we got in the water there were so many mosquitoes and horseflies we practically had to swim underwater. What a production when we had to get dressed! We had to take turns, with two of us shaking towels to chase away the insects while one got dressed. On our return trip through the woods I puffed on my pipe constantly to keep the mosquitoes away. The porches of the houses were all protected by mosquito netting, and we should have suspected something. Although that was our first encounter with these insects, unfortunately it wouldn't be our last. It is strange that, in this country, where it is so cold, such creatures can survive the harsh winters, and then come out on nice days and spoil what little summer we have.

Our stay at Fort McMurray lasted a few days, long enough for a few of the Brothers to finish building three scows on which we set out for Fort Chipewyan and then on to Fort Fitzgerald, where we had to go over a portage to Fort Smith. All along the route on the Athabasca and the Slave rivers I gave a hand on the scows. We were under the eye of our Bishop, who may have noticed that I didn't worry too much about anything, and that the work was no trouble. He once said to me, "Now tell me, you don't seem to worry too much about things, do you?" And I replied, "Why worry? Everything is going well. We've seen worse." Was it that attitude that got me chosen to go to the Arctic coast? I don't know, but the fact is that, when we arrived at Fort Smith, I was busy, like the others, loading the barge that would take goods all along the river as far Tuktoyaktuk, on the coast. There is a large stretch of rapids just before Fort Smith that makes the river impassable, so everything had to be conveyed there by road over a portage from Fort Fitzgerald – one of those sandy roads that created choking dust when the weather was dry, and turned into a kind of gumbo when wet. I made quite a few of those trips, accompanying Brother Berric, also a Breton, from around Brest. One day we young recruits were called one by one to see the Bishop, who assigned us stations at missions in the Mackenzie District. Father Max Ruyant and I were the lucky ones – we were headed for the Coast, and life among the Inuit. My dream and wishes were coming true, and I was very happy.

We started off again, this time on board a tugboat and a barge, the *Sant'Anna*. The boat belonged to and was fully manned by the mission – captain, engineer, mechanic, men of all trades and of an extraordinary calibre, who knew the rivers. They were also architects, builders, hunters, and fishermen. Electricity, plumbing, they were afraid of nothing. As for Max Ruyant and I, we were the deckhands, giving a hand to the pilots and mechanics. We each took a shift, six hours in a row, then a break. The boat stopped at all the missions along the river and large lakes. Since the main destination of this voyage was the Arctic Coast, we had very few things to unload, except at Aklavik. At that time, Aklavik was the centre of all activities on the Coast, a sort of capital for trappers in the Delta, and for the Inuit from Tuktoyaktuk and even farther away. At Aklavik I met Father L'Helgouach, a priest who had spent many years on the Coast and knew the Inuit language so well that the people said maybe he knew it better than they themselves did. He came with us to Tuk as an assistant and a guide. It was at Aklavik that I saw the Liberation of Paris on film! Father L'Helgouach was pretty proud to show us the film, explaining that he had bought a 16 mm projector with money he and the boys at the boarding school had earned from hunting muskrats.

I was in a hurry to see the coast. It was now early July, and we had already experienced the Midnight Sun – once we crossed the 60th parallel the sun was no longer setting. In those days it was every man for himself. The route along the river wasn't marked, so you had to know the landmarks: a broken tree here, a pointed spruce there, a rounded hill. We arrived without incident – we didn't even hit a sandbar, although there are plenty of them in those waters. The whole population of Tuktoyaktuk was on the dock when we disembarked in front of the mission, the first one on the Coast. The Moccasin Telegraph had already announced our arrival.[5] How many people were there in Tuk at that time? Maybe only a hundred, but they were most friendly to us.

Aboard the Mission boat Sant' Anna on the Mackenzie River, going to Tuktoyaktuk, 1946. Father Le Meur is in the middle, front. On his left is Father Max Ruyant, and on his right is Brother Kraut. Standing on the upper deck at the right is Father L'Helgouach. (Le Meur Family Collection)

Tuktoyaktuk Harbour in the 1940s. (Archibald Fleming Collection/NWT Archives/N-1979-050: 1224)

Everything was brand new to me, of course, the country, the people, the customs, the fishing, the hunting. But I was in the land I would come to call home, especially after a few years, when the Inuit themselves would tell me I was one of them, speaking their language, living their philosophy

Father Le Meur on arrival at Tuktoyaktuk, 1946. (Le Meur Family Collection)

and listening to their needs and questions. Of course, that took me some time, and there were moments that were perhaps difficult from a human standpoint – waiting patiently day after day, month after month, or even years, is hardly easy. It seems that we have so much to give, but we have to be content with watching and listening too. Bishop Fallaize, who had ordained me, had also given me advice, just one piece of advice – be patient with time, and patient with people. When we finally arrived on the Arctic coast, I promised myself that I would give all I had, learn all I could about the Inuit, and live faithfully and, above all, honestly. My goal was not just to visit for a short time, but to stay among them as long as they would let me, and as long as my strength allowed.

Chapter 1 Notes

1   *Forces françaises de l'Intérieur* (French Forces of the Interior) refers to French resistance fighters in the later stages of World War II. The German army learned that false documents were produced at the La Brosse Montceaux seminary, and that weapons were hidden there, and raided the seminary on July 24, 1944. Two priests and three brothers were tortured, and when they refused to talk they were executed. In addition, 86 priests and brothers were arrested and were in the process of being sent to concentration camps in Germany when the war ended. Father Le Meur had left the seminary prior to that time, and was serving as a parish priest in Notre Dame de Sion.

2   Ordainment as a Priest of the Oblates de Marie Immaculée normally occurs after six years of religious training.

3   The 'Pétain' was a suit made of coarse blue military fabric, cut in a civilian style, issued to discharged soldiers of the French Army.

4   During the Second World War, Marshal Philippe Pétain was the head of Vichy France, the government of France that capitulated to Nazi Germany. General Charles de Gaulle headed up a competing government, 'Free France', that was based in England. The *Forces françaises de l'intérieur* were French resistance fighters loyal to Free France.

5   The 'Moccasin Telegraph' is a local term for information that is spread by word of mouth.

2

My Apprenticeship Begins

Father Robert Le Meur returning from the Hornaday River near Paulatuk, circa 1946. (Le Meur Family Collection)

My arrival at Tuktoyaktuk in 1946 marked the start of my work as a missionary, and my apprenticeship with the Inuvialuit, learning their language, and about their history and their culture, how they lived. Gone were many of the conventions I was familiar with. Here, people regulated their own lives, their meal and rest times, and what they ate. Inuit logic is based on practical living. Can an instrument regulate your stomach? This way of life – eating when you are hungry, sleeping when you feel the need – is well suited to a land where so much depends on the weather and the cycles of animals and fish. But here, as elsewhere, everything is changing. These customs are disappearing, overtaken by the development that is entering the Great North with giant strides. But when I first arrived the old days and the old ways still prevailed. Little by little, I came to realize where I was and what I had to expect. But I was young, and determined to learn and to persevere.

I took my first lesson in the Inuvialuit language with Father L'Helgouach. I can still see him at the Tuktoyaktuk mission, walking back and forth in the main room, saying slowly to Max Ruyant and me: "*Takusukgaluaripkin* – I would really like to see you; *taku* – root; *suk* – suffix; *aalluar* – modifier, qualifier, tense; *ripkin* – inflected ending." Listening to him speak, I wondered how I would learn the language and, in particular, how long it would take me. We were also learning another language – half French, half English. We'd say "*passe-moi* le hammer", and so on, but we learned very quickly.

But there was more than just studying. There was work to be done before going to Paulatuk, the mission station I was assigned to. We visited the nets every day, sometimes by motorboat,

*John Elgok (**left**) and Father Tardy (**right**) in a boat with water barrels and a fish. Tree River area, circa 1940s. (Holman Photohistorical Society/NWT Archives/N-1990-004:0126)*

and sometimes rowing. What a boat, and what a motor! We called it the *"putt-putt"*. Even the Inuvialuit knew that expression. But it served us very well at that time for checking fishnets and for finding wood, and for getting fresh water. It was an old lifeboat that had belonged, I think, to the *SS Mackenzie* – one of the Hudson Bay Company's paddle wheelers – so not a new boat. Father Franche bought it for about twelve dollars, his entire fortune. The motor, an old DuBrie, had been stuck in the sand on the beach. It was one of the things that were used for tying up the dog teams, an old engine, yellowed by time perhaps, and certainly by the dogs who sprayed it constantly. Father Franche was a mechanical genius. He cleaned and polished it, took it apart, and the only thing that cost him anything was the magneto.

That first summer I spent in Tuktoyaktuk I also had some lessons in taking things as they come. There was the time that Jack, an Inuvialuk, and I went to get a supply of fresh water for the

Our Lady of Lourdes (Roman Catholic Mission boat) docked in front of the Mission warehouse at Tuktoyaktuk, circa 1950. (Terrance Hunt/NWT Archives/N-1979-062: 0027)

mission's schooner, *Our Lady of Lourdes*, from the other side of the bay. Sometimes we could get water from a small river there, but this time because of the wind and tides the river was salty, and we had to portage overland to a small lake. The weather was fine to begin with, just a little light breeze – welcome because it kept the mosquitoes away. It's a lot of work to fill the barrels, pail after pail, and it takes a fair bit of time. The wind came up, a west wind, a real storm. To get out of the

10

small river I was steering the rudder and Jack was standing in front of the motor, trying to protect the boat against the heavy sea. We were soaked to the bone. The magneto got wet, and the motor started to choke and eventually stopped altogether, and we were blown to the shore. Proceeding on foot we reached a camp of Hudson Bay Company employees who were repairing one of their boats that had been driven ashore the year before. We had a cup of coffee with them, and after waiting a few hours we went back to the boat. The wind had dropped a little, and after cleaning the generator we managed to get back to port, despite the rolling and pitching. As for the water in the barrels, well, it had been so inundated with saltwater that it was undrinkable. That's the way it goes.

Eventually everything was ready on *Our Lady of Lourdes*, and we set sail in the direction of Stanton and then on to Paulatuk, which was to be my mission for the next four years. On the schooner were Father Franche, the captain; Billy Thrasher, the pilot; Brother Kraut, the mechanic; Brother A. Josset; and myself and Father Max Ruyant. We also had on board two carpenters who were going to the Anderson River to build a house. A herd of domesticated reindeer had been established there, and the Government decided to have a residence built for the superintendent, Malcolm McNab. On the deck was piled a mixture of cargo, lumber, barrels, even a dog, a gift from Father Sarreault at Fort Chipewyan to the Paulatuk mission, a magnificent animal, half wolf.

Our bishop, Monseigneur Trocellier, was also on board. Nearly every year he visited the missions on the coast by schooner. He always had his spot reserved forward, where the galley was located. During these voyages he was the chief cook, and a good one at that. I don't know where he could have got used to the sea in the Corrèze region in France's interior, where he came from, but he had his sea legs and was never sick, even in bad weather and storms. Always forward, smoking his pipe, he was sometimes knocked to the deck when, without any advance warning, skipper Franche had to hit the ice hard enough to clear a path.

The trip to Stanton was uneventful, with good weather and no ice on the sea. We unloaded freight at the good Father Léonce Dehurtevent's place. After we said goodbye to him he promised to come to Paulatuk in the winter by dogsled to bring us the mail. From there we went to the Anderson River and, if I remember correctly, we had trouble finding the channel and we had to navigate by sounding, since the estuary was not very deep and had a lot of sandbars. But I was experienced now, having operated the sounding line frequently on the Mackenzie River. After many detours and hitting sandbars, often making our way through the mud on the bottom, we finally succeeded in reaching the reindeer camp. We unloaded again, mainly lumber and other building materials – nails, tarpaper for the roof, insulation and other items. Without delay, we set off again, and headed

Father Léonce Deheurtevent and Inuvialuit women and children on board Our Lady of Lourdes at the Stanton mission, circa 1940. The woman in the middle is Jean Tardiff, and the woman at the right is Bessie Steen. (Missionary Oblates/Grandin Archives at the Provincial Archives of Alberta/OB.32236)

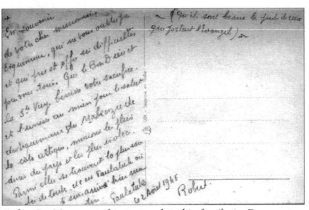

Father Le Meur sent this postcard to his family in France upon arriving in Paulatuk on August 2, 1946. His message in English is: "In memory of your dear Eskimo missionary, who does not forget you and prays and offers his toils for all of you. May God and the Blessed Virgin bless your sacrifice - and unite with mine for the salvation of the Mackenzie Eskimos of the Arctic, the toughest in the country and most isolated assignments. Among them is the most isolated of all and that is Paulatuk where I arrived yesterday morning. Paulatuk. August 2, 1946. Robert."[1] (Le Meur Family Collection)

to Paulatuk, the location of Our Lady of Lourdes Mission, which would be my home for four years and where I would begin to learn about the people, the land and the animals of the North.

The name Paulatuk was given to the area by people who had been hunting geese one spring. On the banks of the Hornaday River they had found some pieces of coal, which they put in their fire. One of the women had just got a brand new tent made of white canvas. The wind blew from the south and brought all the soot onto the tent. When she came out and saw what had happened she exclaimed, *"Paulatuuq"* – "Does that ever smoke!" And that's how the place got its name.[2]

The wind and the coal are two things about Paulatuk that stay in my mind. *Pignangnaq*, the notorious south wind that blows there, comes up suddenly, without any warning. Nothing could withstand that wind when a storm blew. Small dogs disappeared when they were picked up by the swirling wind. At the mission, when I fed my dogs and the wind was blowing all I could do was put pieces of blubber in their mouths. It was pointless to put food on the ground, since the wind would carry it off. Many times while crossing the Hornaday River and travelling against the wind and blowing snow I was forced to crawl in front of the dogs, anchoring myself to the smooth ice by driving my knife into it, and pull on the lead dog.

We used coal that we dug from the banks of the Hornaday River to heat the mission buildings.[3] I became acquainted with the coalmine as soon as I arrived at Paulatuk, and came to know it by heart, I would even say from top to bottom. We went there by boat with an old one-cylinder engine, a DuBrie, that sputtered and struggled the whole time. Each upstroke of the cylinder shook us so much that we wondered if the bottom of our boat would still be there the next time our engine heaved a wheezy sigh. The coal seam was perhaps a metre from top to bottom and not very deep, but to mine it we had to remove the ground above and go in from the side as well. What a chore! Everything was frozen, of course, and our picks didn't last long at this work. We

Loading sacks of coal dug from the banks of the Hornaday River near Paulatuk, circa 1946-1951. (Le Meur Family Collection)

constantly had to sharpen them with the file, and back at the Mission we would forge new ones for the next trip. Then the coal was put in bags and, that done, we piled the bags on the shore. When we had enough for a load, the real hard labour began. We rolled the bags to the bottom of the slope, and then carried the heavy bags– the thawed coal was wet – on our backs and walked in water up to our thighs and deposited them in a small boat, which was a boat in name only, it was more like a square box. Then we rowed to the other boat, which was a bit bigger, while trying not to lose our balance, with the full bags taking up all the room. Then it was a gymnastic exercise, standing and picking up the bags in the small boat and depositing them in the bigger boat, then it was back to the shore. It was non-stop work once the loading began, because we had to take advantage of the good weather. If the wind came up while we were loading we started back to the Mission as quickly as possible, even if we only had half a load. Only during the trip could we rest a bit. Once we reached Paulatuk the bags of coal had to be immediately unloaded onto the beach, high up, so that they wouldn't be buried again in the sand. That's how the summer went by – fishing and coal, coal and fishing.

In spite of the suffering and fatigue, we had some good times at the mine. I spent time there in the spring or the fall, sometimes alone. To relieve the monotony, and just for a change, we could walk in the surrounding area. On the lakes were a few ducks, and on land a few ptarmigan, and from time to time some caribou. Since it was only a short distance from the river, we put in nets, which provided us with Arctic salmon and whitefish.

Fish was the basic food at Paulatuk, and we ate it every day – in soup, boiled, fried, and even raw and frozen, as well as dried and smoked. From time to time, we varied the menu of course. It was during one trip to the Hornaday River that I first ate ground squirrels – *sik-siks*, small rodents wrapped up in a beautiful yellow-orange fur with small dark spots. If I recall – and do I ever – it was one of those beautiful fall days. I'd visited the nets with Edward,[4] and then I was resting in

Arctic ground squirrel, or sik-sik. (Denali National Park and Preserve)

front of my tent, sitting and reading or making notes, not in a hurry to prepare my meal. I had all the time in the world. One of my friend's children came up to me and said something in Inuvialuktun, and to make sure I understood, he made a sign that we were going to eat. Okay. I headed for their tent, which was very close to mine, and I sat down on the ground, like all the other members of the family. The weather was so nice that the table, a simple piece of cardboard, the remains of some packaging, was laid on the sandy shore. The utensils were there too. Everybody picked up an enameled plate and cup and a spoon. My host invited me to serve myself first. A large pot was there in front of me, with a big cup that served as a ladle. The soup was greasy, a thick layer of oil lay on top of the broth. I stirred the pot before serving myself. At first I took almost nothing but broth, so I dipped the cup in again. That's where the surprise came in. I noticed something black and hairy sticking up through the oil on the broth. It looked like claws, very long ones, and in fact it was paws. Of what? I didn't know yet. I sat there, thinking, and in response to my host, who urged me to take more, I said that the soup seemed very good. "It's squirrel," he said, "squirrel soup." Both my plate and my mind were full. Squirrel. Not a problem, it was new to me, but it went down okay. The soup was delicious, in spite of all my misgivings. I finished that serving quickly, even before all the others, which prompted my host to say that I seemed to like it. I took some more soup. The broth had gone down quite a bit in the pot, and when I served myself I saw another part of the anatomy of the famous *sik-sik*. This time it showed me its furry face, a long nose and small mouth, its splendid whiskers – still stiff, or perhaps even more so cooked than alive. They had cooked the animal whole – head, tail, and all the rest as well. How would I get out of this? My friend urged me to take a piece of meat. "It's wonderful," he told me, "even better than the soup." "Oh, yes, very likely, but I like this soup, it's delicious," I gave him to understand. With a somewhat embarrassed gesture, he took another piece of cardboard and deposited the squirrel on it. Ah, what a relief! I smiled to myself and breathed a little easier. The squirrel was there in front of me, where I could see it. The head and legs were covered in hair, but the rest of the body had been properly shaved and the inside completely emptied. More than likely the story of my first Inuit-style meal and how much I liked that soup was related to others, because, since I was by myself at Paulatuk and busy fishing, a kind old woman who stayed nearby prepared me a squirrel for supper almost every day. Sometimes she cooked it herself, and other times I found it on my table at the Mission, ready to be put in the oven or in the pan.

The coal, the isolation, the fishing and the hunting, all of it constant, made Paulatuk the hardest mission of the Vicariate, in my opinion. We didn't complain. After all, we'd come here to have a rough time of it, and the Oblates were known as the specialists when it came to the most difficult missions. It was part of our tradition, and of our training, to go where no one else wanted to go. Paulatuk certainly met that requirement. When one winter ended, we were already preparing in spring for the next winter. At Paulatuk, not being prepared meant being cold and hungry,

14

and wandering about looking in every corner for fish and meat and coal. I couldn't help but think, while musing, of the big trees I'd cut down at La Brosse Montceaux: why so many years of philosophy and theology, and not the a single thing about mining? I should have learned a little about handling dynamite and powder. It was too late to think of that now. Since I hadn't come to this land to starve or freeze to death, I went to the school of life and survival.

It was also at Paulatuk that really I began learning the Inuvialuit language, and English as well, and began to understand the need to be able to communicate with others. It's something you have to go through yourself to realize that simply having goodwill, a strong desire, and a smile are not always sufficient to meet the human needs of friendship and understanding. A few common words to begin with, in Inuvialuktun or in English, would be enough to make myself understood, but I wanted to increase my lexicon and my vocabulary very quickly. I was always armed with a pencil and a notebook, in which, without really knowing the sounds, I wrote words and short sentences. What patience the people showed! What kindness they showed in accepting me and showing me all aspects of their life, and the ways and customs of the country!

*Father Le Meur's companions Father Maurice Metayer (**left**) and Brother Kraut (**second from right**) in the front of Our Lady of Lourdes Mission at Paulatuk, circa 1946. Others in the photograph include Joe Thrasher, Nora Ruben, Mary Evik Ruben, Ang'ngik Ruben, Dennis Ruben, Bertha Ruben, Sadie Ruben, Billy Ruben, and Mabel Ruben. (Le Meur Family Collection)*

Chapter 2 Notes

1   At the end of his message on this postcard, Father Le Meur wrote: ~ *Qu'ils sont beaux le pieds de ceux qui portent l'Evangile.* This is a French translation of the message in Latin on the front: Quam speciosi pedes evangelizantium, ('How beautiful are the feet of those that preach the Gospel'). This phrase is often used in reference to missionaries.

2   The traditional name of the community is *Paulatuuq*, meaning 'Place of Soot' – *Paula* in Inuvialuktun. The spelling on modern maps is Paulatuk.

3   Coal was plentiful at Coalmine (*Aludjiqpik* in Inuvialuktun), but of poor quality. Five bags a week had to be dug from seams along the banks of the Hornaday River, and hauled 30 to 40 kilometers to the Mission.

4   Father Le Meur is probably referring to Edward Ruben.

Our Lady of Lourdes

The Roman Catholic Church Arctic Mission's ship, Our Lady of Lourdes, 1978. (Illustrator unknown).

Many visitors to Tuktoyaktuk today come to look at a schooner sitting next to the church, and want to hear her story. She is *Our Lady of Lourdes* – the Roman Catholic Church Arctic Mission's vessel. Having served from 1931 until 1957, she is now resting from all her adventures, a reminder of past days at sea, a kind of history lesson and a souvenir of a time not too long ago when ships owned by Inuvialuit, the church, traders, the police and others braved the sea and the ice.

Before I begin my story of how *Our Lady of Lourdes* got to her resting place, let's take a closer look at the ship. She was no trans-Atlantic liner, of course, but she was a beautiful, good schooner about 20 metres in length and five metres wide, with a draught of less than two metres, and registered to carry 31 tons. Her hull was built of yellow pine, and up to the water line the hull was covered in ironwood, which helped her to resist the pressure of the sea ice, and to ram and break the ice when required. Because she was so solidly built, she could be safely hauled up on land or even left in the ice for the winter. She had a 70 horsepower Fairbanks-Morse diesel engine, and a winch on the deck run by a 5 horsepower gas motor that was used to raise the anchors and to load and unload cargo, and sometimes to assist if the ship became grounded. She had two sails, a main sail and a jib that helped with steering in heavy weather. With the engine running and the main sail up she could reach up to 10 knots an hour. The large mast rose some 16 metres from the deck and there was a ladder leading up to the crow's nest, which looked like a barrel cut in half. From there, sailors had a good view of the sea ice and look for passages through it. The winch, two anchors and anchor chains occupied the forecastle, and at the stern was the pilothouse. There was a helm in the pilothouse, and another helm on the roof above it, which was useful when travelling in ice and on the river to watch for sand bars and floating logs. Electric bells connected these control stations to the engine room. Below the deck at the front was a triangular galley, which also housed five fairly comfortable berths and had space for food storage, plus a small oil stove, a water tank, and a table that could be stored away under one of the beds. An air vent had been installed in the galley to draw in fresh air, too much at times. The room next door was used for storing cargo. Past a bulkhead at the other end was the engine room. Then came the pilot's room, where there were also two berths and a tiny bathroom in the corner. There were two fresh water tanks on board, one in the galley and the other on the quarterdeck, where there was also a diesel fuel tank.

In general, the ship was fully loaded when it set sail, and I would say she probably carried at least 45 tons at that point. It may seem strange to think of a ship registered to take 31 tons setting sail with 40 or 45 tons on board, but in the land of the midnight sun and ice the sailing season is very limited – a maximum of two months, sometimes less – so safety was often compromised to supply the missions along the coast, and the load it could carry was determined more by the amount of space it took than the weight. There wasn't much free space on the deck once it was loaded. To get from one end of the boat to the other, you had to clamber over all kinds of cargo – barrels of fuel and gasoline, boards, sleds, and other items – all well secured, of course.

When Monseigneur Bishop Breynat, Vicar Apostolic of the Mackenzie Region, decided in the 1920s to increase the number of missions along the Arctic Coast he needed to ship construction materials for the mission buildings, and then each summer send a year's worth of provisions for those stations. Other boats wouldn't take our supplies, because our missions were outside the shipping lanes, and also for political reasons, at least in the beginning, so we had to organize our own independent transportation network on the Mackenzie River and along the Arctic Ocean.[1] In 1928 he purchased the *Nokatak*, a real 'bucket' that proved to be unsuitable. So Monseigneur Breynat got in touch with Captain C.T. Pedersen, a sailor who was probably more familiar than anyone else with sailing in Arctic waters, to purchase a new boat for the Arctic Mission. After being a captain on whaling boats for several years, Pedersen had switched to the fur trade. Every

summer, he left San Francisco on board his ship, a three-masted whaler called the *Patterson*, with all kinds of cargo in the holds, and often with boats on the deck – boats that had been built in San Francisco under his watchful eye. Since he knew the Arctic and the hazards of the ice, Captain Pedersen ordered an extra solid boat for us, one with a rounded hull. In a letter Captain Pedersen wrote, "You may find that she rolls a lot, but I promise you she'll never get caught in the ice. If you're ever in a jam, the ice will lift her up onto the pack ice." These words were prophetic. We would have liked our boat to be a bit bigger, but it had to fit on the deck between two masts of the *Patterson*.

That is how *Our Lady of Lourdes* arrived at Herschel Island in August of 1931. A few of the older Inuvialuit still remember that day, and they told me that they watched her being unloaded. They said she seemed so heavy that

Captain Christian T. Pedersen on the deck of the Canalaska Trading Company supply ship, Patterson, 1934. (Inuvialuit Social Development Program/Bessie Wolki Collection)

The schooner North Star of Herschel Island aboard the Canalaska supply ship Patterson, circa 1935. Our Lady of Lourdes is similar to this schooner, and was brought north the same way. (Mrs. Peter Sydney Collection/Library and Archives Canada/PA-027649)

the *Patterson* listed a bit when she was put in the water, using blocks and pulleys. The mast and cordage and the sails were installed right away. The engine was in perfect shape – it had come from Chicago and the shipbuilder had installed it himself. All she had to do was start providing the services expected of her. She would very quickly become known all along the Arctic coast and earn a well-deserved reputation. There were some troubles, difficulties and hard times, but we managed to get supplies to the missions every year.

Our Lady of Lourdes travelling on the Mackenzie River near Aklavik, 1942. (Charles Henry Douglas Clark Collection, Fisher Rare Book Collection, University of Toronto)

Because *Our Lady of Lourdes* was delivered late in the season, that first year she sailed just from Herschel Island to Aklavik, and then up the Mackenzie River to Fort Resolution, along the way picking up guests going to Father Fallaize's consecration as Coadjutor Vicar Apostolic of the Mackenzie Region.[2] On this, her first voyage, she certainly didn't know what the future held. In 1932, after coming back from Fort Resolution where she had spent the winter, Our *Lady of Lourdes* began serving the coastal missions. For a few years she travelled between Aklavik, Herschel Island, Tuktoyaktuk, Letty Harbour and Coppermine,[3] then a few other places were added to her route as new missions were established at Paulatuk, Stanton, Burnside River, and Holman Island. This little vessel would spend some winters at one of those missions, but other times would winter alone, lost in some remote, wild spot or caught in the ice, unable to move. She wasn't an ocean-going freighter, or an icebreaker, but she served both functions for the cause. Passengers and cargo of all

*Some of the members of the Roman Catholic Church who served in the Diocese of the Mackenzie: Brother Tesnière; Brother Kraut; seated (**left to right**): Father L. Deheurtevent; Father L. LeMer; Father L'Helgouach; Monseigneur G. Breynat; Father A. Binamé; Billy Thrasher; Brother Guèrin; Father Griffin; Louis Bisson, circa 1937-1939. (Missionary Oblates, Grandin Archives at the Provincial Archives of Alberta/OB. 32237). Note: Father Louis LeMer (shown in this photograph) is not to be confused with Father Robert Le Meur.*

kinds, including dogs, would fill her hold and the deck. Many times she had to push and break her way through the ice. One time she even travelled on top of the ice, as its prisoner.

The Roman Catholic Church relied on Fathers and Brothers to operate its barges, tugs and schooners. They doubled as engineers, mechanics and pilots, as necessary. It was really quite a feat. It is thanks to their determination, intelligence, know-how and immense faith that the Arctic missions could operate. The first captain of *Our Lady of Lourdes* was Father Griffin, an American, a phlegmatic type with a clear and keen eye. After spending a few years in the Arctic, he went back to his native Texas. He said he'd had enough. On his way back, through Edmonton, he said it was like being released from prison. When the Bishop invited him to come south for his annual retreat, he responded, facetiously, "You're joking, aren't you? A retreat? I'm on permanent retreat here at Paulatuk!" Then there was Father Antoine Binamé, a Belgian, the genuine article, who, when he had a choice of two paths, two ways of doing something, always chose the most difficult. He also had a sense of humour. One time at Tuktoyaktuk a VIP from the Hudson's Bay Company came on board. The wind blew his hat off and into the water. Without missing a beat, old Antoine grabbed the boathook and presented the visitor with his hat, making sure to scoop up some seawater while he was at it. The next Captain was Father Franche, a Parisian, who would remain at the helm of the *Our Lady of Lourdes* until her final days on the water. He was a real handyman, unflappable, always true to form. In the engine room, taking care of the engine, there was Brother Kraut, a German, very conscientious, a bit slow perhaps, some thought, but once his engine was tuned up, it never failed. Alongside him there was Brother Auguste Josset, a real Navy man, a graduate of the *Jeanne d'Arc*.[4] His calling had come later in life. He was a Breton, from Rennes, strong as a horse. Once he tightened a nut or a bolt there was no undoing it.

Billy Thrasher at the helm of Our Lady of Lourdes, 1942. (Charles Henry Douglas Clark Collection, Fisher Rare Book Collection, University of Toronto)

At the outset, they recruited an Inuvialuk, Billy Thrasher, a real sailor, practically born on a whaling boat. He was a handsome man, with a square build, solid as a rock and strong, and at least six feet tall. He was on board from 1931 until 1950, with only a few brief absences, and he was always equal to the task. His previous experience operating schooners had made him familiar with the dangers of the sea and the ice. Sometimes, though, he had trouble leaving Tuktoyaktuk harbour, because his wife would threaten him – she didn't care for his long absences. He was a loyal companion and very helpful and would pass on his experience as a pilot and his knowledge of the coast to others. Two other Inuvialuit were usually hired as deckhands to complete the crew. They would work on board all season from late June until the end of the sailing season, which was usually the middle or the end of September. Add to this a few passengers such as the Bishop, coming to visit the missions on the coast, priests arriving or leaving or changing mission, and you have quite a good idea of the boat's operations. Everyone worked on board, loading and unloading provisions, taking or relieving the watch. When he was aboard, our Bishop, Monseigneur Trocellier, took charge of the galley.

Most years *Our Lady of Lourdes* made three trips each summer, taking supplies from Aklavik and Herschel Island to the coastal missions. The first trip of the year was to Stanton at the mouth of the Anderson River. That trip served as a trial run, and was undertaken as soon as the ice allowed enough room to manoeuvre, usually around July 20 to 25. The second trip was to Paulatuk, and the last, to Coppermine, Burnside River, Holman Island and the missions farther east. Some years, when there was little or no ice, everything went smoothly. In other years, the crew would have to push and break the ice, turn half-circles, head away from land to find a passage, or come closer in and practically hug the shore and thread their way between icebergs and land. Our schooner was invaluable and very practical in these situations, because her shallow draft meant she could sail fairly close to land. This gave us a big advantage over larger ships that couldn't afford to take chances like that.

20

Our Lady of Lourdes supplying the Roman Catholic Mission at Stanton, 1942. (Charles Henry Douglas Clark Collection, Fisher Rare Book Collection, University of Toronto)

While many trips were uneventful, others involved hunger and cold, sweat and anxiety. If you sail, if you love the sea or if you just like true adventures – not imaginary, but real, human adventures – then I invite you to read about two of the journeys that are described here, without the writer's flourish or the filmmaker's imagination, but just as they happened, taken straight from the travel logs of the participants themselves.

I will begin with an account by Bishop Pierre Fallaize about the time that the crew and passengers of *Our Lady of Lourdes* had to be rescued at Paulatuk. In 1935 the ship was assigned to help with the establishment of the mission at Paulatuk. The Diocese had operated a mission at Letty Harbour on the western shore of Darnley Bay since 1928, but church authorities had decided that Paulatuk, at the bottom of the bay, was a better location. The seams of coal along the banks of the Hornaday River provided an economical alternative to coal shipped from the south for heating the mission buildings, and fish to feed people and dogs were plentiful in the river and nearby lakes. After transporting staff, supplies and building materials to the new location, *Our Lady of Lourdes* spent the winter of 1935-1936 at Letty Harbour, frozen in the ice. Here is the story, as told by Bishop Fallaize:[5]

Bishop Pierre Fallaize and an unidentified Inuvialuk in front of the new church at Paulatuk, late 1930s. (Missionary Oblates/Grandin Archives at the Provincial Archives of Alberta/OB. 09614)

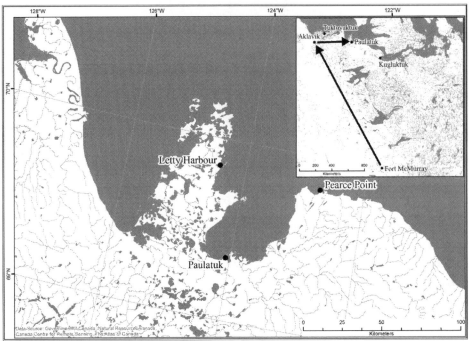

Locations of places mentioned in the story 'Rescue at Paulatuk', and the route followed by the rescue airplane.

"The voyage in the summer of 1936 had an auspicious beginning. *Our Lady of Lourdes* left Letty Harbour on July 21 and reached Aklavik on July 28 – only a week's travel, which wasn't too bad. The crew wasn't expecting to do that well. The residents of Aklavik didn't expect to see the boat so soon either, and when the school children said they could hear the noise of the engine, no one believed them, until someone spotted the boat at a turn in the river. After a day of rest and talk – it had been a year since the last visit – we began loading supplies. There wasn't much freight to pick up at Aklavik, as most of the provisions to take to the missions that summer had already been sent to Tuktoyaktuk."[6]

"We arrived at Tuktoyaktuk on July 31 and started loading immediately. We would have liked to have taken the provisions for all the coastal missions to avoid having to make another trip, but there were 70 tons, really too much, and we decided to take only the cargo for the Coppermine and Burnside missions. At that point, we could see that it was still too much – the hold was bursting at the seams, and lumber and other materials filled the deck. We had to unload some precious coal to lighten the boat, which, in spite of everything, still sat below the waterline mark. After working so hard and so long, we received a radio message from Coppermine telling us that Coronation Gulf was completely choked with ice. What were we to do? Unload again and go to Paulatuk for the first trip? This would be safer and wiser, and perhaps the sea would clear in the meantime. But we were tired, and all agreed that conditions change quickly in the Arctic. The entire crew felt that we should head east and place our trust in Providence."

"And so, we set off on the evening of August 1. On August 2, after a quick and uneventful trip, we reached Baillie Island, where we dropped off a few children who were coming back from school at Aklavik. At the request of the Royal Canadian Mounted Police, we picked up a widow and an orphan bound for Coppermine. We were in a hurry to leave, but the weather suddenly turned windy and foggy, and the ice was so close we could feel the cold from it. Since we were sheltered at Baillie Island we waited there for the storm to die down. On August 3, about 3 o'clock in the afternoon, we set out again. Oh, the wind was still blowing, but it wasn't as strong and it would even assist us, so we hoisted the sail. We could see the ice on the port side, but there was nothing in our path because the wind had pushed it out to sea. From time to time we went through patches of mist, but that didn't bother us. It was a good night, fairly calm, and in the morning we saw the rocks of Cape Parry, the Diamond Rocks. They are quite steep, and birds, like the small penguins, the murres, nest there. You certainly don't want to be blown towards land in that area. A little farther on, we spotted four schooners operated by Inuvialuit who had spent the winter on Banks Island and were making their way westward through the ice to Tuk and Aklavik."

"On August 4, around 3 o'clock in the afternoon, we sailed by Pearce Point, which is easy to recognize by its high cliffs and its rocks in the bay. It had been smooth sailing to that point, but as soon as we passed Pearce Point it was ice, ice and more ice, as far as the eye could see. Then, from out of nowhere, came a black and white dot, a mast – it was the Hudson's Bay Company schooner, *Margaret A*, which had been trying for several days to find a way through the ice to Coppermine, but without success. They'd seen us as well and came to join us, feeling there was safety in numbers. The ice was coming our way, a mass of ice, kilometres wide, so we beat an honourable retreat for some 30 kilometres and took shelter in a cove. The ice continued to pursue us, and pieces were driven into our shelter. It forced us to move out, but this was easier said than done, as a large piece of ice had become attached to our large anchor. We tried in vain to get it off, using the winch and the engine. There was nothing we could do. In the end, the chain gave way. We broke free and withdrew about another 20 kilometres."

"Looking out from the crow's nest, there seemed to be open water channels in the middle of

Murres nesting at Cape Parry, 2013. (Photo credit: Matt Drennan)

The Hudson's Bay Company coastal supply ship Margaret A at Coppermine, circa 1940s. (Margaret Oldenberg/Arctic Institute of North America)

the field of ice, and so we plunged in, pushing and breaking, counter-attacking, and finally, after much effort, we had managed to advance about 50 kilometres, and we anchored ourselves to a submerged iceberg. The *Margaret A* had also left, but we couldn't see her for the fog. Once she was notified by radio of our position she came and joined us again. It was Sunday and we sang a Mass. On the afternoon we set off again. Since our boat has a shallow draft, we tried to make our way between land and submerged icebergs, a difficult and dangerous game. The pilot gave directions to the helmsman from the crow's nest. It was exhausting for everyone, from the helmsman to the man in the engine room. There were orders and counter-orders – ahead, astern, neutral – and it went on non-stop, accompanied by the infernal racket of ice breaking and pack ice grinding against the boat. We moved forward cautiously. The *Margaret A* had more trouble than we did, but she managed to join us four hours after we dropped anchor behind an iceberg."

"The next day, August 11, we set sail again. The Captain of the *Margaret A* asked us if we really wanted to continue. When I said 'yes', the old salt just shrugged his shoulders, which could mean just about anything. We made another difficult 50 kilometres of headway, while the *Margaret A* managed only 20 kilometres. There was nothing but ice farther out, with just a thin strip of water between the icebergs and the shore, and that is where we were travelling. The danger lies in rounding the points that jut out into the sea, as they generally hide reefs that reach far out from shore. We said our Masses every morning. That ocean has never heard so many Masses! A Norwegian trapper in the Inman River area advised us not to try going any farther, because the water was shallow and there were a lot of submerged rocks. But nothing would stop us; we were determined to carry on. We did strike rocks, but with some manoeuvring we got ourselves out of them. Then, farther on, while we were anchored in a bay in the fog, the west wind came up. It was a bad position for us to be in, and we had to get out of it. Fortunately, the boat responded well to our commands and we managed seek refuge behind an iceberg. All around us there was nothing but ice, and what massive pieces of ice they were – hills, mountains – it was like being in a port."

"Since we were trapped, Billy Thrasher walked out onto the ice and killed some seals for food. On August 15, the Feast of the Assumption, there was still no change. We heard on the wireless that there was a big storm at Tuktoyaktuk that would probably head our way, reaching us in a day or two. Meanwhile, ice was piling up everywhere, being pushed by the wind and the tide from the west. From August 15 to 20, we were at a standstill in the wind and the fog. The *Margaret A* was trapped at Inman River because she didn't have enough fuel, and she asked the *St. Roch*, the RCMP boat which was in Coppermine at the time, for help. But the *St. Roch* was also trapped and had to wait like all the others, even though she was a larger, more powerful vessel. Finally, on the 20th, the wind rose from the east, gently at first, then gathering speed. The ice started heading west, so we set out on. But we were too late. The wind shifted to the northwest, becoming violent, forcing us to reverse engines again and take shelter behind an iceberg. After constantly moving from place to place, we finally took refuge in a bay, in deep water, which we didn't really like to do, because icebergs can drift in, trapping us against the cliffs. But we had no other choice. We could only hope and wait. There was no way out of our situation, but a few excursions on land served as a distraction, helped us to relax, and calmed our frayed nerves."

"August 23 seemed like it could be our lucky day – the wind dropped and Billy Thrasher reported from the crow's nest that the ice was starting to move out of the bay. We quickly weighed anchor and set off. Would we finally be able to get round that infamous Cape Bexley, which we'd seen ahead of us for several days, and beyond which we could make out a strip of clear water along the shore? In spite of urging the boat on, and running at the ice with all our might, we weren't able to get around the cape. The wind shifted again to northwest, and we had to beat a hasty retreat to our original refuge. It wasn't until the next day, the 24th, that the Cape Bexley barrier broke and we were able to get past it and make our way through the ice floes to Bernard Harbour. But we couldn't enter the harbour, because there was too much ice, so we dropped anchor about 20 kilometres away. The next morning we continued on, making headway through the drifting ice. We passed Bernard Harbour, where the *St. Roch* was trapped by the ice. The whole day was spent pushing and breaking the ice, and around 9 o'clock that evening we ran into another barrier, but this one was too much for us. After anchoring the boat in the notch of an iceberg we had to resign ourselves to yet another retreat, because the ice was starting to move and icebergs and ice floes were piling up and colliding with each other. We anchored near the shore, but had to keep watch, because the current produced a constant parade of ice and icebergs, and all that coming and going kept us on our toes. It was just a few feet away, a bit too close for comfort. On one side, there was the moving pack ice, and on the other, sharp, hard rocks. This went on all night, and there were times we were very close to a disaster. As soon as day broke we tried again, and managed to get into the shelter of a cove."

"Once again, we spent the whole day waiting for things to change. There wasn't much we could do – we were prisoners of the ice. It had followed us and blocked the entrance to the cove, but at least we were safe. While we were there, we learned that Coppermine was completely blocked by ice, and that the *St. Roch* had managed to leave Bernard Harbour to go and assist the *Margaret A*. The *St. Roch* took on all her cargo, which they would deliver to Coppermine. August 28 started out foggy and rainy. Billy Thrasher noticed an old net in the water. He pulled it in and was surprised to find a seal in it. It was pretty far along, and quite ripe, like a piece of very old Camembert cheese, but he hauled it up and threw it on the deck anyway. It would be useful for feeding to the dogs.

Coppermine, 1942. Our Lady of Lourdes is anchored offshore. (Charles Henry Douglas Clark Collection, Fisher Rare Book Collection, University of Toronto)

Then we set sail once again, starting off slowly because of a thick fog and the ice. That afternoon, the sky lifted and cleared a bit, and the pack ice also seemed to loosen a bit. We zigzagged our way through that puzzle very carefully. Around 7 o'clock that evening, we were in the Coppermine Gulf, among the islands. We were only 10 or 11 kilometres from the village, but once again, we had to be patient, as we were surrounded by ice. We made the best of it and dropped anchor in a sheltered spot behind an island. We stayed at anchor the next day and went ashore to explore the island, where we found wild berries – blueberries, black crowberries, and other plants that looked like gooseberry. We picked everything we could to add a little variety to our regular menu."

"Late that afternoon, the pack ice began to move and we set off again, but darkness and moving ice forced us to drop anchor again for the night. We left on the morning of the 30th. But new ice had formed, forcing us to stop at an island just four miles from Coppermine. Then the *St. Roch* appeared. We quickly fell in behind her, but she decided not to go any farther because of the mist and the numerous sandbars. It was another disappointment, and we even considered unloading the provisions on the island. We were able to visit while alongside the *St. Roch*, but our visit was cut short when the ice started moving and we became separated in the fog. It wasn't until the following afternoon that we finally managed to reach Coppermine, despite some mist, and drop anchor. What jubilation! Ours was the first boat to get through from the west. But there was little time to rest. We had to unload the boat, and transfer provisions destined for the Burnside mission onto another schooner that would take them there."

"On September 6 we departed from Coppermine, heading back west and trying to reach Tuktoyaktuk. We now had on board four children we were taking to the school in Aklavik. The journey had been so long that we'd run out of provisions for the return trip, so we asked Father Buliard, the missionary at Coppermine, for some beans and flour, and counted on finding some seals and polar bears on our journey back. We got off to a good start, and when we left the islands

26

around Coppermine we found the sea quite clear of pack ice, and we covered in 12 or 13 hours what had taken eight days on the way there. Around 6 o'clock in the evening we stopped behind a small island past Bernard Harbour."

"On September 7 the sea was calm. There was ice on the horizon, but it wouldn't bother us, so we continued on our way. Although the number of ice floes was increasing, we moved at a good clip. Before reaching Inman River we met up with another ice barrier, the most solid, tight, and imposing one we'd encountered so far. We tried to go round it by heading out to sea from shore, but it was endless. Even our pilot, Billy Thrasher, with his sharp eyes couldn't see any opening from the crow's nest. So after going about 25 kilometres north, we turned back. We thought it was safer to stay near the shore than to venture out into the unknown around Victoria Island or Banks Island and get caught up there. So we headed back the way we'd come, and dropped anchor for the night on a moving iceberg."

"On September 8 were on constant alert all night long and had to move twice. With daylight, we got closer to land and managed to make our way through to and into Inman River, where we delivered a dog to the Norwegian trapper who lived there. The dog probably wouldn't have been delivered if there had been a clear route at sea. We left again quickly, planning to use the same tactic as on the way there – staying close to shore and making our way between the pack ice and the coastline. But the conditions had changed in the meantime, and the wind and the current had pushed the ice onto the shore. We were able to drop anchor close to shore and held our position there all day, overnight and the following day, September 10, because we were prisoners of the pack ice. The days were quickly getting shorter, the weather was cold and calm, all the lakes were already frozen, and the ice was already thick. It would soon be winter. We had to hurry, but the weather was foggy and rainy. We weren't able to get going again until September 12, and until the 20th we sailed a grand total of only about 60 kilometres, working our way through the ice. Morale was good, but not as good as it could have been, which is understandable. And the food left a lot to be desired – beans and more beans, no fat, because there wasn't a seal or a bear in sight!! We resigned ourselves to cooking and mixing in the old seal we had hauled up in the net and kept as dog food. It was horrible!"

"On the 21st an opening appeared in the sea ice, leading to open water ahead of us. We would have to head for it, but this was easier said than done. We pushed our schooner, first in the young ice, then against the barrier in our path, attacking the pack ice head on, with two men at the helm and two on the engine. At the sound of the bell, the engine roared at full throttle and *Our Lady of Lourdes* charged forward and climbed onto the ice, her weight crushing it. We backed up and took another run at it, head on, port side, starboard side, for eight long hours, but we managed to get through to the open and clear water. The children on board jumped for joy – freedom was almost within reach now. There were only a few large icebergs that the boat wouldn't be able to break, but might be able to dislodge and move a bit, just enough to get them to float. We called on our brave vessel to make one more effort, and she pushed the pack ice, creating a channel to the open water. We sailed another 30 kilometres before anchoring behind a gigantic iceberg. The following day we got a bit further before being blocked by ice once again, but the wind started blowing from the east in the evening, so there was hope for the next day."

Blue Fox and Only Way in the sea ice between the mainland and Banks Island, circa 1937. Tom Kalinek is standing at the rear of Only Way. (Mrs. Peter Sydney Collection/Library and Archives Canada/C-38542)

"However, September 23 was a disappointing day. We managed to draw up near Pearce Point but couldn't get into the harbour, because the entrance was blocked by large masses of ice. On September 24 we noticed that two of the four lugs from our propeller were missing. This wasn't too serious and we could have made the repairs, even here, but we had no provisions left. The sailing season ended then and there for *Our Lady of Lourdes*, far from her home port and without much protection for the winter. But at least we had the satisfaction of knowing that the missions in the east got their supplies for the year."

"We had to haul the boat up on shore as best we could. We were out of food, so decided that we would travel overland to the Paulatuk mission, some 120 kilometres away, carrying our rifles, sleeping bags, pots and other equipment that we would need for the trip. However, at the end of the bay we were fortunate to meet up with the Kalineks, an Inuvialuit family from the Delta, who were also stuck there at Pearce Point with their schooner, the *Only Way*. They had some bear and caribou meat, and with no concern for themselves they gave us a lot of food, and even offered us two sleds and two young people to help us to reach Paulatuk. The mother took charge of the four children we were taking to Aklavik until we could return for them. What a big help! How could we even begin to thank them for their kindness and devotion? They didn't have much, but they were rich in human and divine value."

"Thanks to that unexpected help, we reached Paulatuk in two days. But when we arrived, there was another big disappointment. The fish that had been cached for the winter, a few thousand Arctic char, were gone. Brown bears had eaten them all, and there was nothing left, not even the smell. Luckily, there were still a few pieces of caribou meat left in the ice cellar and that, along with a few pounds of flour found at the Mission, saved our lives. The Inuvialuit around Paulatuk weren't much better off, as the bears had raided them as well. So we had to get organized and find food. We found Father L'Helgouach, who was in charge of the Mission, fishing at a lake,

Matt Berry (pilot) and Red Scharfe (radio operator) with four children from Coppermine standing in front of the airplane that had been sent to pick them up. Paulatuk, 1936. (Rex Terpening/NWT Archives/N-1987-030: 0228)

but his catch was barely enough for himself and his dogs. Some provisions had been left at Letty Harbour when the Mission and the Hudson's Bay Company post there were shut down, so Father L'Helgouach and some Inuvialuit went there and brought back a few hundred pounds of flour, beans, rice and other supplies. The rest of us spread out, some going to the lakes to fish, and others to the mountains to look for caribou. We also needed to get coal to heat the mission house from a place a day's trip away where we could dig it from the ground. We then fetched the children from Pearce Point, and also brought back the wireless set from *Our Lady of Lourdes*. As soon as we were settled in at the Mission we let the Aklavik Mission know what our situation was. Everyone was concerned for us, and Bishop Bryant had been making arrangements for an airplane to search for us on the coast. It would now be sent to Paulatuk to pick us up."

"We had to wait because of bad weather, but the airplane finally arrived on December 10. One of the first things it did was to go to Letty Harbour and pick up the remaining provisions for Fathers Griffin and Binamé, and Billy Thrasher, who would remain at Paulatuk and bring *Our Lady of Lourdes* back to Tuktoyaktuk next summer. Then, on December 19, after a ten-day wait for good weather, the four children, Brother Kraut, Father L'Helgouach and I took off by airplane for Aklavik. The first day's flying didn't last long. The wind and snow forced us to land on a lake. We had only a mouthful of food each, and we had no fire, and so with almost empty stomachs we settled down in the dark to spend a long, wakeful night. The aviators made themselves at home in the cockpit of the plane. Brother Kraut and the children spent the night in a tent set up under the fuselage, and Father L'Helgouach and I spread our sleeping bags out under the engine. We were able to resume our flight the next day, arriving at Aklavik just before we were about to run out of fuel.[7] This marked the end of a long and difficult journey."

Left: *Repairing a broken stern bearing on 'Our Lady of Lourdes', Coppermine. (Margaret Oldenberg Collection / Arctic Institute of North America)* **Right:** *Father Roger Buliard takes a turn at the helm of Our Lady of Lourdes. (Le Meur Family Collection)*

Many more stories could be told about *Our Lady of Lourdes*, about battles with storms, and delays due to weather or the sea ice. Many times it took weeks to make a trip that should have lasted only a few days. Many times the schooner would have to be turned around if the head wind was too strong, and sailed with the wind behind it, because the motor didn't have enough power. Sometimes it had to be hauled on shore to make repairs. But that gallant little vessel always came back the next season, brave and in fine fettle, its spirit unequalled. That persistence earned it a reputation that was unique in the annals of northern navigation. But for now just one more story, this time from 1947.

I was at the Paulatuk Mission. Summer was late arriving – in fact, we really hadn't had any summer by the time *Our Lady of Lourdes* arrived on August 8. I was still able to travel by dogsled, and there was ice in Paulatuk's sheltered harbor. The boat was unloaded right away. All the provisions were there, but the mail had been forgotten at Tuktoyaktuk. What a pity! We'd already been six months without mail. Would we have to wait another six months? From Paulatuk, the boat was to go to Holman Island to drop off Father Buliard.[8] He was coming back from vacation, and was quite anxious to see his Mission again and get ready for winter. We would have liked to keep the crew a few days. They were our only link with the South, and with our other colleagues, and bearers of the news. In any case, they left right away, some reluctantly, others happy to continue and anxious to get home. As for us, after we had arranged our provisions and opened a few surprise boxes, we took up our life and the collar again. We had to get ready for winter – there was coal to be mined and brought back to the house, and fish to be caught for us and our dogs. We had other things to think about besides the *Our Lady of Lourdes*. We had said, "goodbye, see you next year", and a second visit was the furthest thing from our minds.

So imagine how surprised we were to hear a motor in the distance on September 14. No doubt it was an illusion, and yet it really did sound like the *Our Lady of Lourdes*. I went to the corner of the house, a spot sheltered from the wind by our workshop, and listened. There was no doubt about it, it was the boat. This was confirmed when some children came running up and danced around me, saying, *umiaqpak* – "big boat". Sure enough, a short time later it could be seen not far from shore and coming closer. It's quite difficult to describe all the thoughts that could go through our heads at a time like that. What's happening? Is it in trouble? Is there some serious news? We understood as it arrived. The mail was on board this time, and more food and provisions. It was truly a year of plenty. I wasn't complaining, the way things were at the time – only a few fish had been caught, and the weather was bad. Anything we could get was welcome, no matter what, even the canned food we called 'canned monkey'.

All at the same time, and one after the other, they told us their story, about the truly exceptional navigating they'd done, the dangers they'd faced, and the delays they'd encountered to come here for this second trip. Here is what happened according to what Brother Josset, the ship's engineer, and Father Franche, the captain, told us:

~ Hitching a Ride ~

"After leaving Paulatuk on August 8, we travelled in light sea ice towards Pearce Point. From there we began the crossing to Holman Island. But after a few hours the wind caught us, a strong wind with snow, at least 100 km/hour. Visibility was limited, and when we tried to come back the wind was far too strong for our boat. We were surrounded by ice, but in spite of that the sea was rough and the boat was difficult to control. Nearby we spotted open water, a kind of lake. As we got closer, we saw a narrow passage just wide enough to let the *Our Lady of Lourdes* through. Once inside this small enclosed sea we kept going in circles, sailing round and round, hoping against hope that we wouldn't be trapped and crushed. Then the inevitable happened. The ice that had kept us safe for a few hours surrendered to the hurricane and started to move, closing in on us. The patch of open water was getting smaller, and our movements were being restricted. There was nothing we could do. Slowly but surely, the vise of ice and snow tightened around us. Was it going to crush us? Was it going to push us under the ice? We turned the bow of the boat to face the field of ice that presented itself to us, choosing a spot lower than the others in that uneven and hostile mass. Little by little it tightened around us. And then, as if thrust forward by a big wave, the boat was deposited on top of the pack ice. It leaned to the port side, while on the starboard side blocks of ice rose as high as the pilothouse."

"We shut the engine down," said Brother Josset, "and in the quiet of the engine room the wind could be heard howling and whistling in the ropes. The ice around us was moving and piling up around and under the boat. There we were, well and truly prisoners of the ice. In the days that followed we were one with our jailer. From August 9 to 18 we were at the mercy of the wind and the current – our fortune was tied to that of our dry dock, the pack ice on which we were resting. It's strange when you find yourself in such an abnormal situation. The blocks of ice that trapped us merged together, forming a huge iceberg with *Our Lady of Lourdes* right in the middle. Billy Thrasher distributed the lifebelts. When he handed me one", said Brother Josset, "in spite of the danger we were in, I couldn't help but laugh. 'Unfortunately there's no water around,' I said. But Billy advised me to take it anyway. 'You never know what can happen in these situations,' he said. Anything was to be expected, and nothing was impossible. Having come together in the pilothouse, the first thing we did was to say a prayer of thanksgiving because we were safe and sound on the ice, and to ask for special protection in the coming days. Never were prayers said more seriously and sincerely, and with so much devotion! But what disturbed us the most was not knowing where we were, or in which direction we were drifting. The weather had deteriorated so much that we couldn't see more than a few feet in front of us."

"We drifted like that for a week at the mercy of the wind and current, moving this way and that but mainly to the east," said Father Franche. "There was no more danger of being crushed by the pack ice, because we were perched firmly on top of it. A bit too firmly for our liking. The days went by, one after the other. We could walk around the boat out on the ice, but we had nothing much else to do but wait. As for food, we had no concerns in that regard. After all, we had all the provisions for Holman Island – fuel, canned food, ammunition. And we drew from them royally and generously, with Father Buliard's consent, given somewhat reluctantly of course. Every day we worked at freeing ourselves from the ice on which we sat, breaking the blocks of ice around the boat, especially around the propeller. We even tried blasting the ice that surrounded the boat, with powder taken from the precious cartridges intended for Holman Island. A warning – 'Look out! Dynamite!' – was given, but the result was laughable, nothing more than a fart. We can laugh about it now, but at the time, it wasn't funny. It was really serious, and how! We wanted to get free of the pack ice, and Father Buliard was counting the number of cartridges and bullets he would be without for his seal and duck hunting."

"Sometimes the waiting was hard on the nerves. When we were drifting towards islands, or towards a cape, we wondered if we would run aground in shallow water. But no, our iceberg calmly continued on its own course while we broke the ice around the boat. Once the propeller was freed and the engine started, water formed behind the boat and the hole got larger. But under the keel, there was so much ice, and it was so thick, that there seemed no end to it. All members of the crew were free to offer their ideas and opinions, but none could beat the work of axes and picks. Attempts to pull the boat into the water proved futile, even using the winch. It was almost discouraging. Still, every day we continued to loosen some of the ice, keeping our hopes up."

Navigating through the ice from the crow's nest of the schooner 'Eagle', October 1945. (L.A. Learmonth/ Hudson's Bay Company Archives/1987/363-E-393/1)

"By August 18 we had drifted more than 500 kilometres to east and were getting close to Coppermine. Billy was making his daily visit to the crow's nest, high up on the mast, when he shouted, 'Hey, there's a boat passing not very far from us'. It was the *Fort Ross*, the Hudson's Bay Company boat! As if arranged in advance, a thick, black cloud of smoke escaped from our furnace. Someone on the *Fort Ross* saw the smoke and thought it might be a signal. It immediately changed direction and came towards us, through the ice floes, and the captain called to us, 'Hey, what the hell are you doing there?' He didn't realize that we were on top of the pack ice, because beside us and in front of us there were some ponds. We replied that we were trapped by the ice. With that, he passed us a cable and began to pull us. On the first attempt, nothing happened, but on the second, we slid into the water. Apparently nothing was broken or damaged. The engine worked, and so did the propeller. So we set off behind the *Fort Ross*, a large vessel of at least 300 tons, following it to Coppermine. But what a job that was, and what a headache! It was a real nightmare for the pilot and the engineer. We had to practically stick to the *Fort Ross* like glue to take advantage of the passage it was breaking in the ice. Billy, at the top of the mast in the crow's nest, was calling out orders, 'full speed', or 'look out, half speed' when the *Fort Ross* reduced its speed if the ice was too solid. Then we had to avoid being caught by the ice it had broken and cut, ice that came out of the water and back to the surface, and that would have obstructed our path."

"Those last hours, those last kilometres to Coppermine were difficult, but still we were happy. That vessel that had pulled us from the ice had left Tuktoyaktuk two hours ahead of us, and we were almost at Coppermine before it. No one could believe our adventure on the pack ice, a unique event in northern navigation. Boats before us and since have been caught in the ice and drifted with it. But on top of the ice – no one had ever heard of or experienced such an adventure before. Captain Pedersen had actually told our bishop this could happen: 'This boat I'm selling you will never be crushed in the ice, it will climb on top of it.' He had seen things clearly, and the crew had nothing but praise for the qualities of the boat and the vision of that old sea dog Pedersen."

That wasn't the end of the season for *Our Lady of Lourdes*. It went, as planned, from Coppermine to Holman Island, dropped off Father Buliard and the provisions for the mission, then came back to Tuktoyaktuk. Since fall, if not winter, could already be felt, it didn't go all the way to the east, but came back to Paulatuk for a second trip, this time bringing our mail. But the difficulties of that year took a toll on the boat and on those who sailed it. One of the mechanics, already getting on in years, asked to be relieved, and Brother Josset alone took on the responsibility of on-board mechanic after that trip.

That summer of 1947 was etched in the memory of all those who experienced them in the North. Of all the boats that set off for the trading posts and missions in the eastern regions of our part of the Arctic, *Our Lady of Lourdes* managed to make one trip, and the Hudson's Bay Company's supply ship *Fort Ross* also made one, but others failed to reach their destinations. They were driven ashore or caught in the ice, and at Cape Parry, not far from us at Paulatuk, one of those schooners, the *Lady Richardson*, sank beneath the ice in a matter of minutes.

Eventually it came time to retire *Our Lady of Lourdes*, and after 1957 she never again set out from Tuktoyaktuk with provisions, mail and passengers for the coastal missions. Fearing that the elements and vandalism would destroy the schooner, or turn it into a hazard, I decided to do something with it, something useful and of historical value at the same time, something that could also help to enhance Tuktoyaktuk. It was perhaps presumptuous on my part to dream of renovating this boat, and it may seem sentimental, but I felt that the schooner's history made it worthwhile.

So I began talking to some friends at the Distant Early Warning (DEW) Line and the Northern Transportation Company Ltd. camps about my project, and asked for their help. First, I would have to get *Our Lady of Lourdes* up and out of the ice, and then move her to a spot near the mission house and the church. The DEW Line Station Chief promised me the help of tractors from his camp, and we set a date for a Saturday morning in April. The tractors showed up, as agreed. One pushed from behind and the other pulled on the anchor chain, which was caught in the shore ice. Another small tractor gave the boat a good shake from one side. *Mon Dieu!* I'd never seen the mast move like that – it swung from left to right, shaking under the force of the tractors. After some maneuvering, we managed to free the schooner. Once it was resting on its keel on top of the ice one tractor was enough to pull it. What a sight! It swayed back and forth from side to side on the ice, as if it were at sea. Everyone was standing on the shore watching, a bit like the old days. It was taken like that on the ice to a spot beside the Mission. A cable was then attached around the hull. One tractor pulled from the shore, while another was behind the boat, but despite all their efforts, nothing budged. Only a few yards from her resting place, the brave ship had become stuck, as if reluctant to leave that ice and that sea she knew so well, and against which she had fought so valiantly. It was the smooth ice on which one of the tractors was skating that made it very difficult to haul the schooner up onto land. So we decided to put off the operation until the following Saturday. Meanwhile, two young Scotsmen who worked for the Hudson's Bay Company came to see me, and the boat. "You gave me quite a shock," one of them said to me. "I had just got up – maybe the noise of the tractors woke me – and when I looked outside, I saw a ship on the ice and, what's more, it looked like it was sailing. We'd had a party, a good time, the night before, and I wondered if I was still feeling the effects of the alcohol. I couldn't see the tractor, so the schooner seemed to be moving on its own. 'My God!' I said and went to wake up my friend and told him to come and see, to reassure me that I wasn't hallucinating. We came outside, and since the boat had rounded the point by that time we could see the tractor towing her." Quite the story!

All week I worked at cleaning up the inside of the schooner, removing snow, ice and dirt. It was easy to get it out, because the portholes and doors were all gone. I wondered whether I wasn't trying to bite off more than I could chew. But since everyone knew about my project by then, I had no choice but to keep going and finish the renovations. The following week we had no trouble hauling her up the slope, with one of the tractors pulling on the winch and the other pushing. Today she's still in exactly the same spot we took her to that afternoon in April. We raised her using powerful jacks, then put some square timbers under the keel. I spent several hours every day clearing out and discarding all kinds of things from the boat, scraping the bottom, removing grease and mud and oil and who knows what else. Then I took the engine apart. I really had a hard time of it – those engines are indestructible. Once or twice I'd tried using a heavy sledgehammer, hoping to make the job easier, but it was like hitting a spring. The sledgehammer bounced off it. So I had to be patient and remove bolt after bolt, and piston after piston. I moved the engine parts around myself, but volunteers helped me take out the large engine block. We hoisted it up out of the boat, using pulleys attached to the mast.

In May, when the weather improved and the snow began to melt, I started fixing up the exterior of the boat. The paint had completely worn off, and the wood was showing signs of wear. Here again, another company that had always been good to me supplied me with paint. Northern Transportation Company Ltd. gave me portholes. Their workers got them ready for me, and all I

Left: *Lowering Our Lady of Lourdes.* **Right**: *Our Lady of Lourdes resting on the ground, Tuktoyaktuk, 1978. (Le Meur Family Collection)*

had to do was install them. To make a long story short, it took me until July to finish painting the interior and the exterior. Dome Petroleum prepared a foundation for her to sit on. She looked the way she used to, and really became a landmark for Tuktoyaktuk. She is a monument to be visited, and there is no shortage of visitors. Everyone wants to hear all about the *Our Lady of Lourdes*, about her adventures and how she ended up on land. I would have liked to put the boat's story down in writing, but there was no time. So here it is now. It's a fantastic but true story that we can be proud of, and that bears comparison with the story of any expedition on the Arctic sea. Especially knowing what they had to work with, it's impossible not to admire the crew – who had no professional training and were, by Navy standards, unqualified – for their work, determination and courage in sailing and plowing through the water and ice every summer but one, from 1931 until 1957, without loss of human life or cargo.

Our Lady of Lourdes may have represented a mystery to some, an intrigue. In the vastness of the Arctic, and surrounded by vessels owned by Inuvialuit trappers who used them for their work and for their life, and by other vessels owned by commercial companies, our schooner stood out, as did its crew. And as for our presence in the North, people would often say to me, "I don't understand the meaning of your life and your presence up there at all." The presence of an RCMP boat is, of course, understandable – Canada's sovereignty must be visible, and the laws obeyed by everyone. No explanations are required to understand the presence of boats operated by men from the south who have come with one ambition, to make money. And the presence of the Inuvialuit schooners, which carry them to their fishing, hunting and trapping places, is also easy to understand. But our boat? Just to bring isolated missionaries their mail and the things they need to get through another winter? It also brought them – although not every year – a visit from their leader, a very brief visit, but one that gave meaning to the life, like a signature, the recognition that we are at our post. As our Bishop Monseigneur Trocellier said during one of his visits, "I bless all your endeavours". But why spend all this energy in personnel, a personnel that is qualified, not professional, but capable, and with a depth of soul equal to any test, real men, Inuvialuit, and from all continents and countries, from France, Belgium, Germany, Poland, Canada and the United States? For one single purpose, to bring a message of peace and love, humanity and brotherhood, and a bit of the divine as well, in keeping with the order received from Pope Pius XI to go to the ends of the earth and spread the Gospel and the good news. That is why *Our Lady of Lourdes* is so popular, even now that it's on land. It's not our boat. It belongs to the people of the North, and of Tuktoyaktuk in particular. And I took the liberty of hauling it up there on shore as a souvenir of the past, a memory of the Arctic.

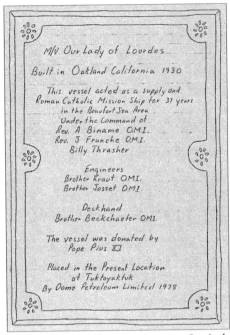

The bronze plaque that commemorates Our Lady of Lourdes, drawn by Father Le Meur.

Chapter 3 Notes

1 The Hudson's Bay Company and the Government of Canada were reluctant to support the Roman Catholic Church's coastal missions, perhaps fearing that the influence of the church would affect fur-trapping activities.

2 Pierre Fallaize, who was consecrated as Vicar Apostolic of the Mackenzie Region (essentially, an 'assistant bishop') at a ceremony held in Fort Resolution in 1931, was the Bishop who ordained Father Le Meur in France in 1943.

3 Coppermine is now known by its traditional name, Kugluktuk.

4 *Jeanne d'Arc* was a ship used by the French Navy to train sailors.

5 Father Le Meur based his version of this story on "*Memoir de S. E. Mgr. Fallaize, O.M.I. sur le voyage du 'Notre-Dame de Lourdes' dans l'Océan Arctique 1936*".

6 The Hudson's Bay Company had begun to build a post at Tuktoyaktuk in 1936 and a Roman Catholic mission was established there soon afterwards. From that time on Tuktoyaktuk was the major transshipment point for supplies for the church missions, and from 1940 on it was the home base for *Our Lady of Lourdes*.

7 Rex Terpening, a member of the air crew who rescued the party stranded at Paulatuk, tells his version of this story in his book, "Bent Props and Blow Pots".

8 Holman Island is now known by its traditional name, Ulukhaktok.

4

Hunting for Food

Winter caribou hunt. (Library and Archives Canada/E3525180)

For people in the South hunting is a sport, but for us it is a necessity. Until our schooner, the *Our Lady of Lourdes*, arrived in summer with supplies for the missions we were short of just about everything – flour, coffee, lard, the basics. Often all we had was whatever we found in the country itself. Hunting trips are no picnic. Oh yes, we enjoy it, especially if the trip is successful, but they can be full of danger and, if nothing else, very tiring. The least appealing part of the hunt is hauling the game back, especially when it is rough going because of weather or the land that we had to travel over, and the distances we had to travel.

A community caribou hunt in the high hills above Paulatuk I took part in shows some of the difficulties we often encountered. It was March, and the days were fairly long, but it was often windy in that area. Many times while setting out to travel somewhere I had turned around in a head wind, and come back to the house without reaching my goal. I knew those storms that lasted for days too well to try to brave them. This time, the wind caught us on the first night up there on one of the plateaus. There were caribou around us, but the storm hid them from our view. For three full days we wandered about in the area, always in the wind and blowing snow. Another day and we would have to go back to the house, because the food we carried for ourselves and the dogs was running low.

On the last morning of our hunting trip we set off again. Going downhill towards a lake we had a narrow escape, a near-tragedy. I was travelling beside Sam Green's team, his dogs ahead of mine by perhaps the length of a sled, no more, when suddenly his sled and the dogs just disappeared. At the last moment Sam threw himself from the sled and yelled, "Look out! Stop!" I had already

Sam and Marion Green with four of their children, Paulatuk, circa 1946. (Le Meur Family Collection)

thrown down the anchor, and my leader made a sharp turn at the edge of a crevasse in the middle of a huge snow bank that had formed on the shore of the lake. It was the first time I, or any of the others, had encountered such a phenomenon. We approached carefully and cautiously. There, at the bottom of the crevasse, was the whole team. A few of the dogs were hanging in mid-air, because the anchor had got caught on the wall of the crevasse. We had to get them out of there as quickly as possible. Attaching ropes around our sleds, we lowered Sam to the bottom of the crevasse. After bringing the dogs out one after the other, we pulled him and the sled up too, and the incident was over. But that day we were on our guard when approaching lakes.

'A future hunter' playing near a dog sled. At the bottom of the photo is a sled anchor, date unknown. (Provincial Archives of Alberta/OB 32282)

After hours of rough going and having nothing to eat or drink we headed back to Paulatuk, still without any caribou. The weather began to clear, and right away we came upon a herd of caribou, about 30 in all. It was just what we needed. There were five of us hunters, and five dog teams. The caribou were in a small valley, and we surrounded them. Only a few escaped. Two that had run off were wounded and the Inuvialuit, in spite of their fatigue, immediately chased after them. Altogether we had 27 animals. That gave us five caribou each to carry, a good load, and two for our supper and for the dogs. We wanted to feed the dogs well, as they had a hard day's work ahead of them the next day. Since we were short of fuel, we held a quick consultation. First, we emptied all the stoves and collected every drop of kerosene. This gave us enough fuel to make a little tea that evening and for the next morning. For cooking we made a fire by burning wood grub boxes in a half-barrel used for cooking dog food, first punching holes in it to provide draught. We then got down to work, cutting up the meat and preparing the load for the next morning. It was awfully cold that night. We survived by huddling together in a tent, the heat from our bodies and from bits of candles keeping us from freezing. I must say it was a tight fit, but no one complained.

In the morning we set off for home. I must admit I didn't really like the first part of the trip. We sometimes came on places with very steep slopes, and then it was hard to control the sleds, especially with a full load of meat. One after the other, we headed down these bad spots after putting a chain at the front of the sled to slow it down a bit. When my turn came I found myself at the bottom of the slope very quickly, but with my lead dog under the sled. As soon as the dog was free I moved away from the spot, and it was another team's turn. The last team also ran into trouble. The dogs were pulling a short toboggan, and the load was high and poorly balanced, not easy to maneuver. The sled began turning end over end, down to the bottom of the slope, the dogs tumbling and twisting too, the harnesses all tangled.

Later, on another lake, we saw some more caribou. A bit curious, they came towards us, noses high into the wind. We stood on the backs of our sleds and let the dogs run. It was surprising how fast those dogs galloped, in spite of pulling heavy loads. But there were more surprises to come. Once we were close to the animals we got off the sleds and started firing. The caribou took off across the lake and up the slope on the opposite side. Our dogs ran after them, pulling the heavy sleds without drivers. We weren't afraid for them, as we knew they would stop at a dead caribou. When the shooting was over we went on foot to find the dogs. Mine had stopped beside a dead animal and were hungrily tearing away at it. One of the dogs, though, was nowhere in sight. It was a dog we had received from the famous Captain Henry Larsen, the Royal Canadian Mounted Police officer who had travelled through the Northwest Passage on the *St. Roch*. This dog, Arpa, had gone right inside the caribou and was eating the intestines. I couldn't help but laugh when I brought him out. Instead of white, as he should have been, he was now red, covered in blood. As soon as he was out the other dogs started licking him and giving him a good cleaning.

We didn't waste any time. The caribou were cut open, just that operation, we would come back later to collect them, and then we continued on our way. Paulatuk wasn't very far, a one-day trip there and back. One small effort was still required to get home. Travelling a few kilometres over uneven ground, we went up, came down, skirted a small hill, crossed a lake, and there was the final descent onto the sea ice. We stopped at the bottom of the slope to catch our breath and rest. The dogs took advantage of this to eat a little snow to slake their thirst, rolled around in the snow that was softer there, shook themselves and waited, ready to set off again for the Mission house. For them, the going on the flat terrain would be easier – no more of that jolting, that abrupt tugging on the back and neck. There would be a little rest and relief for us as well – no more pushing, no more shouting at the dogs. We set off again, sitting on the loaded sleds, peaceful and relaxed. The dogs already felt at home, in a familiar landscape, and trotted happily on the ice. Soon we had arrived. There was the grotto, and the Mission buildings, some tents and a little farther along the cliff, a large cross marking the cemetery, buried under snow.[1] Smoke was visible now, rising straight up to the sky as there was no wind. The few dogs that were too old for long trips barked loudly, and the young dogs rushed to meet us. That was the signal – the women and children came

Lennie Inglangasuk's dogs and sled beside a caribou carcass, Paulatuk, date unknown. (Martha Harry Collection/Inuvialuit Social Development Program)

out of the tents and stood by the doors. "Fast, faster," we said to the dogs. Then we were on top of the slope, me near the Mission, and the others near their homes. There were handshakes and glances at the loaded sled. "How much have you got?" "How was the trip?" The questions flowed as we unhitched the dogs and the women and children led them to their usual places. After a last look back at the mountain and the hills, becoming mere shadows in the dusk, we went inside to have a good hot cup of tea and a snack, and to go over the details of the hunt – the territory covered, the number of caribou, the crevasse – everything down to the smallest detail. Then we put away the meat, and the days were forgotten.

The shrine at Paulatuk, with the statues of Mary and Saint Bernadette, 1950. (F.E. Ferrar/Inuvialuit Cultural Resource Centre)

On another trip, this time when I was using a toboggan, I still wonder how I got back in one piece. All winter the wind out of the mountains to the south had brought us hurricanes and squalls, blowing constantly, non-stop for six to nine days at a time. It had swept away everything in its path. Even our snow porches were gone; the wind had eaten into them and carried them all away. On the bay, in front of the Mission, the snow banks looked as if they had been cut with a knife, and what's more they now formed deep troughs, like waves of frozen snow. We were constantly going up and down, and it was really hard on the dogs, who were constantly being jolted by the up-and-down motion of the sleds. Going towards the hills south of Paulatuk it wasn't too difficult, since we had light loads. But after the hunt, on the way back, things were different. First, there was quite a lot of snow in the pass down to the first plateau. It was a strange kind of descent.

In that soft snow, we had the impression we were sailing on water and cutting across the waves. The snow blew in our faces and covered us, blinded us. We picked up speed and my toboggan was becoming more and more difficult to control. Eventually, about halfway down, I slid past the dogs and, after doing a complete about-face, found myself in front of my team. The dogs were slipping, being carried along by the weight of the toboggan, now facing uphill, as was I, going in reverse. What a performance! The dogs were very helpful to me, because they were grabbing at the ground and acting as a brake. We reached the bottom of the slope without incident, and with no damage – just a few harnesses to untangle and we were back under way.

We could breathe again, the hardest part of the trip was behind us now – at least that's what we thought. Alas, it was just an illusion, one that ended a few hours later as we sledded along a chain of small lakes. This route was a bit longer, but it was a level stretch and the going should be a lot easier. But we had cause to regret our decision. No sooner were we on the lake than we began a series of movements that wouldn't end until we got to the house. The wind had been hard at work in this area too, and the lake, like the sea, was nothing but a succession of north-south troughs, the result of those notoriously violent south winds that are so frequent around Paulatuk. The troughs were deep, and the bottom reached the smooth ice of the lake. As for the distance between them, they were too far apart for the sleds to reach across and slide over top of them, but too close together for comfort. There was no point in crying or moaning about the situation. I sometimes stayed at the front of my toboggan to prevent it falling into a trough, or quickly moved to the back and used my shoulder for support, to prevent it bending too much and breaking in two. What an ordeal! And this went on for several kilometres. By evening, we were worn-out. Constant effort had left us completely exhausted, and my shoulder was black and blue. The dogs had also suffered a lot, from the jolting of the harnesses loosening then suddenly tightening up again. A big, extra helping of food rewarded them in the evening. As for us, we took a philosophical view of the events. As the Inuvialuit say, "*suviittuq* – we can't do anything about it", and "*sila atanirput* – the weather is our boss". In such a land, anything is to be expected.

In the old days, when the Inuit hunted with bow and arrow, they were experts at attracting caribou. Sometimes they attached a kind of flag to a stick or to their bow and waved it, lowering and raising it to simulate a caribou's walk. Nothing was wasted. The intestines and stomach were kept, and even the stomach contents were eaten – a kind of green salad. Even caribou dung was put to use, to feed the fire. In some parts of the Arctic the muskox – like the caribou – was also a blessing, not only for the meat it supplied, but also for the skin. They are strange looking animals, their short legs barely visible below the long hair that covers their hide, and it's a mystery how they can start running and move away at a gallop. According to the elders, hunters would approach them with only bows, spears and knives for weapons. The few dogs the people had were let loose, preventing the muskox from escaping. As soon as they were skinned the meat was cut into pieces. Weather permitting, some was set out to dry, and some was cached

Inuit hunter with a bow and arrow, circa 1930s. (Jack Woods/Nunavut Archives/ N-1988-041: 0137)

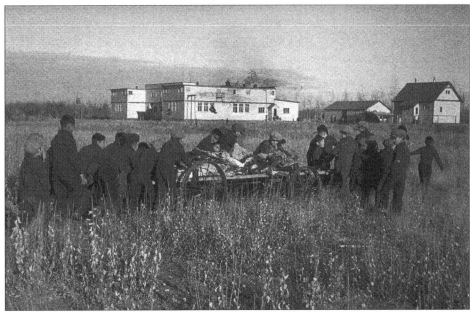

Boys pushing a cart loaded with reindeer meat toward the Anglican school, Aklavik, circa 1940s. (Mary Saich/NWT Archives/N-1990-003-116)

under rocks. As for the skins, an old man told me they sometimes were used for emergency shelters. If someone was caught in bad weather the skins were placed over willows, if there were any, or just over a hole dug into the ground.

Speaking of these journeys and camping and tents, one of my great friends was Father Binamé, a Belgian, a tough nut. He was the first priest at the Paulatuk Mission, and later was the Superior at the Aklavik Mission, where we'd had a school since 1925 as well as a hospital run by the Grey Nuns. The school and the hospital received a number of reindeer every fall from Reindeer Station, where there was a reindeer herd managed by the Department of Northern Affairs. But it wasn't enough, and the Fathers and Brothers also hunted on the mountains overlooking Aklavik. During one of those hunts, Father Binamé and his companion became separated. The weather was very bad, with wind and blowing snow, and visibility was practically nil. Father Binamé realized that he wouldn't find the camp in the storm. The only solution was to stay where he was and wait until the weather cleared up. But evening came with no improvement, still windy and blowing snow. He was starting to feel hungry, so he cut a piece of meat from a caribou carcass and ate it. He then skinned one of the largest caribou, removing the skin carefully and wrapping it around himself for the night. When he awoke during the night, he got a strange surprise. Trying to turn over and change position, he noticed that the skin was completely frozen and that it was holding him so tightly he couldn't get free. In the morning, his companion came to look for him. He'd had a bad night thinking about Father Binamé, although the Father was no greenhorn and had been in worse situations. Arriving near the caribou carcasses laid out on the ground, he heard one of them calling his name, as if one of the animals had somehow been transformed into a human being. He couldn't help but smile when the prisoner, in a pleading voice, asked him to stop laughing and help him out of that sleeping bag. This goes to show that survival tactics in the North don't change, and that even nowadays we sometimes have to adopt them.

We are told that the caribou have declined in number ever since rifles were introduced. At the risk of being contradicted, I dare say that if there were sometimes great slaughters, it wasn't very often. It's possible that instead they changed their migration routes. Some years when supposedly there weren't any caribou I saw thousands of them in March in the hills above Paulatuk, heading towards the coast. Two weeks later, when other hunters set off to kill some, they saw only a few individuals. Similarly, in the vicinity of Kuugaaluk, a few hundred kilometres from Tuktoyaktuk, there were a lot of caribou, but from high up in the air the game wardens in their planes couldn't see them. How could they when the animals were in amongst the trees? So the situation shouldn't be exaggerated.

I fully understand, having experienced it myself, the anger and the resentment that Inuvialuit feel when they are forced to comply with regulations and orders that adversely affect resources that are reportedly almost extinct, such as caribou and polar bears. Around 1951, there was even talk of limiting the number of seals that could be killed. The Inuvialuit apparently were asked to limit themselves to a certain number, and to feed their dogs fish instead of seals. They are feeling more and more constricted, as if a net was falling over them – restrictions on land, more restrictions at sea.

With the Inuvialuit, and like them, I had to fight against so much nonsense and absurdity. In high places we were taken for poachers and outlaws, people who wouldn't submit to the country's laws. From time to time, our bishop would remind us that he had been informed by the Ottawa authority that some missionaries on the coast weren't paying much attention to the hunting laws, that the land was being depleted of geese and eggs. Of course we were collecting a few, after all there were no stores around the next bend. Whatever we could gather and harvest from the land was greatly appreciated. After eating fish and more fish, meat and more meat, for so many months, with no vegetables or eggs, we weren't about to pass up other food, a bit of variety, for anything in the world. For example, if we came upon a ptarmigan or goose or gull nest, we ate our fill, then hid the rest under hundreds of fish in our icehouses, holes dug by the sweat of our brows in the frozen ground. Just try and find them then! Not because we had a guilt complex, but to show that we were no greenhorns and wouldn't be caught.

The chief game warden came to visit me a number of times when I was at Stanton. He wanted to make sure that we were doing nothing that was illegal. Making childish excuses, he went to check the icehouses, and I took malicious pleasure in seeing him go into one where we had spread out blankets of seal blubber. Going back after his visit, I found some matches that hadn't been able to burn – in our icehouses there sometimes isn't very much oxygen in summer – and it seemed that he had slipped on the blubber. Another time, having arrived by plane he wanted to visit the icehouses and even the houses of the Inuvialuit when they weren't even home. That was a bit much, and I sent him packing by asking him if he had their permission, or a search warrant.

That was the end of the first round. He came back again later, but I paid no attention to him or to what he was doing, and I had made myself a promise to cure him in the northern way. After a while, he came up to me and asked if he could have a cup of tea, he and his companions. It was summer and the weather was quite warm. I made a pot of tea and served it to them, but nothing else – no sugar, no little cakes, no bread. I was short of everything that spring anyway, and was waiting impatiently for the boat. They left by plane for Paulatuk, but after an hour or two they were back. I'd heard the plane first, and then I'd seen it make a pass over the sea. The sea was rough now; there were too many waves for a small floatplane, so it had to land on a small lake a few miles away. I continued with my work, and eventually my visitors arrived, dripping in sweat, sleeping bags on their backs. They must have had a hard time of it, because on the land around Stanton there are lots of mosquitoes.

I'd already lit the stove and made some tea. After greeting them again for the second time in one day – for an isolated place that was a record – I asked them if they were hungry. They were all famished. The walk must have whetted their appetite. Where we live, we eat fresh whenever we can. I put my canoe in the water and I picked out the biggest of the herring that were caught in my fish net. I cleaned them at the water's edge and put them, still half alive and jumping, in a frying pan greased with beluga whale oil. Cooking is really much simpler when you are short of provisions. My guests didn't seem very pleased, because it was both the appetizer and the main dish, and there was nothing else. It was all washed down with many cups of tea to remove the taste of the oil from their white man's palate.

Everyone stayed the night at the Mission house. For breakfast there was more tea, and the choice of dried or cooked fish. As they were leaving, when the game warden was saying goodbye and thanking me for my hospitality, I couldn't resist asking him if that experience had opened his eyes to the country's lifestyle and way of living. After that adventure, nothing more was said about laws or regulations or our way of living. Still, he had a sense of humour, because the next summer, during another visit, he offered me a cardboard box he'd brought with him, and in it were sandwiches, some tea and coffee, and a little sugar. Perhaps he thought there might be a forced landing, and that way he would have something other than fish to eat. I kept the contents of the box until the next day, just to be safe. Then, since no one reappeared, I did the honours, all the while having a good laugh to myself.

Chapter 4 Note

1   The Paulatuk grotto is a shrine to the Virgin Mary that commemorates visions of her by Saint Bernadette in 1858 near Lourdes, France. Mary afterwards was sometimes referred to as 'Our Lady of Lourdes' and this name was give to both the Mission ship and the church at Paulatuk.

Ilittualuk – 'He Who Knows'

(Photo credit: Mike Spurell)

We named him *Ilittualuk* – 'He who knows'. I encountered him when I was stationed at our Mission in Paulatuk. What a piece of work! What an animal! He stood 1.75 metres or more standing upright on his hind legs. Stretched out to full length, on long legs with his tail hanging in between, long neck stretched to the limit, nose to the wind, head always in motion, from right to left, forward and back, Ilittualuk was impatient to eat up the miles. Behind him he left tracks huge prints and claw marks that looked like commas, even in hard-packed snow. If all he had done was leave signs of his passing all would have been well.

Yet, not completely. The men thought about him – what a trophy! The women dreamed about him – what an *itirvik*, that band of fur surrounding the hood of their parka! An *itirvik* of wolverine fur interlined with part of a wolf's mane causes quite a lot of envy. Yes, in the end all of us, men and women, dreamed about him. But that was all we could do, the most he would allow us, a dream, a hope, a wish. He always got away from us and took malicious pleasure in outwitting us, and we wondered if he didn't also have magical powers to elude us and make fools of us. I should add, he even had a sense of humour. It was a challenge between him and us. I would really like to have actually seen and heard him – if he could have spoken – after one of his master strokes, and after he had made fools of all of us who had set traps and tried to catch him unawares! I can just imagine him relishing his victory by howling to the four winds, and even smiling smugly to himself. Unfortunately for us, we were never given the opportunity to see such a sight.

We first met Ilittualuk, or rather noted his presence, one fine fall day. Or, I should say, it was he who made his presence felt. Where was he coming from? Which way was he going? Such

Unidentified child wearing a parka with a hood trimmed with wolf and wolverine fur, Paulatuk, circa 1940s. (Le Meur Family Collection)

questions went unanswered. He was there, that was all. He had a way – his way, his own special way – of drawing attention to both his presence and his passing. We learned this at our expense. In the fall, we had set up our fishing camp among some willows that grow along the bank of the Hornaday River. This is a small river, about 200 kilometres long. Its source is a long inland lake where the Arctic char of our region spend the winter. Each spring when the ice melts the fish swim down river from the lake to the sea, and each fall they swim back up the river.

We didn't go that far up the river for our fish, which we caught mainly in winter. There are places close to the mouth of the river where the current isn't very strong that were choice places for netting fish. As soon as the ice was thick and strong enough we lost no time setting the nets under the ice, and it was always a joy to check the nets the first time. I liked to stretch out on the smooth, bare ice, to watch the fish, since the freshwater ice was transparent, like glass. Whitefish were easy to catch, but not char, which were guided by their instinct. As soon as they touched the mesh of the net they moved a bit farther along, then set out again, encountered the net again, and repeated these maneuvres over and over until they reached the end and found the way to freedom. All this was exciting to see, but a bit disappointing. We weren't there to study the fish, but to catch them. We needed a large quantity for ourselves and for our dogs. So we tried nets that were dyed blue, and the results were wonderful. The colour couldn't be seen at all in the clear water of the river.

I liked fishing in the late fall. Usually the weather was nice, not too cold yet. A little snow on the ice made the trip easier for the dogs. There by the river, close to nature, we could rest in the peace and quiet. The setting was ideal for that, with the tent in the midst of the willows and just our dogs for company – our friends in good times and bad.

That fall at the Hornaday River we had a good catch, and we were really glad, because it didn't look like the hunting would be very good. It's strange how, each year, either one or the other was good or poor – a law of the Arctic, I think. But that time there was plenty of char and whitefish. We were in a good spot, protected by the willows, and there was not too much work, just visits to the nets, and occasionally a little trip here and there to hunt willow ptarmigan. After visiting the nets I put the fish in a pile and covered them with water, which froze immediately. This protected them from the gulls and crows, and from fox and wolves. At least that's what we thought, quite naively, although it's true our Ilittualuk hadn't yet appeared on the scene.

On Sundays I went back to the Mission to take a load of fish, to say Mass and to benefit from my companion's presence.[1] We needed God, and without our Mass I wonder if we would have persevered in that land. A visit to the Mission gave us some comfort, as imperfect and poor as the house was. Come Monday morning, it was back to the fishing camp.

Checking fish nets on the Hornaday River, circa 1946. (Le Meur Family Collection)

It was on one of those Mondays, while pulling out the nets, that we became aware of the presence of an evil creature, a thief of extraordinary size, shrewdness and flair. He had already left his mark, his signature, a long yellowish trail, wolf writing, in which with a little imagination a few letters might be made out. After devouring a large quantity of fish, but not the whitefish, oh no, only the char – it seems he was an authority, a connoisseur, nothing but the best for him – anyway, after eating his fill he had sprayed the rest with urine. We were going to see many of his misdeeds after that, and always signed the same way. That day, of course, we had no idea, and we could only blame ourselves for the lack of foresight, our error in judgment, and our hurried preparations. From another point of view, we were also pleased – a wolf in the area, what a windfall! We were bound to get him before long. Some traps were bound to do the trick, and since he seemed to have a preference for char, we would offer them to him as bait. We placed a few traps here and there along the trail marked by his tracks, plus two or three around the fish cache. There again, on second thought, we separated the fish, putting the whitefish on one side and nothing but char on the other, all of them covered, of course, with a thin layer of snow sprayed with water, which turned it into quite a solid cement that was hard to break through. To add a realistic touch, there were some scattered patches of blood, and some scraps, a few heads and tails, also left lying around the traps. And all of it fresh, if you please. For this wolf, only the best would be offered.

Satisfied with these arrangements, and feeling confident, we could sleep in peace, and dream of wolf skin gloves and trim for our parkas. But the dreams that filled our heads while we slept were nothing but illusions. This just goes to show the truth of the old saying, "don't sell the bearskin before you've killed the bear". Maybe Ilittualuk had filled his belly on his first visit, and was still sleeping! Or maybe he had found other camps in the area. There were some around, some distance away, but for wolves distances don't mean much. Their only real problem is to satisfy their hunger. Whatever the reason, he didn't come near us for a few days, and when he did decide to come back he left us another message. He seemed to want to say, "Hey, who do you take me for?", all written in yellow ink. He ate all the scraps of fish, managed to make the spots of blood on the ice disappear by sucking them, and after daintily and carefully using his big claws to scrape the area around each of the traps he sprang them. Next he ate the bait, absolutely everything. Then he sprayed the traps. After this evil deed he undertook to reduce our fish cache as well, leaving us and our dogs short. We went to do a little investigating. Our tour opened our eyes and taught us about our evildoer's craftiness and cunning. I imagined him – and this is no more than a reconstruction of the crime – drawing closer to the camp, slowly – the tracks were there to prove it – his nose to the wind. Then he had made a wide detour, retraced his steps and, finally reassured, calmly and confidently trotted towards the caches, where calmly, in safety, with no risk, he had done his wicked deed. Once again, we learned that the wolf we were dealing with was no ordinary wolf.

All we could do now was come up with some new plans, make new arrangements, and act as quickly as possible if we wanted to keep our fish. Before going to bed that evening we talked it over amongst ourselves, trying to find the best solution, the best tricks or schemes to use. If only we had some poison.... Unfortunately Paulatuk was much too far from any centre for us to get some. Nothing to be done about that, so let's look at another solution – a gun, well placed, set up the same way as for polar bears on the pack ice. We made our plan and discussed everything down to the last detail. The next day, we set to work right away. Since the ice wasn't too thick yet, we used the hatchet to cut a few blocks, which we froze onto the clear ice to form a kind of wall, cementing the blocks to each other with snow and water. This new cache would also serve as protection for our fish. We put a rifle through the wall and cemented it with snow and ice. We put bait at the end of the barrel and ran a piece of iron wire from the bait to the trigger. Once we took the safety off everything was ready to go. If the wolf touched the bait, he would shoot himself in the head. To warn any people who might be passing that way, we added a small flag made of rags. That's a sign everybody knows, meaning there is danger. Before finishing the operation we were careful to put a few caribou hairs into the mouth of the barrel, to prevent snow from getting in, in case of wind and blowing snow. Before leaving we took one more look at the setup, then, feeling confident, we went back to the camp for the night, and the next day went to Paulatuk, confident and sure that this time Ilittualuk would be caught. How foolish of us! That was counting too much on our tricks and hopes, and not enough on the instinct and experience of our wolf. It was, it seemed, a challenge between him and us, a kind of chess match, where two opponents come face to face and patiently wait for the other to make a mistake.

On the trip back to the fishing camp we thought about Ilittualuk a lot. We were anxious to see the results of our efforts, so instead of going directly to the camp we made a detour to the fish cache. How can I express our feeling of defeat when we got there? The bait on the barrel of the rifle had disappeared. Just the wire was there. On the rifle itself were some yellow streaks, the frozen remains of a certain yellow liquid. Inside the ice walls of the cache, what a sight! Some fish were missing, and whatever was left – in fact, everything in the cache – had been sprayed, and this time even some excrement was added. We stood there speechless, stunned, not knowing what to say. There was no denying the evidence. Ilittualuk had made fools of us yet again. He had beaten us, outwitted us. First he had tripped the rifle, made it go off by jostling it a little, and once the shot was fired, he had calmly and peacefully finished his work. As for us, we admitted defeat. There was only one solution left: take the fish back to the Mission, load by load. Of the all wolves we met, I must say, in all honesty, that Ilittualuk was the master.

Was Ilittualuk the wolf that got caught in a trap later on? Everything seemed to point to it, although we have nothing to support this. It happened on the Hornaday River once again, at the start of winter. The people of Paulatuk had a camp up river, and I went to visit them and spent the night there. During the night the dogs woke us. They were barking and seemed very excited, but nobody jumped out of bed – after all, it meant facing a temperature of 30 to 35 degrees below zero, even inside the tent, and it was so nice in the sleeping bag. But we had cause to regret this decision the next morning. Tracks around where a trap had been set showed that it had caught a wolf, and a big one at that. He had struggled, turning and turning, over and around, tearing the trap from its anchor, and had trotted off. His tracks were there in the snow, and blood, and there were marks left by the trap clamped onto his paw.

We gave chase, but after several miles the dogs suddenly stopped. There on the snow was something black. We took a look. Was it a surprise? Not really. We could expect anything of this Ilittualuk. Tired of dragging this millstone around on his paw, he removed it himself, cutting a toe off with his fangs, leaving behind trap, chain, and a small part of himself. The tracks were very clear there on the snow, as if someone had taken a photo, and were enough to reconstruct what had happened. Even the spot where he lay down was still very fresh. But there was no wolf on the horizon, nothing. No longer shackled, he had regained his freedom, all his agility, and his confidence, and had simply vanished into the great white silence and the vast empty spaces, his kingdom.

All was quiet for the next month, no sign of Ilittualuk, no misdeeds to report, none worthy of him in any case. It was so quiet on all fronts and in all the camps that we thought he had learned his lesson and had decided to go elsewhere. We should have known better. In fact, it was only a period of calm before another match that was to be played. It took place in late November or early December, a time when it gets very cold, and when trappers have already set their trap lines and visit them regularly before January's short days and bad weather. The trappers were very active, because white fox were abundant. This was the time that Ilittualuk chose to reappear, thinking perhaps that trap lines had been prepared just for him. Ilittualuk took malicious pleasure in eating the fox caught in the traps. Skin and meat, he swallowed everything, leaving only a few skeletons here and there. Always alert, cautious and on the lookout, he also discovered the traps that were set for him – big traps, far too big for the slender foxes. He managed to uncover all these traps as well. Poor trappers, there was nothing they could do. As long as a wolf is on the lines, they have no chance of catching anything at all. The wolf must be destroyed, if possible. Once again he was the uncrowned champion of the tournament. But he grew tired of this game, and maybe of the food too – white fox all the time? The fact remains, he disappeared just as he had come. Where he went, nobody knew. But he wasn't gone for long.

Was it him again – always the watchful opportunist – who stole a large part of our meat, up there on the mountain? In any case, we put the blame on him, and his reputation only grew as a result. On our fall hunt in the high hills behind Paulatuk we had killed about 15 caribou. Luck had been with us, as there weren't many caribou around. There were wolf tracks everywhere, and the poor animals had absolutely no opportunity to eat or rest with the pack of wolves after them, and so they had left the area. Only a few individuals remained, perhaps lost or bewildered. Whatever the reason, they were of great service to us, because elsewhere the country, although vast, was empty of game. But 15 caribou was too much for two dog teams to take back in a single trip. After cutting them into pieces and setting aside a good portion for our load, we now had to make a cache. But where? There was a little snow, but a snow house didn't seem adequate as protection. We could haul the load down to a lake, cut the thick ice and build an icehouse, but it was a long distance to travel to the lake.

As we thought this over and looked all around, a ravine in the hill on which we were standing brought us back to reality. What on earth were we thinking? This ravine indicated the presence of a stream that ran in the spring, when the snow melts. We should be able to find some boulders there. We dug into the dry, frozen streambed and removed enough rocks to build a cache. What a job! Everything was frozen, and we had to hit the boulders with the back of the axe to loosen them before taking them out. When the hole was deep enough, we put the meat into it, and then we began covering it with rocks. On top we put a very large, heavy rock that two of us had trouble moving. It would serve as a trap. If some animal managed to penetrate the cache – something we couldn't imagine – the rock would fall on it and crush it. When we had finished the cache looked like a small fort.

A few months went by, two months, I think. We were short of meat, and so headed up the mountain to get some from the cache. Fortunately, we knew exactly where it was, because in this whole snowfield our little cache was buried under the snow, and the snow was hard. With shovel and snow knife we began digging, and soon we struck rocks. This was the place. But then, dumbfounded, we saw the large stone on the ground beside the cache. Only a wolf or wolverine could have got into this cache, and then only by a tremendous effort, by creeping into the streambed, shoving aside the rocks, and digging out the snow. A wolverine had in fact been the first to take the risk, and paid for this with its life. The slab of rock crushed it – we found only a piece of the animal's tail to confirm what had happened – and then Mr. Ilittualuk, probably, had arrived on the scene. Everything was ready for the second act. The second visitor had eaten the wolverine, dug through a little snow, and gone under the rock into the cache. He had even settled in there, sheltered from the wind and the cold. In a corner, we saw the place where he had lain down. But what a situation awaited us in the cache! The little meat that remained was completely spoiled and covered in animal waste, both liquid and solid – our friend Ilittualuk's usual signature. What can anyone do in a case like that? Where we live, we're philosophical. We simply waited until the caribou came back in spring. Still, this return match was a bitter pill to swallow.

The next fall it was our turn to strike, and to get some satisfaction in our battle with the wolf. What revenge did I take? Inhumane to some perhaps, revolting or offensive to others, I ate wolf meat, in this case a wolf cub, hoping that it was one of Ilittualuk's young. As we approached the fishing camp on the Hornaday River one time our dogs started to gallop, forcing me to hold on tightly to the sled to avoid being thrown off, and there, through the willows, I could see an animal caught in a trap. A young wolf, already quite a good size, probably about four to five months old, was there, motionless, crouched on the ground, on the snow, trembling. Taking a closer look, we noticed a trail in the still-soft snow, the tracks probably of a female wolf that had brought the young wolf a ptarmigan to eat – the feathers lying around were evidence of this. What would we do with it? Keep it and domesticate it? No, it was already too big for that, and besides, the dogs wouldn't adopt it. It growled and bared its teeth when we approached. There was only one answer – it had to be killed. My companion shot it with the rifle. It had a beautiful pelt, soft and smooth.

That evening, after visiting the nets and having only fish to eat, we talked about meat. Yes, why not make a wolf soup or stew? After all, it was young and ate only good things, even ptarmigan, as the area around the trap showed. No sooner said than done, we cut off a piece of the back and into the pot it went – with no vegetables of course, we used a little rice instead – and when it was cooked, we ate some. Delicious. With a little imagination I had the impression of eating lamb or mutton. Sweet revenge, although not without a touch of sentiment.

I'm not the only one to have eaten wolf. A good old Brother who spent 50 years in the Great North on the shore of the large lakes south of us had also served it for dinner. A female wolf had been trapped by one of the Brothers in the area around their fishing camp, and they had brought the skin and the carcass back to the Mission. The skin was stretched and left out in the wind and sun to dry. As for the carcass, it had been laid out on a shed roof. Back at camp in the evening, tired and famished after lifting nets all day, the Brothers sat down at the table and were served a stew. What a change, after eating fish every noon and evening! The caribou were still absent and the moose were keeping well hidden. No meat, not even ptarmigan. They all appreciated this change in their diet, and they congratulated the good old Brother who was doing the cooking. No one had even thought of asking where the meat came from, or what it was. Fatigue and hunger probably slowed their ability to think. It wasn't until the next day at noon, as they were eating their frugal lunch – fish again – on the shore of the lake, that one of them said to the others, "Hey! Where on earth did he get his meat? Nobody's killed anything yet, or caught anything, or we'd have known about it. The good Brother must be laughing up his sleeve. He probably served us wolf, without us noticing." When they got back in the evening, the fishermen looked up at the roof, nothing in sight, no sign of the carcass. To make sure, they went into the shed and there, under the roof, where, in fall, the meat – when there was any – was kept, they found pieces of the wolf, all cut up and neatly laid out. At supper, after the first mouthfuls, one of the Brothers called the cook over and asked him what meat he was serving. "Um, um, um... is it good?" "Yes, but we want to know who gave you this meat." Finally, after much hemming and hawing, the Brother admitted that it was too tempting to look at that carcass and that meat all covered in fat, which was going to dry out in the cold and was going to spoil – a crime in this country, he said.

And then there was that wolf that Sam Green, a friend and a fellow hunter, missed because he wanted to shoot it in the head so as not to spoil the fur. This happened during a trip, one of the hardest I was ever on. The two of us left from Paulatuk in late October to hunt caribou. The weather was quite good, but the ground had just a very thin covering of snow here and there. We'd been hoping for snow and had delayed the trip, but it was already late fall, and if we wanted to have meat for the winter we had to move quickly. Because the traveling was hard with so little snow we had decided to take just one team

Father Le Meur travelling by dog team over ground that is barely covered with snow, Paulatuk area, circa 1946. (Le Meur Family Collection)

with our best dogs, the strongest ones. We were hoping that up there on the mountain there would be more snow, and that it would be thicker than along the seashore and in the valley. We reached the summit after three long days of walking, hard work and constant effort, helping the dogs, pushing the sled. But what a disappointment when we looked around us! It seemed as if all the caribou had already left the country. Although there were caribou tracks everywhere, they weren't very fresh. Our caribou had vanished. There was no doubt in our minds, the annual migration of the caribou to the south had already taken place. There appeared to be no stragglers. The many wolf tracks around and in the midst of the caribou tracks told us that the herd had taken off at top speed, driven by the wolves. Wolves give the poor animals no rest, and their pursuit is so well organized. Some give chase while the others rest, following but not pushing, and from time to time they change places. All the caribou that slow down from fatigue and find themselves cut off from the herd are instantly killed and devoured.

Still, we hoped to find a few animals. We went a bit farther on the sled, and our efforts were rewarded. In a small valley we came on four or five caribou in a group, huddled together. It was a stroke of luck for us. In an instant it was all over, the killing, the cutting up of the meat. With our dog team we brought the meat back near the tent. Taking only enough time to drink a cup of tea and swallow a piece of bannock, my companion set off, rifle over his shoulder. He wanted, he told me, to lie in ambush over there, in amongst the rocks, on the opposite hill. Some fresh wolf tracks gave him hope that he might see one. Their taste for fresh blood and fresh intestines should bring them out of their hiding place. I didn't have any objection to that. I still had to finish preparing the meat and choose a few pieces that we would take back right away – not a lot, because the trail was still very bad as no fresh snow had fallen. Once again, we had to resort to leaving some meat in a cache, which we weren't very happy about, because we knew that wolves and other animals were going to be coming into the area. But it would only be for a few days. As soon as there was more snow, we would make another trip to take back the rest of the meat.

I watched Sam until he disappeared behind the hill before getting down to work. Some time later I heard two or three gunshots, and the dogs began pulling on their chains and barking furiously. Then there was silence, and I saw Sam coming back, quietly. Once back at the tent, still not speaking, he raised both arms in a gesture of despair and shook his head, a little smile on his lips. As he put his rifle down at the entrance to the tent, he said, "What an idiot I am. He was right there, close by, in my sights. No doubt about it, a child could have had him easily. The wolf was sleeping after a big meal, and seeing him so close I told myself I should kill him cleanly and not spoil the fur. I wanted a square shot to the head. I whistled to make him lift up his head, and the animal took just one leap, as if he were released like a spring, already in full flight and immediately hidden by the big rocks. I fired once or twice to make him go onto the plain, but he didn't appear. And now he's on the run." All the way back to Paulatuk his thoughts returned to that wolf and how stupid he had been, and he an experienced hunter too.

Chapter 5 Note

1   Among Father Le Meur's 'companions' – other members of the clergy – who were with him at Paulatuk were Brothers Kraut and Tesnières and Father Maurice Metayer.

6

The Man Who Became a Caribou

*Sam Green (**left**) and Father Robert Le Meur, Paulatuk, circa 1946. (Le Meur Family Collection)*

The trip back to Paulatuk was no picnic. The lack of snow, even at higher elevations, made things very difficult for us. Taking turns, one of us walked ahead of the dogs to encourage them while the other pushed the sled from behind whenever our team ran into problems. How we sweated, especially in the valley! In spite of the cold, we took off our parkas and walked in our shirtsleeves the whole afternoon. At each lake and stream we crossed, the first thing we did was break the ice in front of each dog, to give them a chance to drink. Then we knelt on the ice and drank the icy water to quench our thirst too. We wanted to reach a camp on the Hornaday River that evening, and we pushed our dogs and spared no effort ourselves the whole day. When arrived on the shore opposite the camp we fired the rifle into the air to attract the attention of the people on the other side, as we didn't know the condition of the ice. A few minutes later a young man came to us and showed us a way across. But the news was bad – no caribou. And Sam related the story of his misadventure again, in detail – no wolf either. Meanwhile, the women were busy cooking a piece of caribou. Sam and I drank cup after cup of tea. It seemed we were completely dehydrated, and I was almost ashamed to keep drinking and drinking. It wasn't a very late night, since we were exhausted, dead on our feet. My hosts suggested I stay with them, in their tent, but I preferred to put up my tent and sleep alone. I couldn't quench my thirst, and I knew that during the night I was going to want some more to drink, which would have disturbed my hosts. I got my tent organized, and before going to bed I went out onto the river and got a few pieces of ice. It was the right decision – all night long, I was drinking hot tea, which I made on my oil stove.

The next morning, as I continued on my trip back to the Mission, I narrowly missed going through the ice. It was the first time that had happened to me. After reaching the shore of the bay that sits between Paulatuk and the valley of the Hornaday River I set out confidently onto the ice. After all, I'd been gone almost a week, and when I'd left the bay was already starting to freeze over. Once we were some distance from shore I stopped my team and checked the thickness of the ice, hatchet in hand. Everything seemed okay, so I let the dogs have their head. They made the trip along the bay often, and knew the way to the Mission house. I settled in on the sled, sitting sideways, with my legs hanging over the edge. The dogs were running well and didn't need any encouragement. But my dozing came to an abrupt end. Something didn't seem right. I had an uneasy feeling, a sense of foreboding. Instinctively, the first thing we do here in the North when we get that feeling is look all around us, and that's what I did, to the right, to the left, in front. The ice on which we were travelling was dark, and when I turned around I understood why. A kind of wake, full of ice, was spreading out behind me. There was no doubt – I was cutting the ice as I went. I was facing a dilemma, and had to act immediately. I tried to find out how the ice was underfoot by stamping my heel. The ice broke right away. I had to go to the left, towards shore, so I started shouting at my leader and at all the dogs – "*dja! dja!* go left! go left". The more I shouted the faster they went, which was all I was asking of them. If even one of the dogs stopped, it was game over, and I would certainly fall through the ice. I had a few anxious moments, but not for long, because the dogs also realized that they were in danger. They turned their heads from time to time to look back at me, but changed direction and dashed for the shore. I breathed more easily.

Once we got to shore we had to climb a slope, and that was no small task. But it was also a pleasure, because it was *terra firma*, and solid ground was certainly welcome. We still had about five kilometres to go, but that was nothing now. The dogs had caught the scent of the house and pulled as hard as they could. Within minutes, they would be able to rest and would be with their companions again. When I arrived I was told that the water in the bay had frozen just one or two days before. The people from the river, who arrived at Paulatuk after me, had a few bad moments when they saw the tracks of my sled, and the trail of open water left by the runners. They thought I had gone through the ice.

It was during another trip on the Hornaday River that I learned about beliefs that the people of the Great North have about the reincarnation of souls, the spirits of the dead who live again in others in either animals or humans, that they passed on from one to the other. That Fall the weather had been awful, with one storm after another. It wasn't unexpected, because the only summer we'd had was the one marked on the calendar. The ice was still on the bay beyond the spit that protected our harbour, and pieces of ice had been driven ashore in front of the Mission. In one way this was a windfall. We put the pieces of ice on wooden boards, leaving them in the sun or in the open air, and when they were full of holes – we call that candle ice – it was pure and fresh, and good for drinking since the warmth flushed the salt from the ice.

The ice didn't make it any easier to get around by boat, and at least once I got trapped on my way to the coalmine. I knew it was a risky trip, because the northwest wind was quite strong, but I thought I would be able to thread my way through the sandbars in the bay and the ice that still drifted around. There was at least one advantage – there weren't many mosquitoes that summer. And so I made up my mind to go. With the weather the way it was I could always pick away at the

Waiting out a storm, Paulatuk area, circa 1946. (Le Meur Family Collection)

coal and get a few dozen bags. But when I reached the first sandbar I was forced to stop. There was too much wind, and the ice was obstructing the channel entrance. There being no way out, I decided to stay there and wait. I secured the boat to the sandbank, set up the tent, and settled in as best I could. The wind didn't drop. On the contrary, it picked up, going from bad to worse, and the pieces of ice beyond the bay ground against each other and piled up. I wasn't the least bit worried, because in front of the sandbank where I had pitched my tent the water wasn't very deep, and there was no danger of the ice reaching me. But I could hear the wind, and the grinding and breaking of the ice, an infernal racket, a great unending gnashing of teeth. It was an assault that nothing could stop, kilometres of heavy ice driven by the wind and the current. The ice accumulated behind my tent, forming a barrier.

The weather is our master. 'Suviittuq', as the Inuvialuit say, 'it can't be helped' – a kind of fatalism that seems to be the rule in the North. Since I'd had a good meal before leaving the Mission, and as I wanted to save the small amount of fuel I had for my stove, I spread out my caribou skins, laid out my sleeping bag on top, and went to bed. What woke me up? I don't know. Maybe the wind dropped a bit. Maybe it was hunger or thirst. Anyhow, I made a cup of tea and began to attack a piece of bread and some cooked meat that I'd brought from the Mission. But what a surprise! Both the meat and the bread were full of sand. It was like a file attacking my teeth. In spite of my hunger, I had to stop eating. Even in the Arctic, we have sandstorms. We just can't win! There was only one thing to do – wait. Patience is one of the first qualities any true Northerner must have if he wants to survive and stay among us.

I was starting to get bored in the tent. The wind was dropping a bit and the sand had stopped blowing, so I ventured outside. As far as my eyes could see, there was nothing but ice. Two small barrels of fuel that I'd put near the tent, and to which I'd attached the tent ropes, had no paint left on them. They were both shining as if they were made of silver. This was the work of the sand, which, like a file, had scraped and rubbed and polished the surface for hours. As I walked and meditated I discovered some nests of terns, sea swallows, small birds that emit shrill cries and fly endlessly in groups above the water. There were eggs in some of the nests, and without giving it any thought, I went to collect some. At least there wouldn't be any sand in them – a good breakfast! But I wasn't expecting an attack. A wave of angry terns swooped over and chased me off, coming within a few inches of me, screaming their heads off, beaks wide open. I had to protect myself with my arms and retreat to the tent.

A few hours later I took to the water again and headed for the coalmine, through the maze of sandbanks. But the wind continued, and at the mine I didn't dare put the nets in the water since the ice was continually in motion. Often, from the top of the cliff, I witnessed apocalyptic scenes. For as far as I could see, the white mass would start to move, gently at first, then would seem to pick up speed, and would come crashing to shore at the foot of the cliff.

After working a couple of weeks over there alone, and having filled a few dozen bags with coal, I returned to Paulatuk and then went to the river to do a little fishing. There weren't many fish, and as there wasn't enough ice to bother us, I left the nets and went back to the Mission. The weather turned cold very quickly, and the freeze-up surprised us. That complicated things. I couldn't leave the nets in the ice, but the ice would have to be quite strong before I could pull them out. There was no question of taking the dogs yet, because although the ground was already frozen, there was no snow. The only thing we could do was go to the river on foot. Taking only our rifles, Sam Green and I left for the river, about a three-hour walk over uneven terrain full of tussocks. I had left my tent there, and if necessary we could spend the night. We had to break the ice along the whole length of my three nets, so as not to spoil them, and then we spread them out on the willows to let them dry in the wind. We would repair the holes later, another day. Since the weather wasn't too bad, we decided to go back to Paulatuk the same evening.

On the way back we heard wolves on a hill nearby, howling. As if driven by the wind, we climbed at full speed, forgetting our fatigue. In an instant, we were at the top, and in front of us was a pack of wolves, a large male and five or six cubs. We had surprised them while they were hunting willow ptarmigan. Flat on our stomachs, side by side, Sam and I watched, rifles loaded and ready. The large wolf chased the young ones away before we had time to shoot. The cubs didn't have to be told twice. They disappeared through some small willows, which were plentiful in that area, and the wolf started coming towards us, step by step, in no hurry, staring straight at us with his big eyes. Another few steps and we would shoot. Suddenly he stopped, turned his head sideways to the right, and howled, or perhaps it wasn't really a howl, more a kind of call or moan. And from the other side of the slope came a soft reply, repeated two or three times. The female wolf had just replied that she had understood the message. The male captivated us with his imposing appearance, his size, his *sang-froid* – he was not inhibited at all now that he had warned his mate and the cubs were no longer visible. He had made sure of that by turning his head, with his body still turned towards us. It seemed as if he wanted to intimidate us with his boldness and arrogance. If his eyes didn't leave us, our eyes didn't leave him either, staying fixed on his, as though hypnotized.

A lot of thoughts were going around in our heads at that point. What was he going to do? He kept on coming towards us, slowly, very slowly, lifting one paw after the other and putting it down smoothly, as if to avoid making any noise or leaving any mark on the hard, frozen ground. We waited tensely, not moving a muscle, stretched out on the ground, rifle at the ready, finger on the trigger, right elbow firmly supported by the ground. All of this in silence, a silence that was starting to weigh on us a bit. Without looking at me, Sam whispered under his breath, "Let's wait a bit longer. I'll shoot when he's really close to us. We'll just shoot together if he jumps aside to get away." Perhaps the wolf also had his own plan. He kept advancing quietly, but his lips curled back a bit now, revealing his teeth, real fangs. Another few steps and he was about 10 metres away at most. Boom! Sam shot at his head and the animal fell, struck down and killed instantly. We approached him cautiously and with rifles in hand. You never know what can happen. Yes, the wolf was indeed dead, his tongue hanging loosely between the fangs. We went to look for the other wolves, but saw nothing, just a few fresh tracks. From far off, we heard what sounded like the wailing, sobbing and moaning of the female.

After removing the skin of the wolf we had shot, I was getting ready to leave the place when Sam said, "Hold on, you haven't finished the job." I didn't understand, so he told me that I had to cut off the head too, and not leave the carcass whole. "We Inuvialuit," he said, "always sever the head from the body. Otherwise, the animal's *anirnirk*, – its 'spirit', suffers and can't get free or enter another body." So I picked up my hunting knife again and finished the job as he'd asked me to. This intrigued me, and I wanted to know more about it. We were rested, and the wolf skin had boosted our morale and renewed our strength. We still had two hours to walk, and as we proceeded in the darkness, to break the monotony and the silence, Sam told me this story:

~ *Amirana* ~

"A long time ago, a very long time ago, our old ones were much closer to nature and the animals than we are today. It was said that some could even become an animal or a person at will. There was a man named Amirana, who was often laughed at by his fellow countrymen because he was small, although he was a good hunter. Finally, since they were making fun of him, and perhaps also from spite, he went off to hunt caribou, leaving behind his wife and two boys. He didn't have a clear idea of what he was going to do, but he wasn't going to stay there in the camp any more to be laughed at by the others, who weren't better than him, or even his equal at hunting. While walking he did some thinking, and his head was filled with all kinds of ideas and dreams."

"Suddenly, finding some caribou tracks in front of him, an idea took shape in his mind. All he had to do now was carry it out, although this was easier said than done. He followed the tracks, and walked and walked for quite a while, over hill and dale, always watchful, observing the country, until he saw the caribou far away on the plain. He paused to get his thoughts clear and make his plan. Leaving his bow and arrows there as a sign of peace and to avoid scaring the animals away, he set off again, walking into the wind so that the caribou wouldn't detect his presence. It was a long way, but he was in no hurry and used the time to think over what he was planning to do. After all, a change of life takes careful thought, but he stuck with his decision. He'd had enough of human beings; he wanted to try something else."

"Having come very close to the caribou, but still reluctant to show himself, Amirana waited a moment. The time had come; there was no turning back now. In the midst of the willows, he slowly stood up and, very slowly and with no sudden movements, walked forward, hands open, as if to say that he wasn't coming as an enemy, but as a friend. The effort was wasted. All the caribou ran away, heads held high, galloping to put distance between themselves and Amirana.

He stayed there, rooted to the spot and confused, looking straight ahead, making no noise, saying nothing. What else could he do? In the herd he had noticed a young bull, larger than the others, standing head and shoulders above them all. Huge antlers decorated his forehead. They were as long and large as the willows of the tundra, and they were covered in a skin like velvet. He had taken the lead, and the rest of the herd followed. He looked around from time to time, stopped and stood erect, neck outstretched, sniffing the wind, even seeming to listen. Then, letting the others continue their racing and galloping, he came back calmly, and then ran off again, satisfied with the situation."

"Amirana kept walking towards the herd, not hurrying. They disappeared behind a hill, and were probably heading for the next valley. But not all of them. When Amirana reached the hilltop he saw a single caribou, the largest, the leader. There was no mistaking him. He was standing there upright, neck fully extended, head tilted back, legs slightly spread – a sentry position. Perhaps uneasy, certainly on the lookout, he was standing guard, watching Amirana's every movement. He waited, as if he, too, had made his decision, and since Amirana was still approaching, without hurrying, without any sign of hostility, he seemed to relax. When he drew close to the caribou Amirana stopped and stayed still, fixed his eyes on the caribou, and waited in silence. Their eyes met and they sized each other up, the one an imposing animal, strong, vital, powerful, and the other a man, small and thin."

"The caribou leader asked Amirana why he was following them and what he wanted. Amirana explained that he had chosen to become a caribou because, he said, the caribou is gentle and the most useful animal to men. The conversation continued. Amirana's story called for explanations, and the caribou, the leader, wanted to be sure that there was fair play, no ambushes or trickery. He knew men, he said. He assured Amirana that he believed him and that he was sympathetic to his cause, but said he wasn't the only judge. Before making his decision, he would have to consult his companions. Together, they would make a decision. Before leaving to find the other animals, he reminded Amirana that life as a caribou wasn't always easy. There were many enemies, especially men, and wolves kept them on the move. But Amirana was more and more determined to carry out his plan. The caribou chief then went away and consulted with his companions, and came back a few minutes later to give his answer. They all understood Amirana's situation and wanted to help him. They accepted him as one of them. He should follow behind the leader, and in an instant he would be changed into a caribou too."

"And so it was that Amirana became a caribou. But he didn't feel comfortable in his new state. It was as if his clothes were too small, too tight against his body. In particular, his head seemed heavy and drawn downwards. But he tried bravely to walk and to run, at first very awkwardly, then a bit more comfortably. Since he himself had hunted, many times, he knew caribou behaviour and habits in detail – at least the external, visible ones – but now it would have to come to him instinctively. So he observed the chief of the caribou that had accepted him, and who looked after him. The chief explained how he could find food, lichen, from the tundra and on rocks, but to Amirana it seemed very bland and tasteless. From the chief he also learned how to dig through snow by striking it with his hooves, and what prayers, *irrinat*, to say to the spirit. These prayers had the ability and the power to change the taste of food and to satisfy the animals' hunger."

"What bothered Amirana more, and made him feel humiliated, was that he was always bringing up the rear, trailing far behind his new companions. He tried hard to take longer strides, but it seemed to him that despite all his efforts he wasn't going much faster. It wasn't just a question of pride, but also one of survival. What would happen to him if he found himself behind the herd? He knew very well that he wouldn't be able to escape on his own, and would fall prey to men and wolves. Men would shoot their arrows at him, and wolves would tear him to pieces while he was still alive. Amirana had been to the school of patience, which taught him how to bear cold, hunter, fatigue, danger – everything. He knew that the leader would instruct him and advise him at the right time. He didn't have to wait very long. The herd was going to be travelling quite a distance, and in a land that was unfamiliar to Amirana. The chief asked him how he was doing as a caribou, and whether he was having problems. Amirana told him about his attempts at running and galloping, and he received this response: 'We caribou, we have our protectors way up in the sky, and if you want to be agile and gallop like us you'll have to adopt our method, which you know from observing us. See, you have to lift your head and look up, at a small star, our star, then you'll feel like you have wings that will help you gallop lightly and without feeling the weight of your head.' In the days that followed, Amirana used this method, and he was able to follow the others."

"How long did he stay among his new friends? He couldn't say. Time isn't measured the same way among animals. From time to time, he wondered whether he had taken the right action, done the right thing. Often when travelling on the tundra he thought about his children and his wife back there at the camp. Was it dreaming like that while walking that was his undoing? The first thing he knew, one of his legs was caught in a snare. He didn't try to free himself. He was receiving the answer to his questions, his constant tormented thoughts. He wasn't happy being a caribou; he didn't feel free. Now all he could do was wait for the hunters to come, and hope that they would listen to him. He felt very tired and weary, but his whole being, his spirit, advised him to stay awake, so as not to be taken by surprise. He stayed standing, watching the horizon and tensely waiting. In the distance, he saw two boys approaching, slowly and quietly. With his big, sad eyes, he saw them stop, gesture, point in his direction, and start running. He knew it well, that feeling, that emotion, that joyful glow the hunter feels at the sight of caribou. As they got closer he could see that they were still just children. He could tell by their clothes that they were *Iliapaaluit*, poor little boys, orphans, their clothes in tatters. In his mind he understood that they needed this caribou that he was – the meat, some fat, the skin and sinews. All these feelings were racing madly around in his head, as fast as, or even faster than, the two boys were running and racing towards him."

"The way the boys ran seemed familiar to Amirana, and now their ways and their speech too. No doubt about it, the *nukatpiraaluit*, the two young boys, were his children, Iputik and Kappun. There, just a few metres away, they stared at him, motionless, silent, amazed to find something in their snare. It was as if they realized that everything they'd heard at evening gatherings about the fate of the *Iliappaaluit* – poor orphans of our folklore – was really true.[1] Their feelings – surprise and joy – were obvious on their faces and in their posture. They realized that the caribou there in front of them wasn't moving, that it wasn't arguing, that it seemed unwilling to fight or defend itself. The two boys had also heard about that many times, that animals sometimes let themselves be caught to save men. As for Amirana, he wasn't worried about his safety any more, only about his spirit. For him, it was the end of a mad adventure."

"The elder of the two boys took his hunting knife in hand and, very cautiously, step by step, approached the victim. Just a few steps away, keeping a close watch on the caribou, sure that it couldn't reach him yet, because the snare was very short, he stopped, breathed heavily, even trembled a little. No doubt, Amirana thought, it was his first caribou he was about to kill. And at that precise moment, Amirana reacted and began speaking to him. 'Iputik, my boy – it's me, Amirana, your father, who's speaking to you. Don't be afraid.' On hearing the caribou talk to him, the boy, afraid, let the knife drop. Amirana said, 'I recognized you by your voice first, and then by the bow you were holding. Call your brother now, so I can give you both the instructions you have to follow to free me from this caribou body so that I can become a man again. I can see you still need me. You are too poor and wretched.' As soon as the younger boy arrived, he, Amirana, told them to skin him alive without killing him, being very careful not to spoil the skin, and then to neatly open up the belly without touching any part of the intestines or anything else. He would then be able to come out. The two children obediently set to work, carefully following the instructions Amirana had given them. They were nervous and frightened, but they put all their heart, courage and skill into the operation, and when it was done, they took a few steps back. They waited with some impatience for Amirana, their father, to come out of the animal's bowels. When they all met again, it wasn't too emotional – emotions are felt inside, but they aren't often expressed outwardly. Amirana learned that his wife had died, and listened to the news about everyone and everything, and then he and his children headed to the camp. No one made fun of him. It was as if the word had gone round, and he lived for many more years among his people."

Sam made a brief comment at the end of this story, adding: "I wonder which human or animal Amirana is in now, today." I have found this belief in reincarnation, in spirits that inhabit the living in old stories and even in current thought. In any case, that's why my friend and companion asked me not to leave the carcass whole. I, too, wonder which animal the spirit of that wolf is in now.

The Mission schooner Roger, Paulatuk area, circa 1949. (Le Meur Family Collection)

During my travels on land I came upon many places where the Inuit of old hunted caribou. One is quite familiar to me and firmly fixed in my memory, probably because of the circumstances in which I became acquainted with it. These memories go back to the fall of 1949, I think in September. We wanted to go to Cape Parry, to try out a seal net we'd received from the Mission at Stanton. So Johnny Ruben and I set off on board our little schooner, christened *Roger* because it was Roger Buliard who had got it for us.[2] Oh, it was no pleasure boat, but it was very useful to us at Paulatuk. First it had to be repainted, sealed and tarred, because it was leaky. Then we installed an engine. A benefactor had bought us an air-cooled engine, which really was too small for our schooner. But still, it helped us fetch the coal we dug at the coalmine. The next year a Brother, who was quite a good mechanic, replaced that engine with one that was more powerful. It wasn't an easy job. He had to make a base-plate, mount the engine, and align the shaft and the propeller. We were able to go faster, but what headaches this engine also gave us – a lot of breakdowns, lost time, and constant repairs on almost every trip. Many times we had to rely on the sail to bring us home. When that happened we had to dismantle the engine and repair the damage, which often meant rebuilding bearings. This required melting some metal to remodel and remake them exactly like the bearings that were broken. It took hours and hours to file them and then make the grooves that allow the oil to circulate.

This time everything was in order, both boat and engine, so Johnny and I set off for Cape Parry. The weather was fine, a bit cold maybe, but after all, it was mid-September, and that was to be expected. We camped the first night in a small bay, sheltered from the wind. On arriving we shot two ducks for our supper. The next day, in spite of a little wind, we set sail for Letty Harbour. But along the way, the wind picked up, an east wind, and there was a very heavy swell. Soon we weren't making headway and had to take shelter behind the entrance of a cove, and anchor the schooner. It immediately turned to face the wind and began a continuous pitching. We were protected from the heavy swell, but still we felt the effects of the breakers and the wind. After having something to eat Johnny went to bed and I tried, in vain, to read my Breviary by the light of a pressure lamp. It gave me a strange feeling to see the lines in the Breviary jumping around, the words moving up and down. It was a waste of effort, so I stopped, and laid down for a moment. Then, tired of the rolling and pitching, we decided to go ashore in the dory. Our smaller boat wasn't a lifeboat. It was a square box, with just enough room for the two of us, and that was it. As a precaution, and to make sure we could get back on to the schooner, we attached a long rope to the back of the boat. Once we were on land, drenched and soaked to the skin, we made the rope fast.

It felt good to be on solid ground. It was cold now, and the wind made it even colder, so we went for a walk in order to warm up, and to do some hunting. After going round the bay and zigzagging over the hill, we returned to the small boat. Gathering a little driftwood on the shore we made a cup of tea, and then we put the small boat back in the water. It was already starting to get dark, and we wanted to get back to the schooner. But the small boat wasn't big enough to stand up to the waves, and it was swamped right away. Returning to shore we needed to get shelter from the wind so that we could warm up and dry out our clothes. We pulled the small boat up onto the shore, and propped it up with piece of driftwood. Temporarily, at least, we were protected from the squalls. Next came the job of gathering driftwood and making a fire. We then made some more tea, while presenting the various parts of our anatomy to the heat of the fire, one side burning and the other freezing. If we could have spun around on our heels like a top, our problem would have been solved. But, with some thought, came up with an idea. We chose some stones, the flattest we could find, and put them

Part of a caribou drive system at Iqaluktuuq, near Cambridge Bay, Victoria Island. This row of boulders leads to shooting pits where Inuit with bows and arrows would wait for caribou. (Photo credit: T. Max Friesen)

in the fire. Once they were hot and out of the fire, we spread them out and then lay down on top of them. When we didn't feel the heat any more, we took some others out of the fire. There were two advantages to this: it provided us with a little heat, and it helped to pass the time. I must admit, time does seem to drag a bit under such circumstances. We would spend two nights like this.

The next morning we had a cup of tea or two, without sugar, and off we went to find some food. Fortunately, not all the ducks had flown south yet. Those still there were small, but they weren't short of fat, and in fact they were so fat that they needed quite a bit of room to take flight. We even laughed about it. After flapping and flapping their wings, looking like overloaded airplanes, they stopped trying, embarrassed and disgusted with themselves. We had our rifles with us, and shot some that were in the bay, the wind and sea bringing them to the shore. Dinner and supper for the following days was duck, and duck soup. We had no salt, so we added a little seawater to the broth.

When we were out walking on land we came upon some lines of boulders with spaces between them. Seen from a distance, the whole thing looked like a 'V', quite wide at the beginning and narrowing to a closed point at the end. These were drive lines, used for hunting caribou. Men and women took part in the hunt. After finding the herd, the men, the hunters, hid behind the boulders, while the women, after making a wide circuit, surrounded the caribou and drove them into the corral by flapping their clothes and imitating the howls of wolves or the noises of other animals, and even birds such as the crow. The frightened caribou rushed farther inside the narrowing line of boulders, within reach of the hunters who shot them with their arrows.

I also have heard elders say that before rifles were used, only bows and knives, they sometimes had trouble finishing off a wounded animal, especially if it was a male. In one hunt, a bull caribou had been wounded. An arrow had struck him in the side, and he was starting to move away, when those herding the animals drove him back towards the hunters. Apparently, on that day, one of the hunters

– perhaps it was bad luck, or perhaps one of his companions had cast a bad spell on him – couldn't fire his arrows as usual, and it was towards him that the wounded caribou headed. He waited for it, his bow bent. He took aim, and missed. The caribou had seen him too, and charged the hunter, lashing out at him. The poor man hadn't had the time to bend his bow again before the animal charged. The only thing he could do was grab the antlers of his enemy before it gored him, and that's what he did. Standing to begin with, he faced his adversary, feet planted firmly on the ground, backing up slightly, pushing, gasping for breath, and not daring to loosen his grip for an instant. The onlookers didn't dare to interfere, afraid they might hit the hunter. Struggling, the two adversaries ended up on the ground, but still the man didn't let go of his prey. Finally, one of the onlookers released a dog, which headed for the caribou and bit its legs. But the caribou kept on fighting. Now the hunter's companions were even more powerless to act, as they also had to be careful not to hit the dog. The caribou felt itself growing weaker. The hunter knew it right away, and gained an advantage over his enemy. He got to his feet, and so did the caribou. The hunter continued striking it in the belly and near the liver. He had wounds too, on his head and body, and warm blood was running down his cheeks. But the animal, they say, was making less effort and now started moaning, so one of the other hunters came to his friend's rescue and finished off the animal, ending the fight. Apparently it took all summer for the unfortunate hunter's wounds to heal, and he bore their marks on his face from that day on. They had to have pluck and courage in the old days to live and to survive.

Coming back to our trip... It was too late now to head for Cape Parry, so we returned, empty-handed, to Paulatuk. We would go and seek our fortune elsewhere. In any case, I didn't touch ducks again that winter. I'd had enough of them during those four days.

Chapter 6 Notes

1 Orphaned children are a theme in many Inuvialuit oral histories. These stories often tell how the orphans overcame adversity to become respected members of their communities.

2 Father Roger Buliard was a Roman Catholic Church missionary who was based at Coppermine and Holman (as Ulukhaktok was then known) in the 1930s and 1940s.

Dogs, Our Companions

Children and dog, Tuktoyaktuk, circa 1955. (Bern Will Brown/NWT Archives/N-2001-002: 6215)

When I went to France for my first holiday, one of the first questions one of my nephews asked was, "Where are your dogs? Didn't you bring any back with you?" To talk about Inuvialuit, without introducing dogs and iglus, is unthinkable.[1] They both play such a big part in peoples' lives in the Great North, and although nowadays they have declined in number and importance, they are still, and will continue to be, a part of Inuvialuit life.

Since the beginning of history, we could even say since Time Immemorial – and this is confirmed by archaeological research – Inuit have used dogs. Archaeological digs all along the Arctic coast have proved this theory. Bones found around ancient campsites are attributed to the canine species. Remains of sleds are a commonplace discovery, and I've come across many myself. When the hunter or head of the family died, his sled runners, harpoons, bows, and other implements were all placed on his grave.

Illustration by Harry Egotak (Ekootak) showing people and dogs pulling sleds. (From 'I, Nuligak').

In the very early days, Inuvialuit had only a few dogs – one per family, or two at most – to pull their sleds, and the people would sometimes put themselves in harness as well.

Dogs were often put to work in summer as well. When a hunt on land was organized, some dogs went along, more as pack dogs than hunting dogs. Not all the dogs were taken – only a few who seemed better suited to this type of travel. Packsacks with two big pockets on each side were put on their backs. On the trip out, they carried pots and other items, and on the trip back the pockets were filled with meat. To belong to this transport corps, dogs had to be fairly docile and obedient; they had to follow the hunters and not stray too far away. Perhaps

Dog with a backpack, Bernard Harbour, 1915. (G.H. Wilkins/Canadian Arctic Expedition)

it goes without saying that they liked these outings, which were more interesting for them than staying chained up.

Dogs were treated as members of the family. They had their own spot in the *iglu* or the tent, if they wanted it. Sometimes they were given special food: the females were fed worms, so that they would have large puppies, and the puppies were given beaver teeth to suck on so that they would grow big and strong and have good instincts. They also had names, such as *Amaruq* ('wolf'), *Tuktuvak* ('moose') or *Kulavak* ('female caribou'). Another name, *Ataniq* ('boss'), was reserved for the cream of the crop, those extraordinary dogs people talk about. If our dogs are precious nowadays, back then they were doubly precious, and essential. Without them, how would the Inuvialuit have found *aglut*, the holes in the sea ice that seals use to come up for air? How would they have hunted polar bear and muskox, without the help of their companions and partners? Many times an Inuvialuk's dog, his friend and companion in good times and bad, through thick and thin, saved his life by sharing its animal body heat. This is just one more example of the way in which the Inuvialuit have taught us how to survive in the Great North: the hunter would simply put his half-frozen hands and feet on the animal's belly, and the dog, all curled up, would warm the hunter. Many times dogs have brought lost or helpless travellers back safe and sound in a snowstorm. People often talk about St. Bernards, but if there were medals for these good and humble servants, I would give some to the dogs that I've known and that got me out of a bad or awkward situation more than once.

Louis Unayaq was one of the oldest residents of Holman Island while I was there.[2] Although he was old, he was still a proud hunter, and still independent. Almost every day he came to see us at the Mission to ask if he could use one of our dogs to hunt seals. I had offered him seal blubber and oil for his lamp but, oh no, he wouldn't accept charity. "As long as I'm able to live by my own means, my own resources, I'll keep hunting seal at least. That's the only hunting I can do now. I'm too old to have my own dogs and go on trips, but this I can still

Louis Unayaq. (N-1982-003-0025)

Returning from a seal hunt, Minto Inlet, Victoria Island, circa 1916. (S.T. Storkerson/Canadian Arctic Expedition).

do, and I'm still doing it." He was one of the real old-timers and knew a lot about the past, when the head of a family would go out on the ice, sometimes alone, sometimes with others. They would take the best tracking dogs with them, one or two for the group, or sometimes each hunter had his own dog on a leash. On the ice the dog would head off, nose down, its natural sense of smell made keener by instinct. To the dog, seal meant meat and blubber. As soon as an *aglu* – the seal's breathing hole – was found, it was marked. A seal has several breathing holes, but the dog would find them fairly quickly. One hole or opening would be left untouched, the other breathing holes would be closed off, and the vigil would begin. The hunter would stand completely still, leaning slightly forward over the hole. He would often have a special piece of skin reserved for this purpose, a kind of small mat or rug that stopped moisture from getting into his boots and provided some warmth. When a seal came to the *aglu* to breathe, a few hairs that had been placed on the hole would move as it came to the surface of the water under the snow. Its breathing and the motion of the water were enough to move the hairs. The hunter would then strike with his harpoon, holding tightly on to the line and not loosening his grip until the seal suffocated underwater. After the seal had been brought out onto the ice, the dog would drag it back to camp. Usually, the operation went smoothly and the dog arrived without any problem, and with the catch intact. Only when the line got caught up in bad ice would the dog sometimes begin eating the victim, but that didn't happen very often.

In the past, dogs also played a big part in hunting *nanuq*, the polar bear, the king of animals. They still do, although not so much now as then. After all, these days we have powerful rifles, while in the old days the hunters had only bows, harpoons, knives and a large measure of courage. The dogs were released to chase after the bear, and once they reached it they surrounded it, keeping a respectful distance. Past experience had instilled some fear in them. They kept the bear from getting away by barking and rushing at him, then quickly retreating. Each dog approached in turn from behind, snapping at the bear's rear or his hind legs. But any dog that was too presumptuous could meet a terrible end, since a simple smack of the bear's paw would propel

Illustration by Harry Egotak (Ekootak) of a man hunting a polar bear with the help of a dog. (From 'I, Nuligak).

him through the air. If he landed on his back, that was the end of him. If he got caught from the front, the bear would bite him and, using his powerful neck, give him a good shake before tossing him a few metres away. Mr. Nanuq has formidable power in that long neck of his, which would seem to get even longer then. The dogs put the bear at the mercy of the hunter, who could then get closer. He would shoot his arrows at the bear and then move in to finish him off with a spear or harpoon.

From time to time, by force of circumstances, the Inuvialuit will resort to the old ways of hunting, like Jimmy Memogana did on Holman Island just a few years ago. Jimmy is one of those brave trappers and hunters who use unorthodox methods, such as his method of trapping Arctic foxes. If the weather was good, Jimmy stayed home and hunted seal or caribou, or just worked around his camp. According to him, that wasn't the time to be out on the trap line checking or setting traps. When

Jimmy Memogana preparing a stone block to make prints, Holman (Ulukhaktok), circa 1950s. (Maurice Metayer/Holman Historical Society/ NWT Archives/N1982-003: 0019)

the weather is good and there's no wind, he would say, man's scent stays in the air for a long time and the animal – in this case, the fox – recognizes it right away. He gets suspicious and won't go near the traps unless he's really famished. But when the wind is blowing, the scent of both dog and man, even on the bait, is immediately taken and carried off or swept away by the wind, so you'll have better luck.

One day Jimmy was travelling out on the ice, at the end of his trap line, ready to come home, when he caught sight of a polar bear in the distance. The dogs picked up the scent and away they went, chasing after the bear at breakneck speed. The bear had sensed danger and was running away, trying to put some distance between him and his enemies. For more safety, he took a route through a maze of piled-up ice, where he was king and could negotiate and climb more easily than the hunter and his dogs and, if necessary, hide. But Jimmy, in spite of the hard route, didn't give up. He kept going, pushing his team on. The dogs needed no encouragement, because they knew what to do – they'd done it so often that the excitement of the hunt was in their blood! Here's how Jimmy tells it:

~ *Jimmy Memogana's Bear Hunt* ~

"We're close to land now, and I'm closing in on my prey. I figure I'll be within range any minute now. But I'm waiting for him to go up the side of the hill, where he will have to slow down. And he does. He's starting to get tired too. I have trouble stopping my dogs. They want to keep running, and the sight of the bear so close now isn't likely to calm them down any. I think I only have two bullets left in the magazine. I can't take any chances, and each bullet has to count or I could be in trouble so I wait for *nanuq* to stop on the side of the hill. I have him in my sights and don't take my eyes off him. The instant he takes a break, I shoot. I'm sure I've hit him, because I heard the noise a bullet makes when it hits its target and I see the bear jump, but the bullet probably isn't far enough into the flesh and hasn't reached his heart. Later on, I found it in the fat. I quickly decide to shoot the last cartridge, and this one has to hit the bull's eye. Without hesitating, I take the gun and shoot. *Bang!* I hit him again. He takes a few steps, then stops and lies down on the snow. I don't waste any time, but race towards my victim with the dogs and the sled. Just a few steps away from the bear, I see that although he's got a bad leg wound from the second bullet, he's showing signs of life – growling, biting at himself, rolling around. There's only one thing I can do now. I release the dogs, and they rush at the bear, surrounding him, barking and tormenting him."

"This is the diversion I need to give me time to think and to make other plans. If I go back to camp to get more bullets the bear might get away. I have my tent pole there on the sled, and that gives me an idea. I grab it from underneath the rope used to tie the load to the sled and attach my hunting knife to it. Like the old ones would have done, I'm going to try to kill him using the spear I've just made. I come up to him slowly, from the side, and throw my spear at him as hard as I can. I hit him near his heart. But he gets up, and in spite of the dogs and the pain he starts chasing me, even though his bad leg and the wound in his side slow him down. He grabs the shaft and breaks it with his two front paws and his teeth, and rips the knife off. After a while I stop. The bear keeps coming towards me, but fairly slowly now. I take hope and order my dogs to start fighting again, and to harass our pursuer. The bear turns back, with the dogs all around him. They stop him not far from the place I tried to kill him with the spear, and I see the knife on the snow, still attached to a piece of tent pole. I have to get to it. I weigh my chances, and keep a close watch on my victim's movements. When he turns away from the dogs that are attacking him from the front to defend himself against those coming at him from behind, I rush over and grab my weapon and begin another honourable retreat, thinking the bear is on my heels. I look behind me, and I'm pleasantly surprised to see him in the same spot, still occupied by the dogs. But he's less aggressive and not getting up. He's sitting there on his haunches, leaning forward as far as he can to try and get at his attackers. So I retrace my steps and move in closer too. I realize that he knows the end is near, he's growling, and shaking his long neck and his huge head. In spite of some aversion and fear" – it's difficult to separate these two feelings, Jimmy says – "I run towards him and stab him three or four times, then step back a bit to see what happens. I see the bear stretched out on his side, and the dogs on top of him. I don't need to tell you how relieved I feel. But just to make sure, I stab him a few more times. No doubt about it, *nanuq* is dead. He defended himself bravely and put up a good fight. With a lot of difficulty and effort, I turned him over on his back, put him on the sled and set out for home."

These true stories describe better than any academic essays the large role dogs played in the Great North. There is some question about where they came from, and why there were so few of them in the olden days. Some of the old people say it was contact with Indians that opened the peoples' eyes to the usefulness of having dogs. Or might it have been from Asia, Mongolia or Siberia that they first learned of them? Wherever they originated, the Inuvialuit have had them since time immemorial. As for the small number of dogs, this is easily explained if we keep in mind that, in the past, staying alive was a full-time occupation, trying to find something to eat here and there. It was simply a question of survival – since food was scarce to begin with, the Inuvialuit could not allow themselves to have many dogs. Changes came in about 1900, with the arrival of whalers

Susie Wolki travelling by dog team near De Salis Bay, Banks Island, spring 1935. (Mrs. Peter Sydney/Library and Archives Canada/PA27698)

who provided the Inuvialuit with rifles. This made it easier for them to obtain seal, bear and other meat, and the number of dogs on the coast began to grow. Then came the era of traders. Fox fetched a good price now. The Inuvialuit quickly learned their value and took up trapping. To set and check the traps on their trap lines they had to rely solely on dogs – dogs gave them mobility and let them cover long distances.

We missionaries who lived in the North and adopted the people's way of life also adopted their means of transportation. What would we have done without dogs? What could I have done without them? Out of necessity, I became a dog driver, and fed and raised dogs. It was a lot of work, but it also brought me joy and pleasure. I don't really know how to begin. With the story of one dog's life, from birth to death? With stories of some that were dearer to me than others? How I couldn't have survived without them? How they served as companions to me in my solitude? With Siulik ('Jackfish'), my best lead dog, or Cocoa and Coffee, who gave me so much trouble and played so many tricks? Or Darkie, the swinger, the 'Rock and Roll' dog because of his gait? Or Whitey, who couldn't see a child without trying to eat it? Or Pouf, who ran nearly the whole length of the coast and brought us back to the house in blowing snow? Or César, who almost ate a door of our house? Or Nanuq, the wild one, as big as a Percheron horse, who was uncomfortable inside the house? Where to begin? We owe them so much, a debt of gratitude and honour. Without them, we would have been cold; without them, we would have been hungry; without them, we would have had no means of travel; without them, we would also have had no human contact, no contact with our colleagues. That, in brief, is how important our dogs were in our life up there in the North.

Father Deheurtevant and one of the Mission's dogs, Paulatuk, 1951. (J. Ross Mackay)

My first contact with dogs was at Fort Chipewyan during my journey to the North in 1946. One of the Oblate brothers wanted to present a gift to a priest on the Coast. It was a young female, Bergère ('Shepherdess'), about five months old, a magnificent animal, half wolf, and he asked me to look after her during the trip. Little did

*Father Max Ruyant (**left**) and Father Robert Le Meur in the dog compound, Fort Chipewyan, 1946. Father Le Meur is holding Bergère. (Le Meur Family Collection)*

I know that I'd be taking her all the way to Paulatuk, to the Mission that was also my destination. It was hard not to mistake her for a wolf when she was free – her attitude, her behaviour, her gait, the way she ran, were all very wolf-like and, like a wolf, she had a mane of long hair with black tips. While she behaved well and was dignified, at the same time very affectionate and playful. When we got to Paulatuk she was tied up like the others, but of course she was my favourite. Often I untied her and took her for walks, or I'd let her play with the children, but she was so big and strong that she would knock them down, and then find it very amusing to shake them. I had to stop her, because the children were afraid. Later on, she played lots of tricks on us, proving that she didn't just have wolf blood in her – she also had wolf intelligence. And how! One fall I

"Bergére" our favourite dog doing a dancing step with Mona (Ruben), Paulatuk, circa 1946. (Le Meur Family Collection)

brought her into the house. She felt quite comfortable and at home inside. After dinner, my companion and I went up to the chapel to pray. At Paulatuk, the chapel was on the second floor. That evening as we piously recited our prayers upstairs Bergère stayed down in the kitchen. We'd had soup and boiled caribou meat for dinner and everything was still on the table, along with the tinned butter and tinned milk. When I came back downstairs from the chapel and began clearing the table, I noticed that the tins seemed lighter and that the soup pot was completely empty. I looked around, but there was not a mark or a spot anywhere.

Did Bergère know she was on the hot seat, under suspicion? She was right there beside me, her nose and head turned towards me, her tail in the air, wagging back and forth continuously. I tried to solve the crime. How could she have helped herself to the food without spilling a single drop of milk or soup? Even the butter tin was completely empty.

I picked up the tins and looked at them, examined them more closely. Light teeth marks on the rolled up lids of the tins were our evidence of what happened. Without disturbing a thing or making any noise – we would have heard her, because the chapel was directly above the kitchen – Bergère had lifted the tins and the pot off the table with her teeth. How could I punish her? It was our fault – "lead us not into temptation" – and it was a lesson for us. I couldn't help but admire her. Another time, a young boy came to visit while we were eating our dinner. They come and go as if they were at home, and if I'm eating and there is food left, I share it with them. This time, our visitor was interested in some bread, so I buttered a piece and passed it to him. I can still picture him, sitting on the ground leaning against the door frame. He was holding the piece of bread in one hand, slightly raised, while he chatted to us. Bergère, who was on the other side of the main room, was quick to notice that the little boy wasn't in any hurry to eat his bread. She stood up, studied the situation and slowly, quietly, started moving in. I watched her, without interfering. She was like a cat getting ready to pounce on a bird or a mouse. I had a hard time not laughing as I watched her. One step at a time, she came closer until she was right behind the little boy. She stopped, stretched out her neck, opened her mouth and brought it closer to the bread, and all with such grace. Her gaping mouth made me think of a pair of open pliers, about to close slowly on some object. Sure enough, she slowly closed the vise, her jaws. Once her teeth were in the bread, she didn't tear it away immediately. No, for a second or two she stood there motionless, and our little friend kept on chatting, unaware of her presence. Then, quickly, she snatched the bread out of the boy's hand and leaped out of his reach before he realized what was happening. In one quick motion, the bread had disappeared. "*Alii*," said the startled little boy. That was all. As simple as that.

Bergère never missed an opportunity to prove that she was special and very resourceful. When she had her first litter of puppies, she stumped us again. I gave her plenty to eat, morning, noon and evening. At first, all the food disappeared, but after a few days, her appetite seemed to wane. I didn't pay too much attention, thinking that perhaps the puppies were starting to try food that was more solid than their mother's milk. It wasn't until one day in late September on our way back from a seal hunt that I realized where she was getting her food: she was treating herself to gourmet meals. Our boat was on the side of the bay, a kilometre or less from the house. I had securely stored some food – butter, cakes, biscuits, tea, coffee, sugar and even some honey – in cardboard boxes in the bow. Well, Bergère had found this hiding-place and she was helping herself. All her favourite food was gone. She had also got into the habit of coming along with me to visit the fish nets. She would follow the shore and often arrive before me, because I was rowing over, helping herself to the fish caught in the nets nearest the shore.

With a mother like that I could expect anything from the two of her puppies I kept. Lacking imagination and having trouble finding names for them, I simply called them Café ('Coffee') and Cocoa, because of their colour, one being pure black and the other, the stronger one, more of a chocolate colour. Their personalities were obvious from a very young age – they were aggressive and rowdy, but hard working. The Inuvialuit would say that these dogs knew nothing of laziness. They had to be either beside or ahead of other teams, and to get there they would pull the whole load between them. In those days at Paulatuk we harnessed our dogs two by two, side by side. Since these two were rather hard to control, we put them at the back. That's where they started showing their strength and their eagerness. They were always looking for food, anything edible would do – any fish or bird, feathers, wings, beak and all. Their heads weren't much, but they had strong backs and powerful muscles. After I'd left Paulatuk and moved to Holman Island one of the priests at Paulatuk was going to the Hornaday River to bring back a boat that had been left there on the ice in the fall. He loaded the boat onto the sled as best as he could and set off for the house. Everything was fine on the river, but when they had to climb up the bank the problems began. No matter how hard the dogs pulled, with the priest pushing from behind, the sled wouldn't budge. The poor Father was discouraged, but he didn't want to give up and leave the boat there. Suddenly, he had an idea. If he could just find a bit of fish, he was certain that the sled and the boat would be on top of the slope in no time. He looked inside the boat and found what he was looking for – bits of fish stuck to the bottom. He used his hatchet to pry them loose. Then, putting his plan into place, he took Cocoa and put him in the lead position. I would have loved to see the dog's face when he was promoted! Cocoa knew just one thing and that was pulling and pulling, while watching everything going on around him. Very quickly, before Cocoa got it into his head to start fighting – since the lead dog has more freedom of action than the others – the priest climbed the bank and there, standing a few steps in front of Cocoa, showed him the bits of fish. With no hesitation, Cocoa and the others pulled, and the sled appeared on top of the slope in no time. The famous Cocoa got his reward and was immediately returned to his usual spot.

Café died after eating a piece of cloth. Cocoa was heartbroken without his brother, his comrade-in-arms, but he continued on the same path. He may even have become more brazen, or perhaps it was age that made him more voracious. On trips, we had to be wary when venturing near him to arrange the harnesses of the dogs ahead of him. Once he bit the driver's caribou skin parka, and another time it was a glove that disappeared into Cocoa's stomach. And what a stomach it was, my friends! He didn't die of old age either. In the end, he had to be tied up away from the other dogs because he would howl and howl all night long. It was an eerie sound in the darkness. But eventually he got sick, and one of our Inuvialuit put him out of his misery.

Too often, people look at dog teams superficially, seeing them in a romantic and perhaps nostalgic light. They say "This is great! You're so lucky you can ride around like this!" and so on. But do they realize how much work, preparation, care and time we have to put into maintaining our means of transport? Not just the dog itself, for its whole life, but also the sleds and toboggans, and the harnesses. And although catching enough fish to feed just ourselves would not take long, getting enough to feed six or seven dogs is a year-round job. In spring, there is net fishing on the ice, then in summer we set our nets in open water from the time the ice leaves until it forms again at the end of September. If our summer catch was insufficient for the winter we would fish again on the ice up until the end of December, visiting the fishing nets at least twice a week.

At Stanton, where I moved to from Holman in 1951, the fish we caught in the summer was always sufficient for the winter. Morning and evening, I visited the nets. It was pretty rewarding but also pretty hard work. I stopped only if there were storms. When the fish were most plentiful, fishing went on all day. Between visits to the nets there would be a cup of coffee and a bit of bread, then it was posthaste back to the nets. After the fish were removed from the nets they still had to be packed up and carried on our backs to the icehouse dug into the side of the hill. So don't be surprised if, after all that work on our part, that in winter the dogs in their turn worked for us.

Father Tardy cutting blocks of fresh water for drinking water. (Le Meur Family Collection)

Our dogs preferred being taken out on a trip to being chained up for months at a time, as they were from the end of June to the beginning of October each year. With the first snowfall they start getting excited, knowing that soon they'll finally be seeing a bit of the country again. They prefer the cold, it seems to me. When the weather is nice, in July and early August, they suffer just like us from the heat, and from the mosquitoes. To find relief from the heat and from the mosquitoes and other biting insects they burrow into the ground, lying directly on the permafrost where its cooler. All you'll see of them is the tip of a nose or a few handfuls of hair poking out of the ground. Sometimes, when there were just too many biters, I rubbed their noses and the area around their eyes with the same kind of ointment we use to repel mosquitoes.

When fall arrives, and with it some snow, one of the first tasks is to get some fresh new ice for drinking water. This is done as soon as the ice is about 30 centimetres thick. It is sawn into blocks, and stacked a little distance away from the hole in case water spreads over the ice surface. The blocks are hauled by dogsled back to the Mission, where they are then stacked on platforms prepared for that purpose. One or two blocks are brought inside as needed and put in a barrel in the kitchen to melt. These first trips, from the house to the lake, each taking a few days, served to get the team in good shape after being idle in summer. Other activities, such as hunting willow ptarmigan hauling wood or coal, also were done by dogsled. Practically every day the dogs had a trip to take, and they quickly became fitter.

The dogs had to be made ready for the longer trips that were to come, over the tundra and on the pack ice. Here is how I went about getting them ready. I had a team of six dogs, and in the fall, on the first trips, they were very difficult to control – it's like someone getting out of prison and realizing he's free. During the months of inactivity, my lead dog had perhaps forgotten some of the commands and which direction he was to go. I shouldn't say "forgotten". It's more like a psychological thing that affects students after vacations – they know the rules haven't changed in their schools, but they still have to be reminded of them. I took my lead dog out first, alone. I had to get fish out of the icehouse, and this was an excellent opportunity to retrain the leader. I used a small sled, piled a load of fish on it, made right and left turns, and drove around some obstacles. These exercises went on for hours, accompanied by a chorus of noise from the other dogs who they didn't like their situation, and made their objections known in their own way – barking, howling, and straining against their chains. Next, I attached another dog or two in turn, but always with the lead dog in front. I used the same tactic again, hitching up three dogs, then four, but always changing them after a trip to get ice.

Eventually the big day came. The dogs may have been delighted, but in my case the truth is I had to spend an hour or two getting back into the swing of things myself. One after the other, the dogs were hitched up to the sled, firmly held by an anchor, or even two anchors. I still had to train them to stay calm once they were in harness, because, since I travel alone, I can't afford to have my team take off without me. In this land, it could mean death, or at least a long, cold walk with no food. After harnessing them I'd yell at them to lay down on their bellies. They didn't take my commands seriously the first time, so I had to use both diplomacy and force. I harnessed them just in front of the house, then went back inside and kept an eye on their behaviour through the window. As soon as one of them got up and pulled on the harness, I went out and applied, or I should say pretended to apply, the whip. I cracked it over their heads, just so they felt it a bit, enough to scare them.

This whole exercise could take a good ten minutes before I decided to set out. But the dogs quickly understood that I was the boss and that they had to obey. After that, I had no problems at all in winter. Every morning I harnessed my team, starting with the lead dog, and ending with the dog at the rear, the wheel dog as he's called in English. They waited until I put the chains for tying the dogs in the sled. The whole time, my lead dog would sit on the snow, watching the preparations for departure. He knew them well, and he knew my habits. Slowly, then, I'd head to the back of the sled, to a kind of small platform that was left clear, the driver's spot. I took a mischievous pleasure in watching my lead dog, Siulik. As soon as I was standing on the platform, he would stand up straight, wagging his tail, his face turned towards me. As I reached down to pull the anchor out of the snow, he would start moving. There was no room for error here, because, if we compare them to automobiles, sleds start off in third gear, full speed ahead. If the driver isn't ready, the results can be disastrous, especially when the days are short and there is practically no light, and obstacles are hard to make out.

Despite their faults and what we had to do to take care of them, we couldn't help but love our dogs. They were our companions, and we had so many great trips together. Like Pouf, for example. In very bad weather, when we thought we'd have trouble finding our way back to the house, all we had to do was put Pouf in the lead and, one way or another, he always managed to get us back. How, we're not sure. He probably took the direct route, which isn't always the best one in the Arctic. When he was in his old age and the time came to put him down, I asked someone else to do it. I carried out this difficult job for others as well. It's a very strange and touching moment, even more than that, I'd go as far as to say it's a bit painful. It's as if the animal knows what awaits him. The executioner, with gun loaded, takes the victim away on a leash, dangling a fish or a piece of meat or blubber in the other hand – the last meal for the condemned, the last cigarette. The dog is led out onto the ice and, once far enough away from the houses, he is set free and given his

74

*Father Le Meur (**left**) wearing his mittens made from his dog, Nanuq, 1952. In the middle is an unidentified Inuvialuk, and to the right is Father Ruyant. (Le Meur Family Collection)*

fish. Usually, he doesn't move, doesn't even try to run away. No, he just stands there and sniffs the food on the ice, but doesn't even touch it. Instead, he looks at you, and there is something in his eyes that is hard to define. Is it melancholy? Regret? Sorrow? You quickly take aim and the job is done, while the other dogs howl and howl. They aren't excited, as they usually are when they hear a gunshot. Do they also understand what has happened?

When I was at Stanton, I had to have one of my best dogs, Nanuq, the biggest and strongest, put down. He had completely destroyed the pads of his paws on a trip. I brought him inside the house and nursed him, but to no avail. A friend did the sad deed for me. Afterwards he said to me, "You know, Father, it's a shame to leave Nanuq like that. He's so big you could get at least two pairs of mittens out of his skin. I'll gladly skin him and my wife will make the mittens. You'll have one pair and I'll have the other. That way, you'll remember him whenever you travel, and he'll be there with you and continue to serve you." I agreed, and ended up using the fur of my good servant Nanuq until 1970. I travelled a lot with him.

Once, I almost froze my hands when I wasn't wearing those mittens. I was going from Stanton to Paulatuk, a five-day trip. On the second day, I broke camp and set out very early. It looked as if it would be a beautiful day, although extremely cold, almost minus 50 degrees, with a light breeze. I had worn cloth gloves to harness the dogs. Gloves or mittens made from animal skins aren't as practical for that job. The dogs were in fine form. I threw my anchor onto the toboggan. My dog skin mittens were around my neck, secured by cords, and the cords were laced together and the mittens flipped over so they hung down near my lower back, as was customary. And there I was, on my way, in the dark, before I'd even had a chance to put them on. The dogs were running at a full gallop towards a lake, down a steep slope that I hadn't noticed, and all of a sudden I was flat on my back on the ground, my feet caught in the ropes at the back of the sled, fortunately. There was no point in shouting at the dogs that early in the day. They were too excited. They dragged me onto the lake, onto the bare ice. I tried hard to get back up by pulling on the safety rope, which was attached to the front of the sled and left hanging at the back. The rope serves a double purpose: we can hold onto it to steady ourselves while standing at the back of the sled, and we hold it as we run alongside the sled or the dogs, which we do to warm up during the day. As I said before, it's also a safety feature. In case the dogs try to take off, or if we fall, we can grab onto it from behind and still be attached to the team and the sled. That time, I couldn't get back up until we were on the other side of the lake, but that didn't take too long, thank God. I quickly pulled on my mittens, and tried to get some warmth back into my fingers. They slowly got warmer but, I must say, I suffered for a good hour at least. Feeling returned to my fingers, one after the other, and when the blood started circulating again, oh, what pain! I swore I would never, ever again, pull up the sled anchor unless my mittens were firmly on my hands. There is no better teacher than personal experience. It really makes us wise.

Sometimes while travelling the dog team would take off, perhaps because the driver wasn't paying attention, or because of an accident, or who knows what else. It happened to me once. One afternoon I decided to go out, not for any special reason, just to get a bit of air. I left on a toboggan, taking only four dogs. I wanted to try another dog in the lead position, so a few kilometres from the Mission I stopped the team, and without putting down the anchor I went to unhitch the leader and put the other dog in his place. As I was going back to the sled the team took off without me. I saw the sled go past and tried to jump on as it went by, but missed, and off they went on their own. I sprinted after them, even got within a few steps of them, and tried to get hold of the rope hanging behind the sled. The dogs seemed to be enjoying the game and when I was just a few feet away, they took one look behind them and off they galloped, moving away from me at quite a clip. After several attempts to catch them, I walked back to the village, not quite knowing what to do, and decided I would tear a strip off them if they came back. All I could do was wait, and the time seemed to pass slowly. I had some things on the toboggan – a rifle, some caribou skins, my caribou skin parka – and I was afraid that even if the dogs came back, my things would be gone. One bump along the way was all it would take to tip the sled. I wondered if they would fight with each other, or get hooked on a piece of old ice. That evening, around 6 o'clock, I heard the dogs barking. I went out and saw them there beside their chains. When I went towards them, they were all happy, and kept wagging their tails and yapping with joy. First I glanced at the sled. Everything was still there. My anger and anxiety had also faded a bit – after all, it was my own fault. It didn't seem right to punish them at that point either – they wouldn't have understood why. So I took them out of harness and fed them. I had learned my lesson.

One year I had travelled by dogsled from Tuktoyaktuk to Stanton, leaving on January 7 with the Royal Canadian Mounted Police, who were going for a patrol. I had arranged to meet Father Max Ruyant at Stanton, and the two of us would then go to Paulatuk to drop off the winter mail and make our annual retreat. We would also catch up on some Inuvialuktun language studies. The Inuvialuit told me it wasn't smart to set off with two old dogs and four young ones, only five months old, all from the same litter. They had been born in August and I had raised them and looked after them properly. At four months they were already learning about their life as northern dogs. It was strange, but they took to it right away, with almost no training. My habit was to put the young ones between two older ones. They learned very quickly, but if they didn't keep up, they paid for it. If a young one was being dragged along, the old soldiers didn't stop, they just carried on. It took only a few minutes of that for the new dogs to stand up and start pulling, although a bit awkwardly. But in the case of these young ones, right from the beginning they started pulling like the veterans, as if they knew the ropes. I was even more pleased that they left the harnesses alone, and didn't try to tear at them with their teeth. Perfect. So I decided to set off, promising to send the two old dogs that belonged to Father Franche back with the police when they returned to Tuktoyaktuk.

From the first day, I wondered whether the people hadn't in fact been right. Until midday, there was nothing abnormal in the attitude of my dogs. They were walking well, and I could keep up with no problem. But late in the afternoon they began to tire, and the pace slowed. From time to time my young dogs turned and looked at me as if to say, "So, when are we going to stop?" But they were out of luck. The other two teams were ahead of me, and I couldn't afford to get too far behind or my companions would start having doubts about my team. I pulled in only about half an hour after them at the chosen campsite. As soon as we arrived, my puppies lay down and didn't move. They were bushed, completely exhausted that first evening. I even had to carry them in my arms to the spot where I chained them. The next morning, they were fresh and ready to go. That day was a repeat of the day before: all fired up until midday, and then dragging their feet, but they were brave and kept pulling with all their might, which wasn't much. That second day was longer and we travelled farther, too. On the last day, which promised to be another long one, I tried to keep my team calm in the morning, but in vain. Just like the two previous days, the young dogs gave it their all, and couldn't stand to see another team in front. Perhaps they needed the company of the others. But late that evening – it was pitch dark, although the stars were shining – we were still going. Of course, I arrived at Stanton dead last again. I stopped at one of the log houses, where I knew the people. When I went in, I couldn't see or make out very much, since there was just one candle lighting up the only room in the house. I greeted the woman of the house and quickly asked her where her husband was. Then I noticed there were two children as well. They were standing on the bed in the corner of the room. They seemed frozen with fear and were staring at me. I think my sudden and unexpected appearance was a shock for them. I must have looked quite unreal, like someone or something from another planet; my beard was all covered in frost and ice, and so was my face. When I moved towards them to shake hands, they began to scream and yell. I said goodbye to the poor woman and left as quickly as I could so as not to scare them too much. They must have thought I was a ghost or a spirit of some sort. Five minutes later, I was at the Mission house. A few Inuvialuit were waiting for me. The police and Max Ruyant had told them I was coming. The people came to say hello, and offered to help me with the dogs. But the four brothers wouldn't let anyone else near, and I had to unhitch them myself, and I had to carry them in my arms to be chained. The next day they were in good form again, but we let them rest for a few days.

Once we'd packed everything up for the trip – food, tent, the whole lot, as well as a few bags of mail for the Mission there – Max and I were ready for a week of travelling. The days were still short, and my dogs weren't very strong either, at least that's what we thought, and we decided not to push it as there was no reason to hurry. The police had taken Father Franche's old dogs back with them, so I would use Max's lead dog, Dragon, and we would help each other out. But Dragon wasn't very obedient for me. Some lead dogs are like that – they only obey when they hear their master's voice, and play tricks on other drivers. Dragon was one of those dogs – he walked well with Max, but gave everyone else a hard time. In the end, I told Max it would be better if he took his lead dog back and lent me another one. I would follow alongside or behind. He said he had another dog that could perhaps go in front. It was Siulik, whose usual spot was behind Dragon, the lead dog. We changed over immediately and, after a little persuasion, Siulik seemed to settle in at the front as leader. The next morning, I had some trouble getting him to take the lead, but after that there was no problem. He obeyed my commands immediately and, better still, he hardly ever zigzagged at all. All he knew was a straight line, from point to point. I was very pleased, because I could count on him all day long.

In his typically generous fashion, Max gave Siuluk to me and he officially became my lead dog. Nothing would have made me give that dog up; he was worth his weight in gold. I travelled many, many kilometres with that dog, in all kinds of weather. He knew the way better than I did. I used a little compass in bad weather and snowstorms, and when Siulik became my lead dog, I wanted to see whether he was as reliable. I set my compass on the sled, between my legs, and watched the needle. It hardly moved. He was always right on course. How? I don't know. Instinct, perhaps, or a sense of direction? In any event, he always got me home safe and sound, and would deliver me right to my door. Once he was on a trail, it was as if it was imprinted in his memory. He knew it in any weather, even in fog or blowing snow. I had to watch him the first half hour, because he would stop to unload, a good amount, but after that there was no stopping, even when the others felt nature's call. I don't know how many times he brought me back to the house, or to various camps, on his own. I had taken to always stopping and camping in the same spots. In the spring, when the weather was fine and the days were long, I would sometimes have problems getting past these places – he would instinctively stop there. But once we got moving again, there was no problem. In the fall, when the ice was still young and thin in places Siulik would instinctively avoid the bad spots. If I gave him commands and tried to keep going, and he wouldn't budge; all I had to do was test the ice and I would see that it was bad. In the spring, though, he wouldn't change his route if he encountered water – he'd go straight through it. His nose and his instinct told him that there was a good layer of ice underneath.

Ah, those late spring trips! We could expect anything – snow, rain, water, even patches of bare land. It was a real cross-country course. Once in June I was coming back to Stanton from far up the Anderson River, where I had been looking for wood for my spring camp. On the way back I was caught in a storm – half snow, half rain. I was nothing but ice. My entire sled was a block of ice, and the dogs and the harnesses were covered with a few centimetres of ice as well. That same spring, a few days later, I was going back to the spring camp to stay, again by dogsled. What a trip! On the river ice, everything was fine, but when I saw that the ice up ahead had already candled, and was dangerous, I knew I had to get to land.[3] Siulik didn't hesitate. He threw himself off the ice and into the water, dragging the others with him. The whole team was in the water, with the sled behind it, and me standing on the load, trying to keep my balance. Knowing what the conditions were, I had previously secured two small barrels to the sled. They acted as floats, and that's how we made it to shore. It was a fine, sunny day and I don't know if my dogs had enjoyed this little game or if they were just too hot, but they didn't want to leave the shore. They were pulling in the shallow water and were quite comfortable with its icy temperature. In fact, they really didn't have anything to pull, because there was still ice underneath, anchored to the sand on the bed of the Anderson River, and the sled was gliding along on its own. The pace was good, but after a few kilometres we had to leave the shore and travel on land. There was almost no snow left. I tried the hillsides, travelling there would eventually take me off course. Fortunately, I had a good lead dog. Through willows, over bare land, down into deep troughs filled with water, Siulik led the group, without getting discouraged, and without looking back. For Siulik and the others, this was the last journey of the year.

And how could I not give an honourable mention to the other members of the team? Whitey, named for his beautiful white coat, ended his days working for the RCMP at Tuktoyaktuk. He was a very nice dog and liked playing with children when he was young. Later on, though, he couldn't stand them, especially if they were wearing fur parkas. Why? Perhaps children had teased him. When we arrived somewhere, he always had to be watched if children came up to the team. Titak, a real rascal, had tremendous drive and spirit. Always on the lookout for something or someone he could get at while travelling. His spot on the team was behind Siulik, the lead dog. Darkie, the last one of the group, had quite the gait. His rear was always moving back and forth, ready to go right or left with the sled, which was just behind him, always at his heels. He was a quick study and didn't need to be taught the rhythm and technique. I think he was born to be between the shafts, so to speak. I loved to watch him, and to watch him work. He and Titak were good friends and in fact they had the same style, the same gait when they were in harness. Their first year in harness the team went from Tuktoyaktuk to Stanton and Paulatuk, back to Stanton and to the Anderson River, then back to Tuktoyaktuk before Easter. On Easter Tuesday, it was off to Aklavik via Reindeer Station, then from Aklavik back to Tuktoyaktuk. In all, we covered about 1600 kilometres. For dogs only nine or ten months of age, that was certainly a record year. Needless to say, they were quite broken in by the following year! I continued to travel a lot and never had a problem with them.

Another fact about this team that should be added to their list of accomplishments is their part in rescuing a downed airplane at Stanton. Yes, an airplane. It was the end of March, and the doctor from Aklavik was coming to do his rounds. God knows, I was very happy he was coming, as I had two sick people. The snow and the landing strip marked out on the ice at Stanton were in good condition, but as we learned later the landing gear had somehow been damaged when it was taking off from Tuktoyaktuk. Everything seemed to have gone smoothly on landing, but suddenly the plane tipped forward slightly, appeared to crash down onto the right wing, and spun around a bit before coming to a stop. Mike Zubko, the pilot and an old friend of mine, and the doctor, a man named Christensen, originally from Greenland, were on the ice in no time. No one was hurt, and there was no fire, but the airplane, a Cessna, was in terrible shape. The wings were badly damaged, the tail and ailerons as well, and the propeller was all twisted. Mike looked at it and shook his head. "Too bad it didn't burn up. That would have simplified the insurance investigations. Now how much will I get for it? And how will I get this plane off the ice before the thaw?" He was a bit discouraged. In situations like that, our remedy is always a cup of tea or coffee. Life always seems a bit brighter afterwards. Patience.

I walked over to the plane and realized that there was a way to bring it onto land near the Mission. Why not hitch up my dogs and a few others!! I said this to Mike, and he smiled. "Impossible," he said, "the airplane is too heavy." I asked him if he would let me try anyway, and told him we had nothing to lose. I drove the team over to the plane, where I tied a rope to one of the skis and waited for a Brother to come over with his dogs too. We did the same thing to the airplane's other ski. Then I asked one of the observers to give the airplane a bit of a shake, and we were off. The plane was moving. The pilot couldn't believe his eyes. I brought the plane off the ice and up onto land, close to the Mission. There, the ice and water couldn't get at it when the thaw came. At least Mike's spirits seemed to have lifted a bit. Now he wanted to get back to Aklavik, his base of operations. I told him the police were on their way here and that they could take him back to Tuktoyaktuk. That trip was quite an experience for Mike. He'd never travelled by dogsled before and apparently he thought the trip would never end. Since he didn't have any proper warm clothing with him, I lent him some of my winter clothes. He was short, so my clothes covered him from head to toe. He came back later, during one of my absences, and repaired the plane well enough to get it flying and take it back to Aklavik.

In the North, anything can happen, even the spectacular, or odd accidents, like a plane colliding with a dog team. This happened at Tuktoyaktuk. Once or twice a week, the airplane flew there from Inuvik. Our landing strip on the ice in the bay was marked with wood posts and some small flags flapping in the breeze. After every storm the snow banks had to be broken up and the whole length of the strip leveled out again. In emergencies, if the airplane came in bad weather or at night, a few pots with burning kerosene served as approach lights. But that day it was still broad daylight. The airplane circled overhead a couple of times, made its approach, touched down and began to glide along the ice. Meanwhile, a dogsled was also approaching from the other side of the bay. The driver, a woman with a child on her back, warm and cozy under her parka, was standing behind the sled. She'd been hugging the shore of the island in the bay, which is quite high at that point and cuts off all visibility on the right. The dogs were running along at a good clip as well. As she got to the tip of the island, she and the pilot saw, at the same time, that the airplane and the sled were headed in the same direction, at full speed. The woman couldn't control her dogs, and the pilot couldn't control his plane very well either. Powerless to help, we could only watch from a distance, and pray for as little damage as possible. They collided, and the tail of the aircraft seemed to knock the woman over. As soon as the plane came to a stop, we went to help her. There was more fear than damage, it seemed, as no one appeared to be injured. But since the child had sustained the greatest impact – when the driver fell on her back, the child hit the ice hard – the pilot took the mother and child with him when he went back to Inuvik, to have them checked out at the hospital, just as a precaution. Everything was fine, no one was hurt, but it came very close to being a serious accident.

Coming back to those winter and spring trips, I'd like to finish the story of that year I'd covered so much ground between January 7 and May 8 or 9 with my young dog team. I was back at Tuktoyaktuk for Easter and spent Holy Week there at the Mission. On the Tuesday, I set out for Aklavik, travelling again with Royal Canadian Mounted Police officer. I had my team, of course, and the policeman also had a team with some of their best dogs. I wondered how I would do, and thought I'd probably lag quite far behind him. But that didn't worry me. I knew the way, and the days were quite long. So there we were, on our way, crossing the pack ice to get to one of the arms of the Mackenzie River in the Delta. At first, it was uneventful. My dogs, all fired up, were even in the lead for an hour or two. But then I started to fall behind a bit. This didn't really matter, but Titak, the dog behind Siulik, the leader, didn't like it, so I managed, with difficulty, to stop my team and put Titak in the lead. Oh, it didn't take very long, no time at all in fact, for me to catch up to the policeman. At that point things began to get complicated, because Titak didn't know any commands yet, or the rules of the road. He was happy just to stay level with the other driver. The policeman became exasperated and irritated as Titak happily stayed on his heels, perhaps thinking he might get a few pats. But no, on the contrary, what he got was a few surly remarks. I tried, without success, to get him to move out in front or to the right a bit. Siulik seemed to understand the situation and was pulling hard to the left, but the young dog didn't ease up and stayed beside and level with the other team.

Siulik, meanwhile, without any command from me, was pulling off in one direction or the other to try to pass the other team. I found this little game quite amusing, because the policeman wanted to prove he had the better team and occasionally cracked his whip to get his dogs to pick up the pace. Only then would Titak deign to move aside, to avoid getting hit. He really was a poor sport – he didn't play the game, which required, even on a dogsled, that everyone take a turn leading. But there was nothing I could do. He didn't know the rules of the game, and as for me, I was quite comfortable behind or to the side. I could just ride along and enjoy the scenery! There wasn't much to see at first, just snow, but soon the river brought some changes – its meanderings, its curves, and hills all around. I was enjoying my revenge for the trip in January, when I arrived after the police every night. The policeman really didn't understand any of it, and shook his head from time to time, turning to look at me as if asking me to explain how it was that these young dogs were keeping up with experienced old-timers. I think he was forgetting that although they didn't have the older team's experience, these young dogs had covered a lot of kilometres. They were already tough, and hardened beyond their years.

And so we proceeded on our way to Aklavik, capital of the Delta in those days. Along the way I played a trick on one of my good friends Mike, the local mechanic and handyman at Reindeer Station, the camp connected with the domesticated reindeer herd, which was under government control at that time. There was nobody at his home so I let myself in, put on the coffee and sat

Reindeer Station, early 1940s. Loading sleds to move out to reindeer camps. (A.L. Fleming Collection/ NWT Archives/N-1979-050: 0313)

down at the table to drink it. I had shaved off my beard before leaving Tuktoyaktuk, and when Mike came in, he looked at me, a bit surprised perhaps to find someone in his kitchen, looking quite at home. I said hello, but didn't give my name. He was racking his brain, trying to think who on earth I was. Definitely someone who knew the place and knew his house well, someone very familiar to him, but who? He went out, just for a moment, and came back in smiling. "Well, Father... ," he said. He'd recognized Siulik, and then it all fell into place. I had the same experience two or three other times as well on the last day of the journey, between Reindeer Station and Aklavik. The people we met, some Inuvialuit, would greet the police officer and politely shake my hand, looking me over carefully. Then I would begin speaking Inuvialuktun, and that really surprised them. Who on earth could it be? They knew me and had also heard my voice on the radio, but without my beard I was a different man.

Our route led away from the river onto land. There were trees in the Delta, which was a big surprise for my young dogs, who had never seen trees before. In their curiosity, they left the beaten trail and fell into the soft snow. They were completely buried, and had to do a lot of legwork to get back onto the trail. They learned quickly, and wisely settled for admiring the trees and the vegetation from the trail. Everything in that area was new to them.

That day the policeman tried to break away, to give me the slip, but Titak wouldn't accept that. I had used the same tactic as the day before, putting Siulik in second position on the team. And so we arrived at Aklavik, both teams side by side. To be perfectly honest, I should say that I arrived at the same time as my travelling companion just outside Aklavik. We parted company there, since we were headed in two slightly different directions. He was going to the Royal Canadian Mounted Police detachment, and I was going to the Mission. To make sure I got there safe and sound, I put Siulik back in the lead position for the last few metres to our final destination.

There was a pile of garbage on the river ice. It was the garbage dump in those days. In May, when the ice left, pushing everything – ice and water – to the north and out to sea, all the rest would disappear too. But as I approached Aklavik that day, everything was still there, and there was a lot of it. There were also fat ravens on the piles of garbage. Ravens were a novelty for my young dogs. Titak wanted to get closer too, but that didn't suit me, or Siulik, who was trying, unsuccessfully, to get us to the Mission. For a few minutes, I was being pulled this way and that near the ravens, who weren't in any hurry to fly away. What a performance! The people on shore must have been

A dog team coming into to Aklavik, 1930s. (A.L. Fleming Collection/NWT Archives/N-1979-050: 1181)

quite amused. Still, I eventually got to the Mission, where there were more surprises in store for my dogs. I can still see them too, this time chained to stakes and sprawled out on the snow, observing, watching the ravens out of the corner of their eye. The birds were perched bravely and without fear on top of the stakes, keeping an eye out for something to nibble on. Suddenly, one of the dogs would leap at a stake, reaching it in a single bound, but the bird was always faster. The dogs would bark a bit to scare the ravens, but this had no effect on the birds and they kept coming back. After a number of tries, the dogs just ignored them.

Chapter 7 Notes

1   The Inuvialuktun word *iglu* refers to 'house' or 'dwelling'. Father Le Meur uses the word to refer to a snow house, which is a common use of the term by non-Inuvialuit.

2   Father Le Meur served at the Holman Island Roman Catholic Mission from 1950-1951. In 2006 the official name of Holman, also known as Holman Island, was changed to its traditional form, Ulukhaktok.

3   Candled ice is a form of rotten ice that develops in columns when the ice begins to melt. Candled ice is weak, and cannot support a weight.

8

Bear Stories

'Chicksi (Gerard Siksigaaluk), **centre***, and sons (William and Thomas)', circa 1930s. Gerard Siksigaaluk is wearing boots made from polar bear skin and William and Thomas are wearing polar bear skin pants. (Charles Rowan/NWT Archives/N1991-068: 0478)*

In many places, the lion is considered the king of the beasts. In the North, the king, the emperor, is without a doubt *nanuq* – the polar bear. There is something appealing about polar bears – their majestic demeanour, their skill, their Herculean strength, their finesse and cunning, their boldness. The polar bear has a special place in the lives of the Inuvialuit. Polar bear fur was used to make clothing, and its meat was highly prized by everyone. The polar bear was also used as a medium for casting spells. In many stories of vengeance, people invoke a polar bear's spirit, and bear then kills their enemy. Mittens made of polar bear skins were placed on the victim's grave, beside a hunting knife, in case the dead person's spirit wanted revenge.

This is what one of the elders in Tuktoyaktuk, Felix Nuyaviak, said to me: "Father, *nanuq* thinks like a man, he hunts like a man, he is like us except for one thing – he doesn't talk. You see, we are wondering who was the first to hunt seal? Did *nanuq* give us the idea, or did he adopt our way of hunting? *Nanuq* waits beside the seal's hole, just like us, not moving, crouched down on his big paws, after uncovering just a bit of the seal's *aglu* – his breathing hole. And he is patient, he knows how to wait. Then, when he smells and hears the seal coming up through the water, he stretches out his huge paw beside the hole, and gets ready to strike, just like we do when we get ready to throw our harpoon. Then, with one smack of his paw, he kills the seal. It's nothing for him to then take it in his jaws and throw it down on the ice. And in the spring, when the seals are sleeping on the ice, he watches them from a distance. He takes his time and doesn't hurry his approach – no, he takes a few steps and then stops, staying still. The only black on him is the tip of his nose, and he keeps that covered in the snow. Since he blends in with the white snow the seal

A polar bear on the pack ice.

doesn't suspect anything. And have you seen him on thin ice? He glides, like he is skating. If he walked, he'd break through the ice. At the edge of the ice he stays in the water for hours, patiently waiting until a seal comes along. Whether the seal is big or small, it can't get away. With a single movement of his head and enormous neck, he throws the seal onto the ice, as if it weighs only a few pounds. See how smart *nanuq* is? We Inuvialuit," Felix Nuyaviak continued, "or at least the elders, we wonder if he doesn't think about us as well."

Inuvialuit have many stories about polar bears to tell in the evenings, when everyone gathers around the fire or the stove. Felix Nuyaviak also told me that in the old days the elders sometimes amused themselves with animal skins, with the claws, head and teeth intact. They dressed up in them, and had fun imitating the animals – the way they walked, and grunted. If the animal was a polar bear they even jumped into the water and swam like a bear. The children, of course, were frightened by the game, not knowing if it was real or a disguise (sometimes the old ones used that trick to get some peace and quiet in the house). Once, when the excitement was at its peak, one of the participants, instead of just pretending to bite, seized his opponent's arm and tore it. One of the actors had become a real bear. Since that time, the old ones say, they have used only skins without forearms and claws.

It's not surprising that polar bears are a big part of Inuvialuit folklore. Because they come from the pack ice, polar bears are seen as having a realm over there, far away in a place that man can't reach, because to get there he would have to cross many crevasses and large expanses of open water. But one time, according to legend, a man named Angusiluk did travel to the land of the bears:

Carving by Bill Nasogaluak depicting an Inuvialuit woman transforming into a bear. She keeps a memory of her husband in her thoughts so that she can change back to human form. (Susan Irving/ Prince of Wales Northern Heritage Centre)

This happened a very long time ago, in the olden days when humans and animals were very close. They could communicate with each other, and even trade places. Angusiluk was a good hunter and provider. At his camp the racks were always hung with meat, blubber and fish. There was always good lamp oil, oil that never smoked and always burned with a clear flame. His wife always had work to do, too, since the seal and caribou skins that had to be scraped and sewn into clothing were so plentiful. They lived beside the sea, Angusiluk, his wife and his mother and father. In summer, when the caribou skins were good for making clothes, Angusiluk went hunting on the land. He sometimes spent many days away on those trips. In the evening, he camped in a small tent, alone with his thoughts and dreams. One night, while he was waiting for sleep to come, he saw a fox come into the tent. Strangely, the fox now looked like a dog, and it even had a harness and a leash. It went towards some garbage and started eating it. From outside came a voice, a woman's voice, a beautiful, clear voice. She was calling her dog. Always hospitable, Angusiluk told her to come in too, but she didn't want to, and refused in spite of Angusiluk's insistence. Then, taking hold of the dog's leash, he said that if she wanted to see it again she had to come into the tent. She hesitated for a moment and then came in. Angusiluk was surprised – she was a beautiful young girl. They talked, and Angusiluk asked her if she would like to share her life with him. And with that, they were married.

When Angusiluk decided that he had enough caribou skins they got ready to go back to his house. First, he made two bundles of skins, one with 10 skins and the other with 9. They also took some of the dried meat that his new wife had prepared; they would come back later for the rest. Not only was she beautiful, she was a good housewife and she was also very strong. She lifted one of the bundles of skins as if it was nothing, and even overtook her husband while walking. When they got close to the camp, Angusiluk's first wife came to meet them and immediately saw that her husband had a new acquisition – a second wife. And when she saw how young, pretty and strong the new wife was, she wanted to show what she could do. But she couldn't lift the bundle of skins that Angusiluk had dropped on the ground. Then the new wife took the bundle of skins, put it on her back with the bundle she was already carrying, and continued on to the house.

Angusiluk found himself with two wives – the one he had when he left the camp, and the one he had found while out on the land. There may have been a little animosity and friction from time to time, but nothing serious, just some teasing between the two women, nothing more. Still, the first wife and her mother-in-law had noticed that the new arrival had not only a good appetite, but also a certain fondness for fat, any fat – fish, seal blubber and even caribou. Winter came, and Angusiluk was now quite often absent, sometimes for several days at a time. Hunting and fishing took up a lot of his time. Once while he was away his second wife put aside her work for a moment and went outside. She headed towards the racks to get some food and to eat a few morsels of fat, in secret, without anyone seeing. While she was up there on the rack, she heard her rival speaking and saying to her mother-in-law, "All that young woman knows how to eat is blubber and caribou fat." She was hurt that people were making fun of her, and angry about it too. Still, she went back to the house and finished her work. Then, taking her dog's harness, she walked away from the camp and headed straight for the pack ice. She decided to leave and go back home to her own people.

When he got back, Angusiluk was surprised to see only his first wife and his parents at the house. When he asked them for news of his second wife, he learned that she had left with her dog. Angusiluk understood that she wanted to leave, but he loved her, and didn't want to lose her. After having something to eat and drink, he took his harpoon and set off. He was comfortable walking on the pack ice, because he had taken care to put on his boots that were specially made for walking on ice, with fur on the soles. Out on the sea, he found tracks – not human tracks, but bear tracks, two sets. He followed them for quite a distance, and eventually he saw what appeared to be smoke or a kind of light mist, indicating open water in the middle of the pack ice. When he got there, he saw his wife and her dog. As soon as he reached them he asked them to come home with him, but his wife refused, because she wasn't very happy about being teased and made fun of. Nothing would change her mind, so Angusiluk said he wasn't going back either – he would follow her and live with her wherever she went. She told him he was making a mistake and that he'd regret it later on. The road ahead was very long, with many obstacles. They still had a long walk ahead of them on a very difficult path, with bad ice and open water. And then, how would her people receive him? But in spite of all her objections, Angusiluk simply continued to say that he wouldn't leave her.

They set off – she and her dog, who had turned back into a white fox, and Angusiluk following behind. A crevasse appeared in the ice in front of them. Again, they stopped to talk, and again Angusiluk's wife begged him not to follow. She was thinking of him more than herself, she said. But her husband insisted, and she agreed to take him with her. She told him that, to get across the crevasse, he now had to climb onto the back of the dog – the dog that had just been a fox and had now turned into a bear. He did as she told him, and found himself on the other side of the crevasse. They didn't stop, but continued on their way for some time. In the evening, Angusiluk built an *iglu* for the night and then went hunting. He caught a seal, gave the blubber to his wife and the dog, and then ate the liver. The next day, they continued walking on the pack ice, crossing many stretches of open water. That evening, it was the same procedure as the previous evening – build a snow house and kill a seal.

The next day, the woman told her husband Angusiluk that soon they would see lights in the distance on the ice, but not to be fooled – the lights were still a long way off. In the evening, some lights did in fact appear on the horizon, so small that they looked like stars. They followed the same routine every evening, and at night they slept on the woman's parka to protect themselves from the snow. Angusiluk was feeling a little nervous, and his wife a little excited, because the next day they would reach the land of the polar bears. "Look," she said, "the lights already seem bigger. Tomorrow evening we'll be there. Pay attention and listen closely to me. And don't forget what I tell you, if you want to live. As we get closer, don't worry about me, they know me. You'll see a lot of bears, young bears, coming to meet us, and they move quickly. One is very remarkable, faster than the others, and stronger. As soon as he gets close to you, he'll know that you're a stranger, an Inuvialuk. He'll charge you and try to push and force you to the ground. Don't let him. Be prepared, and as soon as he starts approaching you, go on the offensive and push him down, otherwise all the others will surround you and bite you. Do you understand?"

So the next day, all day long, they continued on their way again, and in the evening they could see the lights, nearer now. The brightest belonged to the woman's family. As they approached, a group of bears started galloping towards them. Angusiluk, remembering his wife's words, was ready, and the first bear that came at him was forced to go on the offensive. The fight was short-lived, and when the others saw that their leader was defeated, they went back to their camp, as did the bear that had challenged Angusiluk. The travellers, taking their time now, entered the home of the woman's parents, and the entire polar bear population followed. Angusiluk was amazed to see the bears, as they entered the porch, take off their skin and fur, and become humans. Visitors and the curious were there. They wanted to see a man up close. They all seemed pleasant enough, except the biggest one, the one who had challenged Angusiluk. Each time Angusiluk felt he was being watched and looked over at him, he turned his head away and looked at the ground.

Polar bear mother and cub.

When the visitors left after hearing the latest news, Angusiluk, intrigued by the attitude of the one who seemed to be his enemy, asked his wife and her parents for an explanation. His father-in-law responded, "Oh, him, he recognized you." "Really? How could he recognize me?" "Several years ago you killed his mother on the pack ice. That wound on your cheek, that scar, identified you – he had seen it, and he told us about it." Thinking back several years, Angusiluk remembered, even though he had killed many bears. It was on the pack ice, a long way from home. He had seen a bear and a cub, and after a long pursuit, he'd attacked the mother first, thinking that the cub would wisely stay with her. But that didn't happen, and he searched in vain for the cub. It had disappeared in the middle of the bad ice, and Angusiluk couldn't find it. "So he was the cub," said Angusiluk "he has grown a lot since then." "And his name is Angimmiq," said his father-in-law.

It was quite late, and they were thinking of going to bed and getting some rest. But that didn't happen. Just as he was about to fall asleep, someone else came into the house. He was, he said, a friend of Angimmiq, his messenger. Angimmiq had given him the point from the harpoon that Angusiluk had been unable to recover from his mother's body. Since Angimmiq had two of them, he had given one to him as a gift. And now he was delivering Angimmiq's message. Angimmiq couldn't stand the fact that Angusiluk had beaten him when he arrived in the camp, so he was challenging Angusiluk to a match the next day, to see who could carry a large piece of ice the furthest. Angusiluk was uncomfortable with the challenge, and didn't know what to say. But his father-in-law nodded to confirm that the contest would take place tomorrow, and indicated Angusiluk's agreement with a "*heh, heh*".

Once the messenger had left, Angusiluk asked for an explanation, which his father-in-law provided right away. "Heavy chunks of ice will be placed on the pack ice, and they are to be carried as far as possible, to the last marker if possible. Usually, men get only as far as the fourth marker, and the bears always win because they are stronger. When I was young, I could reach the fifth marker, but I prepared myself and carefully examined all the chunks of ice before setting off. They are very heavy, and smooth and slippery. But I found a piece that wasn't very well cut, one I could dig my nails into to get a good grip." In the morning Angusiluk's father-in-law repeated his instructions, and told Angusiluk to use one of his outer parkas that was hanging in the porch, the smallest and shortest, dating back to his youth. Then he wished him good luck. Angusiluk put on the parka, and was transformed into a polar bear. But he didn't feel very confident. There was already a crowd on the ice when he got there, and he was the last one to arrive. Everyone stared at him — some were Angimmiq's friends, their eyes full of hostility and scorn, and the others were simply spectators, who gave nothing away in their gestures or their eyes, remaining passively neutral. Angimmiq, full of confidence, went first, lifting his load quite easily, and carrying it as far as the fourth marker. Angusiluk had discreetly looked at the other pieces of ice, and chose one in which he'd noticed some dents. As he started out, some remained silent and others laughed. He paid no attention to them, and when he got to the piece of ice that Angimmiq had triumphantly set on the pack ice, he stopped for a second to let his scorn show, then kept going, farther and farther, until he reached the last marker. Once there, he let his load fall and, saying nothing, turned slightly and started running towards the house. He didn't trust Angimmiq. In fact, he, and could hear the noise of snapping jaws and teeth behind him, and feel his enemy's breath on his neck his neck. But he got to the house just in time.

That was a happy day for Angusiluk. He had won the first round, to the delight of his wife and in-laws, but he knew that other tests awaited him. Angimmiq wasn't going to let things drop without trying some other tactics. He wanted revenge. Every night he imagined that he could hear his mother moaning, begging and crying out for vengeance, telling her son not to fail. She wouldn't be happy until her death was avenged. Angusiluk waited, knowing that the messenger would soon come to see him. And he did come, but this time began speaking right away, without any preliminaries, which was against tradition. Usually, there is some talk about other things before getting down to the matter at hand. Tomorrow, he said, Angimmiq would challenge Angusiluk again. They would dive under the ice, and the one who could stay under the water longest and swim the furthest would win. Again, the father-in-law answered for his son-in-law and accepted the challenge. It was agreed for the next day. Holes would be cut in the ice, and the distances measured. After the messenger left Angusiluk was told about the test he would face the next day. He would have to swim to the fifth hole if he wanted to survive. The old one told Angusiluk that he had been able to do it a long time ago, when he was young. So far, no man had been able to get farther than the fourth hole. So that was the danger. Angimmiq would probably stand right beside that hole to prevent Angusiluk from getting out. Angusiluk would have to get to the last hole. "Here's what I did," said the old one. "When I got to the fourth hole, just when I thought I was going to suffocate, I moved around so that I could breathe along the left side of my harpoon, which was always with me, right up against the ice. After that, it was child's play to get to the last hole and come out the winner."

When Angusiluk arrived on the ice the next day, the whole population was waiting there and, as is the case for any game or fight, they were excited. Angusiluk had again put on his father-in-law's outer parka that transformed him into a polar bear. This time it was his turn to go first. First, he stood at the edge of the hole, all his senses on alert. After looking all around him, and staring at his enemy, he took a deep breath and threw himself into the water and started swimming under the ice. He felt comfortable in the bear's skin, and could even swim just like a bear. As he approached the fourth hole he was feeling weaker, and as if he was going to suffocate. At the edge of the fourth hole he looked up and could see Angimmiq's shadow in the water. He was there all right, standing a little bent over, waiting for his prey. But Angusiluk had thought of everything and planned his route. Bypassing the hole and not making any noise, he got away without being seen and left Angimmiq standing there, brimming with confidence in himself and sure of his success. Now Angusiluk was hurrying to reach the last hole and was wondering, above all, if he could again stay ahead of his enemy when he ran back to the house. He still had a chance to make it, because the last hole had been cut in a place not far from the house, and since Angimmiq was probably still on the lookout for him at the fourth hole, he had the element of surprise on his side. When he reached the last hole, he climbed out, threw himself onto the ice and ran as hard and fast as he could, ignoring the exclamations of surprise behind him, but not being able to ignore the grunting of Angimmiq in hot pursuit. Once again, he managed to reach the house safe and sound, but not a second too soon, because Angimmiq was right there too, and Angusiluk could almost feel the gnashing of his teeth.

Once inside the house he wondered if Angimmiq had run out of tricks and schemes. He also wondered if it hadn't been presumptuous of him to come to this land of the polar bears. But he had to accept things as they came, and play the game, hoping for a good outcome. As for Angimmiq, he wasn't feeling any better and wondered what he was going to do – he hadn't expected such cunning and tenacity from a human. Maybe he should put an end to the hostilities and make an honourable peace, especially since he knew that Angusiluk had not only an advisor but also an ally in his father-in-law. And his father-in-law also had influence within the bear community. But the spirit of Angimmiq's mother wouldn't leave him in peace, and every evening he still heard her cries and calls to avenge her death. He didn't want to be seen as a coward and a traitor, so he asked his messenger to go and see Angusiluk and tell him that the next day he should be on the pack ice again, and that this time they would determine who was the best seal hunter. Once again, after accepting the challenge the father-in-law gave Angusiluk some advice. "The seals in the *aglu*, the breathing hole, aren't the only seals – there are also seals that stay in their dens, safe under snow banks. They may be harder to find, but they are easier to catch. I'd advise you to look for one of those seals."

At the appointed time, Angusiluk, following his father-in-law's advice, put on the parka that was hanging in the porch and went to join all the hunters. They spread out across the ice, all of them looking for seal holes. Angusiluk, doing as his father-in-law had advised, moved away from the others, abandoning the flat and smooth pack ice for the old and piled-up ice. He sniffed the air, trying to detect a seal den. The dens are built in a snow bank near an *aglu*, their hole in the ice. Angusiluk was familiar with them, and had found them quite often, but with the help of a dog. Today, he was on his own, but since he was wearing the bearskin he was acting like a bear, and his sense of smell had developed instantly. It didn't take him long to find a den. He immediately went on the attack, advancing carefully so as not to wake the occupant, and after making sure there was in fact a seal inside, he knocked the roof down. He stunned the seal, as bears do, with a single smack of his paw, pulled him out of the snow bank, picked him up in his jaws, and took off at top speed for the house. Angimmiq came after him right away, but again Angusiluk managed to stay just ahead of him. He felt the same fear, the fear of being bitten by Angimmiq. Having such gnashing of teeth and grunting so close behind him, he told his father-in-law, wasn't very pleasant for him or very good for his health either.

Angusiluk felt trapped, caught in a situation from which he couldn't escape. He realized he was never really given much time to recover from his ordeals. When the messenger came that evening, he wondered what new test, what new provocation, he would have to face. It didn't take long. Angimmiq, said the envoy, wanted to fight the next day. It wouldn't be a contest, it would be combat, biting. Again the father-in-law answered for his son-in-law, but only after a moment of silence. That silence was oppressive, and it was the messenger who had to lower his eyes first, looking at the ground, when the response came. It wasn't an ordinary response, but rather a challenge, and a condemnation. "Oh, so it's by biting Angimmiq wants to live," he said. "Tell him I don't approve of that method at all, in fact I think it's shameful. And if he really insists on it, it's me he'll have to fight." With those words, there was silence in the hut, and the messenger left.

The next day, and in the days that followed for a long time there was peace in the realm of the polar bears. But still Angimmiq didn't let go of his hatred and his desire for revenge, and Angusiluk didn't trust him. He took no chances, although he did allow himself to go out hunting and caught seals like the other bears, sometimes at their breathing holes and sometimes in their dens, but always like a bear, stunning the seals and then bringing them back to camp by dragging them or carrying them in his jaws. Angimmiq was consumed by jealousy, and he dreamed of revenge. He appeared polite, but inside, he continued to plot. One day, alone on the pack ice, he called upon his protector spirits. He was confident that his enemy was within his grasp, and that this time he wouldn't get away. He was far from the camp, completely alone, and along came Angusiluk, out hunting. This was the chance Angimmiq had been waiting for so long. Using his sorcery, he slid under the water, and waited at a seal's breathing hole. When Angusiluk tried to hit the seal, he was pulled into the water, and a kind of skin or blanket immediately covered him. It was Angimmiq's protector spirit. Angusiluk realized it immediately and, struggling, took out his knife and cut and struck and stabbed again and again until he was free and could get away.

During this battle, Angusiluk's thoughts had turned towards his home. Here was his opportunity. Without any reservations, and without thinking back to the time he had spent in the realm of the polar bears, he headed for the coast. For a long time he walked under the water, deep water. When he realized that it was getting shallower and that the ice above his head seemed to be getting closer, he left the water and continued, in human form, on the pack ice. When he got home he was struck by the silence. There was no noise, and no one around. He took a quick look around and discovered a large quantity of whale bones. He also found the bones of his parents. He put them all together in a pile, all the bones, and found some mice, which he put in the middle of the bones. Then he asked his spirits for their help. His father and his mother came back to life, and lived happily for a long time.

That is the story that Angusiluk told his family and friends when he returned from the land of the polar bears.

There are a lot of stories about close calls with polar bears that come around camps. Nothing scares them. They walk right by the dogs, paying no attention to them at all. One time at Baillie Island the Kotokaks were surprised to hear their dog barking in the porch, and then to see the door to their house open and a big polar bear walk in without knocking. He had smelled seal blubber, and how! The Kotokaks were burning it in the stove, and it was the smoke from the stove that had attracted the bear to the camp. The dog wasn't feeling very brave, and escaped to a corner at the back of the room. The adults just stood there frozen at first, the women covering the children with blankets so they wouldn't see the bear and start crying. The elder Kotokak stared at the bear, and whispered to another man to pick up an axe. He told him just to hold on to it, not to use it. On the floor beside the stove there were a few pieces of blubber. Kotokak slowly moved closer to the stove, grabbed a piece of the blubber, and, holding it under the bear's nose with one hand pushed the bear back a few steps, not giving it a chance to turn around. The bear backed out of the house. Once it was outside, Kotokak grabbed a rifle that was propped against the house, and shot the bear.

Recently, a serious incident took place in an oil company camp out on the ice near Tuktoyaktuk. A bear had been prowling around the camp. They had kept an eye on it, but it disappeared and everyone went about their work. Later, the camp foreman was having a cup of coffee and talking to the cook in the caboose. They went outside, and were standing by the door when the bear, which had been hiding behind the caboose, came up behind them. It hit them with his paw, felling both men and knocking them out cold. Then he seized the foreman in his jaws and dragged him a few metres away. A few minutes later the cook regained consciousness and, still a little groggy, wondered what had happened to him. Sitting there in the snow and feeling the cold, he glanced around, looking for his companion and saw a white form only a few metres away, a form that he gradually realized was a polar bear, once his vision cleared up a bit. The bear had one paw on a body – the body of his companion. Now fully conscious the cook rushed into the office, and using the mobile radio he alerted the camp workers and asked them to come right away. The workers quickly arrived on their tractors, and with the shovels lifted halfway they moved towards the bear and cornered it while someone dashed forward to get the body of the poor foreman, which was

Left to right: *Sarah, Ella and Henry Nasogaluak, Annie Cockney, Susie and Joe Nasogaluak, Tuktoyaktuk, circa 1950. (Photo courtesy of J. Ross Mackay)*

already missing several parts. That bear was scrawny, emaciated and starving. Some time later, the police came in an airplane and killed the bear. Felix Nuyaviak explained the bear's attitude and actions to me. He said, "This is what I heard from my ancestors and the elders when I was a child. Some polar bears are born under a bad star and are unlucky all their lives, and can't catch anything when they hunt. They might have been injured by hunters, or chased by dogs. Something stays with them though – the fear of dogs barking, and of sudden or strange noises that they can't explain. Fear haunts them. That's what happens to them. They know how to hunt seal – it's instinctive. In the silence, when they're on the lookout and watching the seal's hole, everything is fine, but when the seal comes into the hole and starts surfacing, there is a noise, a gentle splashing sound, and that's enough to make the bear suspicious. Before even hitting the seal, it runs away, thinking it hears barking dogs chasing it, or even humans. That's why," added Felix Nuyaviak, "those kinds of bears are very dangerous – since they can't survive alone on the pack ice, they move often and prowl around camps and villages, hoping to find some food without hunting."

I've heard several times that, according to Inuvialuit tradition, you shouldn't wish to see a bear. That happened to Kakianaan – Jim Wolki, a good friend of mine – one time when he was camping with his family on Banks Island. They were living in a tent with a roof that he had reinforced with wood and covered with snow. One night before he went to sleep he said to his wife, "It's too bad we're not seeing any bears, because I'd really like to get a big one." His wife scolded him for thinking such thoughts. But Jim told her not to worry, he had his rifle and so there was no danger. Unlike the time he was near Horton River, when he left his rifle at home, against his wife's advice. He wasn't going far, just down to collect and cut a little driftwood. "And," he said to his wife, "my hatchet will be enough if a bear shows up." Well, a bear did show up and he'd had to run for his life. His hatchet had seemed a pretty poor weapon to him then. He'd managed to reach the camp with the bear right behind him, on his heels. Back to the time on Banks Island – they went to bed, and during the night they were awakened by a loud crack, the sound of wood splitting, above their heads. Jim lit a candle and could see a bear's paw hanging down into the tent. He was immediately awake and jumped out of bed. In a few strides, he was at the door and, with a single shot from his rifle, put an end to the escapades of *nanuq*, the polar bear. Jim was satisfied, but he had also learned his lesson.

When I was living in Tuktoyaktuk, Joe Nasogaluak, 'Big Joe', told me that the tradition of not wishing to see a bear is an ancient one that has passed down among Inuvialuit. He recounted the following story as an example:

~ *Nuyaviak Gets His Wish* ~

"I'm telling this story so the young people will remember. It happened around 1900, at the end of winter. At that time, our families lived east of Tuktoyaktuk, around Baillie Island and at the Anderson River. They usually spent the summer in the Anderson River area fishing and hunting moose and caribou in summer, and went to the coast, to Baillie Island and surrounding areas, for the winter. Every day, everyone went out onto the pack ice to look for seal breathing holes. The men waited patiently at the breathing holes for seals to arrive, and then harpooned them and hauled up onto the ice. The women and children took them back to their camp, and cut them up, separating the blubber and the meat."

"When people finally had their supply of seal blubber most left to go to the Anderson River, but this time Nuyaviak and his wife Tassugana, their daughter Arnavigak and son-in-law Angusinauk stayed behind. They wanted to get more seals, just to be sure they had enough. Nuyaviak was a good trapper and hunter, with a reputation as a bear hunter. He had killed a lot of bears with just a harpoon attached to a long rope made of *ugiuk* – bearded seal skins, which allowed him to control the bear and prevent it from getting away. Among the objects that were of great value to him was a hatchet he had bought at Fort McPherson, on one of his trips among the white men.[1] He didn't

Angusinauk, Baillie Island, circa 1925. (Leo Hansen/Danish Museum of Natural History/Fifth Thule Expedition/Neg. 2037)

use it very often, but he stroked, admired and sharpened it, and it cut like a razor blade. Often, in the evening, when stories were being told, he sharpened his precious tool with a file he had got from the American whalers who sometimes wintered at Baillie Island. One evening, when everyone was in the snow house, he was passing the time examining his hatchet, but his mind was far away, dreaming of other things. Their stay around Baillie hadn't been very productive in polar bears – they hadn't caught even one yet. Deep in thought, maybe without even being aware of it, he said, 'If only a few bears would show up, I could defend myself with this hatchet.' His wife, Tassugana, trembled and protested. She didn't like that kind of joke at all. 'Nuyaviak, don't say things like that. It's not a good idea. You know very well that some animals, like polar bears and whales, hear from far away and sense human thoughts.' But Nuyaviak wasn't himself that night, and he reacted strongly. 'That doesn't matter.

94

I'd still like to see one of those bears. I need some of that meat and another bearskin. My pants are getting old and worn, and the fur is gone.' Despite Tassugana's scolding, he kept on talking about the benefits of bears and the bad luck they'd had that fall and winter, not seeing one. Tassugana told him again to stop saying – and, especially, wishing – things like that, especially now that the other families were far away on the Anderson River."

"When Nuyaviak had finished sharpening his hatchet and talking about bears, they went to bed. The next morning, feeling proud of himself, Nuyaviak teased his wife, pointing out what nonsense she had spoken. Tassugana didn't answer, and went out and started preparing breakfast over a fire of wood and blubber. While she prepared the meal of seal meat she thought about the work she was going to finish that same day. There was still a seal to cut up, and a skin to dry. Her musing was interrupted when she thought she heard a kind of squeaking noise, a familiar sound, like sleds sliding on ice. She left her pots and fire at once and rushed into the house to announce the news. 'I think we have visitors,' she shouted, loud enough to wake everyone. 'Who?' she was asked, 'Where from?' Tassugana couldn't answer all those questions. 'I didn't see anything. There's too much rough ice, and too many snow banks,' she answered, 'but I'm going to check.' On her way out, Tassugana tripped over the dogs as they rushed into the snow house. '*Ki, Ki, Ki,*' ('Go on!'), she murmured, angrily. When she stood up she found herself nose to nose with a polar bear. Tassugana fell to the ground again. Crawling on all fours, she went back into the house, making a less than dignified entrance. But while she'd lost her composure, she hadn't lost her voice, and she shouted at everyone, '*He, nanuq tadjva!*' ('Hey, there's a bear here!')."

"Nuyaviak and Angusinauk got up right away and stared at the bear. What's more, something could now be heard walking on the roof, and it wasn't dogs, that much was certain. It seemed there was at least one more bear prowling around outside. The one that had arrived first and had collided with Tassugana was now inside. Everyone was alarmed, and felt it was hopeless because their rifles were outside. Only Nuyaviak had a weapon – the hatchet, as yet untouched by blood. But it seemed pretty ineffective and weak against an animal the size of the bear. It fixed its gaze on Arnavigak. She was pregnant, and the baby she was carrying inside made her look quite big. The bear kept on staring at her. Without daring to say anything, everyone wondered if the bear was going to attack her. She hid behind her husband, frightened, her thoughts turning to the child she was impatient to have. But then the bear, after what must have seemed like hours to the poor prisoners in the house, saw the seal Tassugana had brought in to thaw so that she could cut it up. Instinct was stronger than curiosity. Paying no more attention to the humans who were all around it, the bear bent down to sniff and smell the seal. Satisfied by that quick examination, the bear seized it in its jaws and started to retreat, backing up, and dragging the animal along the ground through the porch, where it collided with two of its companions. They were curious, too. Maybe they wanted to say hello and greet Nuyaviak. Maybe they wanted to tell him they had heard his wish."

"Angusinauk was ready to defend the life of his wife and unborn child at any cost. Without making any noise, he broke through the wall of the snow house where he thought his rifle was, making a hole large enough to put his hand through. On the first try, he was in the wrong spot. On the second try, reaching his arm to the left, he felt the rifle. He grabbed it and quickly pulled it into the house, but before doing that he had taken a quick look outside to avoid being surprised by a bear, which could have bitten his hand. The people in the house still didn't know how many bears were in the area, just that there were at least three. As soon as he had his rifle in his hands – an old model 45-70, but effective and reliable – he got into position, moved a few steps forward and killed the first bear in the entrance to the house. Hearing something walking on the roof, he aimed blindly and shot another bear, just wounding it. Knowing the leader of the visitors was dead for sure, he went outside, rifle in hand, and killed the wounded. He then headed for the drying racks, where three more bears were stuffing themselves with the blubber hanging there. Nuyaviak's dogs were feeling braver, each one barking louder than the next. Angusinauk shot the three bears, one after the other. It was a good day."

Inuvialuit often see a humorous side of encounters with polar bears, at least after the fact. This story about Dick Qaatigaaryuk and his family happened one winter when they were camped on Banks Island. Early one morning they were awakened by their dogs. A female and her pups were creating an uproar on the roof of their dwelling. Why all the noise? There must be a polar bear in the camp, looking for food. But it was too dark to go outside and look around. The mother dog and her pups rushed into the porch, a sort of tunnel made of snow. They heard the intruder grunting and walking around. There was no doubt, it was a polar bear. The dog tried to protect her pups but was silenced, crushed by the bear. Dick's rifle was outside the door in the snow porch, so he rushed to the door and pushed against it with all his might to prevent the bear from entering. He watched through a crack in the door as the bear swallowed one of the pups, hardly biting it. It seemed that the bear didn't like it, though, because it spit it out almost immediately. Meanwhile, the other dogs were hiding on the roof of the tent. The bear went outside, and the Qaatigaaryuks no doubt thought he'd left for good, but he hadn't. Soon there was a commotion on the roof – even the stovepipe was moving, and the dogs were barking. Thinking that the bear was up there chasing the dogs Dick Qaatigaaryuk grabbed the only gun in the house, an old and not very reliable rifle. He took a chance and fired at the sound. The lead shot flew almost everywhere, and even pierced the stovepipe. But there was more noise than danger to the bear. This game of hide-and-seek lasted a while, with more shots fired. Finally, the dogs calmed down and Dick went outside and got his good rifle. The bear was still looking for food around the camp, so Dick shot it. He certainly deserved it. A few days before when he was hunting he only got a polar bear cub, and said he wished he would see a bigger bear. He got his wish.

Stories like these are real, they really did happen. As to how they should be interpreted, I'm not adding anything. I'm telling them to you just as they were told to me. These reflections by the Inuvialuit, who know the animals of the North and their habits so well, prove how close they were to them.

I had some experiences with brown bears (*aklaq*) too. One time at Paulatuk Sam Green and I went by boat to the Hornaday River to move some fishnets. The trip across the bay to our camp at the mouth of the river was uneventful. After pulling up the first nets we continued upstream, crossed over to the other side and took another channel. We were going against the current. The motor we had wasn't very powerful, and our boat was barely moving. At one point we had to get into the water to get past a small rapid where the water was shallow and the current was strong. The water was moving so fast we could barely hold the boat against the current, and we had to stop a number of times to recover our strength, holding on to the boat with a rope. But after a fair bit of effort we got through the difficult spots. That was when we saw three bears on the opposite bank. Fortunately, we had stopped the motor, and the noise of the river covered any noise we were making. Bears have a good sense of smell, but don't see very well. We stopped and observed them, watching them eating blueberries. It was a strange and fascinating sight to see – the enormous animals, a female and her two already fairly big cubs, gorging themselves, getting ready for hibernation. They would shake the small bushes and then, with

Grizzly bear sow and cubs. (Denali National Park and Preserve)

their giant paws, gather up the blueberries they are so fond of, or they would sift through the bushes, blow on their paws to remove the leaves, and swallow the berries without chewing them.

But we were more interested in having meat than in studying bear behaviour. So, without starting the motor, we landed on the opposite shore without being detected by the bears. The wind was in our favour, so there was no danger of being detected by our scent. Once the boat was safely moored we climbed the bank, making as little noise as possible. When we got right to the top of the bank we thought we'd see our bear friends, but there was nothing to the right or left, or in front of us or behind us. They hadn't had time to go very far, though, so we split up. Sam went farther back from the river and I went along the bank, which was quite high in that spot. Our plan was to not lose sight of each other. As soon as we spotted the bears, we would give the signal by waving our rifle.

After only a few dozen yards I saw the bear family lying in a ravine in full sun, on a flat spot that had just enough room for the three of them. I signalled their presence to Sam, who came right away. Lying there on our stomachs, we watched our victims for a minute or two. They were within our reach and there was no way out, no exit – the slope was too steep, and there was nothing but big rocks below. They had to come upward, towards us. We realized it was an ideal spot. Once we killed them, we would just have to push them down to the edge of the river, ready for loading on the boat. So it was in our best interest to prevent them from climbing up. Since they appeared to be dead asleep, we decided to attack and not to wait. First we'd take the mother bear. The cubs would stay with their mother. We started firing. What a rude awakening for them! The female bear leapt up after she was hit by the first bullet, biting herself and turning towards us for just a few seconds, then she fell, rolling and sliding down the slope, crashing onto the rocks below. The two others followed, struck down and riddled with bullets. We went down the ravine carefully, loaded the animals in the boat, turned it around and went back to camp.

It was an easy trip back, because the current was fairly strong. After a good cup of tea at the tent we started to skin the bears, then cut them up. We wanted to finish before going to bed, and eventually we finished our work by candlelight. It was a good supply of meat in case we didn't have enough caribou later in October. While cleaning them, we found their stomachs were full of the berries they had gathered so carefully a short time ago, still fresh, although a bit warm. That evening, after a good bear steak, we even had dessert. We weren't going to miss the chance to eat fresh fruit in a land where, at that time, only a few oranges and apples reached us with the arrival of the mission boat, *Our Lady of Lourdes.*

But coming back to brown bears... Every chance they get, they visit unoccupied camps, tearing the tents, knocking down the racks and opening all the canned food, which they can do with just their claws and teeth. Many times the people have come back to find their camp vandalized and their provisions gone or destroyed – coffee, flour and tea scattered everywhere, the stove ripped apart, sugar gone, canned honey, jam and syrup also gone, just the cans left scattered around the tent or in the tent, cut open or pressed flat by bears. It's obvious why Mr. *Aklaq* isn't welcome in these parts.

Of course, in other parts of the world all of this seems inconceivable – seeing a bear prowling the streets or knocking at your door. But I have lived this kind of life where anything can happen. Just a few years ago, I never went out, not even to visit neighbours just a few metres or half a kilometre away, without my rifle slung over my shoulder. I could have found myself, and in fact did find myself, face to face with wolves or bears. So we understand all the anxiety, bitterness, anger and scorn that people in the North feel towards all the regulations imposed on them by people who live in safety in the South, with red lights and green lights and police at every corner controlling traffic. More and more orders are coming from Ottawa or from Yellowknife – only so many bears can be killed here and there. Do the bears know how to read, or when they are outside the safety zone? As well, the people aren't always consulted, and don't know anything about the new regulations until they get notices from government employees. Last year, on my way to the store, I met a trapper who told me that the polar bear quota had been reduced. When I asked him if the people had been consulted, he said no. I told him that as soon as I got back to the house, I would write a letter and all they would have to do was sign it if they thought it was valid. Was there any prior consultation on that restriction? What is the reason for the restriction? The trappers got together and discussed the issue, and decided to send the letter to the authorities concerned. Their representative on the territorial council, the territorial commissioner, the head game warden, the Minister of Northern Affairs would all get a copy. You have to know how to use blackmail too. The next day, I got a telephone call from our representative on the territorial council, telling me that he was looking into it and asking me why I hadn't warned him earlier by telephone. He said he was going to look after it right away. And I did get a positive response – the quota wouldn't be changed. He clearly suspected that I was behind it. My reason? Simply to help and support the people, at a time when decisions shouldn't be made until after the people have been consulted. There are so many restrictions on them right now, restrictions on the caribou hunt in the reindeer reserve, and restrictions on how many polar bears can be killed in a specific area, and so on. Meanwhile the bears have free rein. I know some people who wondered if they would set traps at their camps, because, they said, "What will I do if the bears come to my camp after the quota is filled? I can't run around shouting to make them go away, or try to scare them off." That doesn't work for bears – they don't usually get scared off that easily.

Sometimes the bear is taken out of its realm. In 1962 a trapper caught a polar bear cub near Tuktoyaktuk. I took him on my sled to show him to workers at the Distant Early Warning Line camp. We tried feeding him bananas and oranges there, but he didn't like our delicacies, so we fed him milk from a baby bottle. And then suddenly, without a yawn, or even a sigh, he dropped to the ground and fell asleep. As we watched, fascinated, one minute he was playing and wrestling, growling at anyone who came near, and the next minute there was nothing – not a movement, not a breath. I was afraid that he might be dead. But no, after about ten minutes he was up on his feet again, exploring and scratching the carpet with his claws. He seemed to be looking for a solid, hard and white surface. The next day he was taken by airplane to Edmonton and then to Vancouver. If you go to Vancouver and you're in Stanley Park, visit the zoo and you'll see him there – his name is Tuk.[2] When I went there several years later he didn't recognize me, and, I must say, he was so big I had trouble recognizing him too.

'Tuk' the polar bear at Stanley Park Zoo, Vancouver, 1996. (Photo credit: Jan Bjorklund)

Chapter 8 Notes

1   Until fur trade posts were established along the coast in the second decade of the twentieth century, Inuvialuit would often travel to Fort McPherson to obtain supplies at the Hudson's Bay Company trading post.

2   Tuk, the polar bear named after Tuktoyaktuk, remained at the Stanley Park Zoo in Vancouver until he died in 1996. He was the last captive animal at the zoo, which closed soon after his death.

Felix Nuyaviak's Memories of the Past

*Felix Nuyaviak (**centre**) at a drum dance in the schoolhouse at Tuktoyaktuk, circa 1956. On the left is Raddi Quiqsaq and on the right is Jim Cockney. (Terrance Hunt/NWT Archives/ N-1979-062: 0064)*

During the time I've been learning the language of the Inuvialuit and collecting legends and stories of first-hand experiences, I've gained a better appreciation of both the value and the beauty of their narratives, their gift of storytelling, their imagination. Often, armed with a tape recorder, I listened for hours on end to the elders telling their stories. They related them without hesitation, their speech flowing like a river. All I had to do was listen and change tapes. It's one of those storytellers that I'll introduce here – Felix Nuyaviak. He is now more than 87 years old, but is still active, and an early riser.[1] He is slightly stooped, but every day he goes around visiting the homes of his children and grandchildren, often accompanied by his granddaughter Sharon. He is a true artisan and still makes *ulus*, the women's knives, although now it's miniature *ulus* he makes and sells. He also belongs to a drumming group that performs music from the old drums and traditional dances in Tuktoyaktuk, and sometimes even in the South and in Alaska. Here is one of his stories:[2]

~ *Memories of the Past* ~

"From my youth, from my earliest years, I have memories. I have happy memories, golden memories of beauty and joy. But I also have others, quite a few, unfortunately sad and unpleasant, that I can't forget either."

"As children, we liked to go hunting, we boys, armed with slings and small stones. I think the birds must have suffered from our actions. Everyone enjoyed it, both young and old. Something was happening every minute, from morning to evening. In those days it wasn't the clock that

regulated our activities. No, the weather was our only master. Our whole life followed a cycle, like that of the animals, those on land, and those in the sea and in the air. There was a time for everything – a time for fishing, a time for hunting whales, caribou and seal. All these activities were regulated by the *angatkut*, our shamans. Summer and winter, we were truly nomads, always on the move, always travelling, a campsite here and another farther on. All our attention and our activities were directed towards finding food – animals, birds, anything that could be eaten. No one dreamed of resting. The elders were in the habit of saying that rest would come quickly enough when it was time to die."

"A period of the year that we all really liked, and that is still etched in my memory, was the white whale hunt in summer. Our gathering at Kitigaaryuit was no picnic at this time.[3] Certainly we enjoyed the hunt, but still it was work. The children could have fun, but the adults worked hard. Rifles weren't in use yet – our weapon was the harpoon – and there were no, or very few, wooden boats, only kayaks. There was a whole fleet of them, all along the shore, one beside the other. Here again, everything was regulated. A hunt leader was appointed, and the lookouts took turns 24 hours a day. It was the time of endless days, as the midnight sun was shining. The lookouts stood on platforms built of driftwood and watched the horizon. As soon as whales were spotted heading toward the river the hunters were alerted. At the given signal they formed a line with their kayaks behind the whales, advancing on a single front, very close to each other. They all paddled very slowly and without making any noise, so as not to attract the attention of the whales. Once the whales had entered the river the leader gave the signal, and the hunters took up the pursuit, singing and chanting as they paddled. Their paddles would move in rhythm now, and very fast, to scare the whales and push them farther in, towards the shallow water and the sandbanks. They struck them with their harpoons, and then struck again to mark them with a special mark.[4] When the commotion was over, when the whales that had been struck were no longer moving, it seemed as if the water they had been pushing ahead of them withdrew and they were stranded on the sandbanks. It was then child's play to finish them off. The whales were then brought back to the camp. The old ones, who were clever people, had a very special method for doing this. Before pulling them behind their kayaks, they blew air into the whale by inserting a wooden tube for that purpose through the skin and the blubber. Once inflated with air they floated, and were easy to

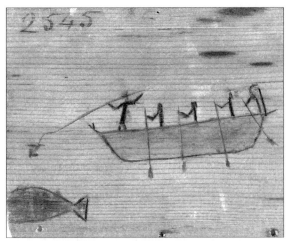

An illustration by an unknown Inuvialuk of a bowhead whale hunt, circa 1860s. (National Museum of Natural History/ Smithsonian Institution/MacFarlane Collection/E2545-1b)

pull. This way, a hunter could tow up to three or four whales without too much effort."

"Next came the bulk of the work, and it was work in which everyone, men and women, and even the children, took part – removing the skin, the blubber and the meat. The meat was cut up and dried. The blubber was put in sealskin bags and then placed in holes in the ground, or in an ice cellar dug into the side of a hill. In my day, in my youth, *maktak*, the blubber, wasn't cooked like it is now. We learned to do that from the Inupiat who came from Alaska, and it seems that this was a habit they'd picked up from the whalers."

"Our neighbours to the east, the *Nuvugarmiut* who lived at *Nuvurak* – Atkinson Point – didn't take part in our white whale hunt. They were more interested in the large bowhead whales that visited their waters. They found that hunt more exciting, and more profitable too. What courage our old ones had! They dared to go out hunting those huge whales, some in umiaks – boats made of seal skin or whale skin, larger than a kayak – and others following in kayaks. As they did in the case of white whales, they threw harpoons, which were attached to floats inflated with air. I was told that they even jumped onto the back of the whale, to thrust the harpoon into the whale at the most vulnerable places. The oldest ones sang their *errenat*, their special song for the circumstances. It's too bad I've forgotten them – I was too young at the time."[5]

"Once the whale hunt was over and all the work completed people went their separate ways again.

An Inuvialuit fishing camp in the inner Mackenzie River Delta, circa 1865. (Based on a sketch by Émile Petitot in 'Les Grands Esquimaux', 1887)

"Esquimaux Dancing at Fort McPherson", 1892. (James MacDougall//Hudson's Bay Company Archives 1987/13/211)

Each one left with his group, formed on the basis of family or other connections. These groups weren't very big. We needed quite a lot of space to be able to gather all the food we needed for a long winter. Some went along the river, others along the coast. Tuktoyaktuk was a good place for fishing, as were places farther east, like Tapqaq and Toker Point. The fish we caught in our nets were cut open and dried in the sun, and sometimes even smoked. The fish eggs were collected and frozen. What a delicacy!"

"Some groups travelled up the rivers and channels in whaling boats or *umiaks* to the trading post at Fort McPherson. We didn't need very much in those days, just sugar, tea, which we'd become fond of, flour and molasses to make bannock, tobacco and a few tools. It was only later, when the rifle had appeared on the scene, that we bought powder and cartridges to make bullets ourselves. The group that formed for a trip was generally quite large, for their own safety and to make an impression. The feuds and hostility with our neighbours, the Gwich'in, in the not-too-distant past was fading, but distrust still ran deep behind masks of smiles and pleasantries."[6]

"September would find us getting ready for winter. Men would gather at the *kadjigi*, a kind of common house or clubhouse. The women and children were not allowed. There, we put the kayaks in order, and got the dog harnesses and sleds ready. This was where the hunters liked to relate their stories and achievements, and to gossip. From time to time the women would bring something to drink and eat – some tea or just water, a piece of dried or cooked fish – and towards evening, before nightfall, everyone went home. There weren't any long evenings around the fire in those days. We went to bed early, but we also got up very early."

"Looking back now, it seems to me that young people showed more respect for the elders and were more obedient. Oh, like all children, we would sometimes make too much noise and commotion, but then if the warning *"Taima* – that's enough" had no effect, then *akłaq*, the brown bear, made

'Old (abandoned) Ka-ja-gi or dance house at Kittigazuit', circa 1909. (R.M. Anderson/Library and Archives Canada/C-023947)

his entrance. Such a visit from the 'bogey man' was enough to restore calm in the house. His jaws were huge, and he said, "*Ah! Ah! Ah!*", and he walked around very close to the children, who hid behind their mothers, pulling their hoods over their heads so they couldn't see, but at the same time peeking out from under them."[7]

"When the ocean began to freeze and frost started forming on the land, the men set out ptarmigan snares. Sometimes they also spread out old fishing nets, ones they could no longer repair, between willow stakes, and then chased ptarmigan into them. We all waited for the first snowfall. Then the sleds could glide over the snow-covered ground, and we could travel further."

"As soon as the sun disappeared for good, family after family from all around made their way to Kitigaaryuit for the winter celebrations, and there were happy meetings and reunions after an absence of several months. The camp filled up fast with laughter and noise, and with snow houses too. I can't give a number, because I didn't know how to count yet – my only school was nature, what I saw around me, and what my parents did – but there were a lot. When everyone got together on the ice for games there were so many people that the water in the water holes moved and shook. And in the darkness, what a fairyland of lights it was – a bit like the Christmas lights nowadays. All those lit oil lamps at Kitigaaryuit and at Kuukpak, the village on the opposite side of the Mackenzie River, shone through the walls of the snow houses. It was really beautiful to see."

An illustration by an unknown Inuvialuk of a snow house camp with fox skins drying on poles, circa 1860s. (National Museum of Natural History/Smithsonian Institution/MacFarlane Collection/E2545-3b)

"Kitigaaryuit in 1909." This photograph was taken seven years after a measles epidemic in 1902 led to the temporary abandonment of Kitigaaryuit. (I.O. Stringer Collection /General Synod Archives, Anglican Church of Canada/P7517-191)

"Hospitality, good humour, generosity, and participation in festivities and games were the rules in those days. The elders saw to it that everyone was happy, that they shared meals and participated in games. They urged us to take part in various challenges, and they often voiced their encouragement, *"Ki, ki* – 'come on, come on' – let's have fun, let's eat". The days were filled with games, challenges, combats and matches, and the evenings were spent listening to stories and, of course, dancing also played a large part. Each person in turn tried his hand at high jumping, arm-wrestling, and leg wrestling, and each of the games ended with a champion being declared. From time to time the elders, past masters in the art of presenting animals as marionettes, bringing them to life, charmed us with their skill and their extraordinary ingenuity, a kind of magic show. They showed us foxes, swans, bears. Those animals made their own sounds, they walked, ate and seemed so alive that they could be mistaken for the real thing. Unfortunately, that art, kept a secret and passed from father to son, disappeared along with the elders who died in the measles epidemic in 1902."

"The festivities ended with the return of the sun, around the middle of January. Then there were special rituals, clearly defined, that had to be followed. The old skins that had served as mattresses inside the houses were thrown away, the old oil was removed from the lamps and replaced with fresh oil, and pieces of blubber were offered to the sun. Before everyone went their separate ways, the dart game, *papigak*, brought all the hunters together, and each one had to make a wager. The object was to throw a dart or harpoon at a piece of blubber set on the snow, attempting to hit it. Then everyone scattered to the four corners of the horizon, all happy to have had a good time, and arranging to meet again in the summer for the white whale hunt."

"In 1902 a great epidemic of measles destroyed many of our people around Kitigaaryuit. Those recollections are still very clear, still very vivid in my memory. What terrible days we lived through then, a true nightmare. So many died in the prime of life, the young and the old, children, youths, overcome by that scourge at a time when we were all assembled for the whale hunt, in July. Death spared no one, young or old, weak or strong. Some died after being sick for only a short time, others lasted a bit longer. They were dropping like flies everywhere, overcome by the disease – in the tents, outside on the shore, some while burying the dead. What hours of agony we experienced. I remember, and I still cry. I still see the dead in my memory, some wrapped in caribou skins, others simply left on the ground, barely covered with a few poles – no one was strong enough to make proper graves. When it was all over, there were only a few handfuls of survivors. Kitigaaryuit, a place that just the other day was full of life and joy, had become a place of death, a kind of haunted place under a spell, an evil spell. A village so full of life and noise was gone – no voices calling, no songs, no movement – and we were frightened. Traumatized and seized with panic, the survivors, myself included, fled. Taking one last look back at the place, I saw the tents standing near the water. The end of a tribe, the end of our race, was what I thought at that moment. The next year, two boats were enough to carry those who had survived that cruel epidemic to Fort McPherson. Once there, we gave the news, and we wept and cried aloud in our grief. Then we invited the people to sing and to dance, to help us put those sorrowful times behind us. And it's me, Felix Nuyaviak, one of the survivors, who is telling you this true story of the past so that you won't forget, and will remember your ancestors, their courage and strength, their great deeds. People of extraordinary worth, of great stature, living in a land where, to live and survive, all the qualities required of humans are demanded to the highest degree. Real people, *Inuvialuit.*"[8]

"And with that, I, Felix Nuyaviak will end my story."

That was one of the many programs I prepared for the community radio station in Tuktoyaktuk, CFCT, in the 1970s. I ended by saying, "Today those people live on in you who are endowed with the same inspiration, and the same spirit and courage. Such a race, such a spirit, can't die in everyone. It will survive in some, a like what happened at Kitigaaryuit. The people left the place because they were afraid of the silence and of death, which reigned supreme, but they quickly recovered and went on living. It is your turn to continue the tradition that is shown to you by people such as your elder, Felix Nuyaviak."

Chapter 9 Notes

1   Felix Nuyaviak passed away in 1982 at age 89.

2   Felix Nuyaviak told his story to Father Le Meur in Inuvialuktun. Father Le Meur translated this story into English, and retold it in his own fashion.

3   Kitigaaryuit, sometimes spelled Kittigazuit, was a traditional village and beluga whale hunting area near the mouth of the East Channel of the Mackenzie River.

4   Felix Nuyaviak may be referring to using arrowheads with an 'owner's mark' to so that whale carcasses could be identified by individual hunters once the hunt was over. A similar technique is known to have been used when caribou were speared by hunters in kayaks at caribou crossings, or after they had been driven into lakes

5   In his book 'I, Nuligak' Bob Cockney (p. 70-71) told of a song that bowhead whale hunters would sing to ensure that they would arrive safely home:

> "You that we are towing along
> Ah, ya ah e ya
> Big whale, big whale
> Stir up the sea with your tail
> E ya ah e ya
> Give us fair weather today
> So we arrive safe and sound on shore.
> E ya ah e ya
> Tug – tug along hard
> E ya ah e ya
> Row – Row"

6   Some Inuvialuit made annual trips to Fort McPherson (originally named 'Peel River Post'), '*Igluqpait*' ('Big Houses') as they called it, to trade furs for European goods at the Hudson's Bay trading post that had been established there in 1840. This meant travelling into the territory of their traditional enemies, the Gwich'in Dene.

7   This practice of imitating bears is also told in Chapter 8.

8   '*Inuvialuit*' means 'Real People' in English. It is the term chosen by the Inuit of the Western Canadian Arctic to assert their identity.

Qilalukkat – **Beluga Whales**

Hunting beluga whales from a motorboat, 1985. (Peter Poole/Department of Public Works and Services/ NWT Archives G-1995-001-4180)

And so life goes on. Not exactly the same life the elders lived – there is less hardship now – but life in the North can still be difficult. Living conditions may have changed, but the land remains the same. Winter is still just as cold. The wind still finds its way back to the icy, frozen plains of the North, and blowing snow still reigns and creates confusion on the flat terrain. The wild animals still come as their instincts dictate. Inuvialuit still harvest the animals, and even with modern technology there is still a lot of work involved.

As they always have, *qilalukkat* – the beluga whales – appear near Tuktoyaktuk in the summer as soon as the sea ice opens up enough for them to swim to the mouth of the Mackenzie River seeking their food, the herring. I remember one time seeing herds of whales while on the way from Tuktoyaktuk to Inuvik by boat. Although the weather was fine, I saw foam just about everywhere as I approached the river. I realized that I was crossing through a herd of whales, and slowed my outboard motor. They were all around me, ignoring my presence. Later on in the summer, after they had been chased by hunters, they were much more cautious, but that time I was able to stroke their backs.

When the beluga whales are due to make their appearance there is excitement in the air. The boats are ready, the floats and harpoons have been inspected, and everyone is watching the weather. On the first nice day, several hunters head out, and often come back after just a few hours, towing one or two whales. Then the excitement reaches a fever pitch in the village.

The first whale brought in it doesn't last very long. People are particularly fond of *maktak*. How can

I describe it? It's a white layer between the skin and the blubber. It can be prepared in different ways – raw, just as it comes, or boiled, dried, or grilled. This is my method: I boil it in water just for a moment or two, take it out of the pot, drain it, cut it like slices of bacon, and then throw it into boiling oil. When I tried this recipe for the first time a whole gang of children cleaned me out of it in no time at all. The next day I took some to the women who were working in the Fur Garment Shop, and there again it was a success. Sometimes we also roast it in the oven. But Heaven help those visitors who eat too much. We who live here are used to it, but I remember once serving *maktak* to some important visitors, an Apostolic Delegate to Canada and a French priest, a Jesuit, who had come to tour the Arctic coast. I was careful to warn them, because it's easy to lose track of how much you're eating, but my two visitors became ill, and didn't want to see any more *maktak* the next day.

Pieces of beluga whale skin, maktak and blubber on a drying rack. (David Stewart/ Inuvialuit Communications Society)

Coming back to the whale hunt... you have to take advantage of every nice day, and there aren't that many of them in a summer. If there is a wind and it creates waves, chasing whales becomes practically impossible. It's also difficult to shoot properly and accurately when the boat is going up and down in the waves. Even if the whale is shot there is a chance of losing it, of seeing it disappear as it sinks to the bottom of the sea before it can be harpooned. Later, it may be found on the shore, driven there by the waves. Or in winter the dogs will find it when the trappers are travelling along the beach. A found carcass is a windfall, or even a double windfall – the meat and the blubber are still good for the dogs, and the carcass attracts foxes, which scratch and scrape everything they can from it. Anyway, in the summer only a few days are favourable for hunting. Two years ago, I counted only six days when hunters could get to the places whales gather. That's really not very many! Also, often when the boats set off in good weather, bad weather takes the hunters by surprise and they might have to quickly take shelter. In order to save themselves, some hunters have had to jettison the whale they were towing, or that they had already cut up and stowed in the boat, because the boat was too heavy and was taking on water. Yes, while hunting can be rewarding, here in the North there is always that element of surprise that lies in wait and catches us off guard.

I remember a time when people set off after beluga whales in whaleboats under sail. Those who took part in such hunts told me that they sailed amongst the whales, without frightening them, and then glided in very close and used only a harpoon to hunt them. But today boats with outboard motors are used. In the boat are rifles, harpoons and empty containers attached to long ropes that serve as floats. A few kilometres from Tuktoyaktuk the hunters are all attention, although usually the whales won't be encountered until they travel farther out. The hunters can see them from quite a distance, tiny white specks away out there in the water. The person steering the boat heads in the direction indicated by the hunter, who stands on the prow, eyes fixed on the horizon, his rifle ready and held excitedly in his hands. The closer the boat gets to the area where the whales are, the more attention the hunters pay. The belugas can be seen everywhere now, travelling in pods of up to six, diving and then after a while coming back to the surface to breathe. That's

A whaleboat returns to a beluga whaling camp at Nalruriaq near Tuktoyaktuk following a beluga whale hunt, 1936. The flag on the mast signals that the hunt has been successful, and that they have a whale on board. (Richard N. Hourde/Hudson's Bay Company Archives/1987/363-E-396-20)

when the hunter will fire the first salvo, to frighten a whale and make it dive back underwater as quickly as possible without getting a lot of air. The boat follows the whale, the motor running a little slower now. If the weather is good, the trail is quite easy to see on the surface of the water, a kind of small wave, a bit oily. The shooter doesn't waste any time. When the whale breaks the surface another shot is quickly fired, and it dives back underwater to escape. It's starting to tire, and the hunters move in closer. The next time there will probably be a hit, maybe not fatal, but the blood will now clearly show the route and movements of the wounded animal. The next time it surfaces there will be yet another bullet, or if it isn't too far away a harpoon is thrown. Then there is no more danger of it escaping – the float attached to the harpoon impedes the whale's progress and all that remains is to finish it off with a bullet to the head. If the hunter isn't able to harpoon the whale before it sinks under the water there might be a chance to retrieve it by snagging it with a hook while circling the spot where the whale went under.

If a decision is made to continue hunting, the dead whale is left there, along with the float. On the way back the hunters will take it in tow. Then, it's back home, where the women are impatiently waiting for the men's return. In the past, a signal was given as the boat returned: a piece of cloth at the top of the mast indicated that the hunt had been good and that the hunters were on their way back with a whale or whales. No flag on the mast meant that they were coming back empty-handed. As soon as they arrive, family and neighbours are there on the beach, the women with their knives, their *ulus*, in hand. The whale is untied from the boat, and the rope is thrown to land and used to pull whale, which can weigh more than a ton, onto the beach.

Once the whale is on the beach the harvesting begins. The skin with the *maktak* and blubber still attached is removed from one side, and the carcass is then turned over onto the other side and the operation is repeated. Then the meat is removed until nothing is left but the skeleton. The work continues, with the meat being cut up into thin pieces and hung on a rack to dry. The

A beluga hunting camp at Nalruriaq near Tuktoyaktuk, circa 1955. Part of the harvested beluga carcass remains in the water. On the drying rack to the left are strips of maktak; to the right are strips of meat and at the far right are large pieces of the outer skin to be used for boot soles. (Bern Will Brown/NWT Archives/N-2001-002: 3909)

maktak and blubber are removed from the skin, and strips of *maktak* are cut in diamond shapes. Some are hung on the drying racks; other pieces are put in the ice cellar, or cooked. Metal barrels are used for cooking pots. A little water is put into the barrel and then filled with *maktak*, and heated over an outdoor fire tended by the women. Some pieces of blubber are also cut and placed in containers, along with some fish or smoked meat, to make *uqsuq*. At every meal a little of this oil would be put into a can, usually an empty lard can, and fish and meat would be dipped into it for a bit of flavour and moisture.

One of our visitors from the Vatican said, "To live in this land, a person needs a strong stomach." Possibly, but I must admit that I didn't dislike that oil, although I preferred seal oil. One year at Paulatuk we had managed to get some that was really great. That spring we had killed several good, fat female seals, and we had made oil with the blubber. We added some smoked char, goose meat and caribou meat to the oil, just enough to give it a smoky flavour. What a treat! We always had some on the table at Paulatuk and Stanton, especially in the evening when we had our supper, which consisted of frozen raw fish, soup, and a little rice or semolina. Once, when our

Boiling maktak at a beluga whale hunting camp near Tuktoyaktuk, circa 1950s. (Provincial Archives of Alberta/OB 32261)

Sam Green (?) with a bearded seal, Paulatuk, 1948. Father Le Meur wrote on the back of this photograph: "A big seal that we killed last spring where the ice was breaking up. It took two people to pull it out the water. While one of us butchers the seal the other looks after the cooking. Behind the seal is a box with food and a teapot on a camping stove. We cut a piece of old ice for water." (Translated from French. Le Meur Family Collection)

Bishop was visiting, he commented that there was a very strong odour in the house. "It smells like seal oil," he said. We answered that we didn't smell anything. "Oh no, of course not," he responded, "you're soaked in it."

A few years ago, the Government attempted to set up a trial whale-based industry. One project was to make dog food by grinding meat, blubber, bones and other remains, and then drying and making them into a kind of flour, which would then only have to be mixed with boiling water to make into a paste. The only drawback was that the machine was far too big for that small project, and it required too much in the way of raw materials. As is nearly always the case in these projects, this one lacked common sense. Another product, *maktak* in a can, has also appeared on the market. Father Max Ruyant gave me two cans. One day when I had two elders visiting me I opened a can for them. Very cautiously, each of them cut out just a small piece, bit into it, and very quickly swallowed it. They were too polite to spit it out, but they told me that it was nothing at all like their *maktak*, and I agreed – that soft, grey-black substance in the can had no flavour. I myself had tried to develop a fried *maktak* filled with cheese, and I had also talked to one of the directors of northern research in Inuvik about it. He tried the *maktak* I'd prepared, and promised he would study it, but so far there hasn't been any follow-up. There is a product for sale around here, a type of puffed cheese. It seems to me that *maktak* could very well be processed the same way, because it puffs up naturally when it's fried. With beer or an aperitif it would probably have enjoyed some small success. In any case, I learned that my *maktak* cuisine was appreciated by both the Inuvialuit and by other people who came through Tuktoyaktuk. In the whale-hunting season I had many visitors who asked me if they could try these delicacies. But that's as far as I went with my experiments with preparing *maktak* French style.

Many other things have also been tried, but without much success. For example, a gun for shooting the harpoon – what a joke that was! The police and some of their friends went out hunting after they received this kind of gun for testing from the Department of Fisheries and Oceans. The first time a whale appeared, the most daring of them seized the gun and fired. Nothing. A harpoon with a good length of line was lost. After it had been examined, another attempt was made, first making sure the line was attached to the gun. This time, the harpoon wasn't lost, but when the line ran out it sprang back, and the harpoon retraced its path, almost hitting a passenger or two. That was the first and last test as far as I can recall.

While the hunting methods have changed, and while the meat and blubber are not as important nowadays – because Inuvialuit can purchase other food in the stores – and while the skin is no longer used for the soles of boots, or for coverings of boats, one thing is certain: the beluga whale still plays an important role in the economy of the people of Tuktoyaktuk and surrounding areas. After all, it is food for which they don't have to pay an exorbitant price. All it takes is a little work, some nice weather, and a bit of luck. But the people realize that with all the changes and the offshore oil and gas exploration activities, it is in danger of disappearing from their life. Recently, the Department of Fisheries and Oceans organized whale hunting camps for the Dene of Fort McPherson. For a while, there was a bit of friction between those people and the people in Tuktoyaktuk, because it was more difficult to catch whales after the Dene had chased them. Another time it was whale researchers who created a problem. From morning to evening they would leave the harbour at Tuktoyaktuk and head out to sea to find whales. The hunt then became harder, because the whales, being very sensitive, fled at the slightest noise. The researchers wanted to learn why the whales that were caught had empty stomachs – but the people complained that they scared the whales, and they wouldn't come into the river to feed!

Before ending this chapter on the beluga whales I'd like to relate something else that happened over which quite a bit of ink was spilled. It angered the people of Tuktoyaktuk, who are realistic and down-to-earth. One fall, at Husky Lakes east of Tuktoyaktuk, a trapper noticed a stretch of water that wasn't frozen yet. Getting closer, he noticed some beluga whales were coming to the surface to breathe in this small open patch of water, the only one in the lake. There were maybe a dozen or slightly more whales, and their activity was preventing the water from freezing. If ice did form, the whales broke it right away. Of course, the news spread through the village and the surrounding areas. The Moccasin Telegraph still works – not always accurately perhaps, but with at least a grain of truth. The regular airplanes that flew over the lake made a pass over it for a better look. This was a novelty, something to see, a real find, and a curious sight. The nearby town of Inuvik seized the opportunity and trips were organized to go and see them, those poor beasts trapped in the ice and prisoners of the cold. The newspapers also picked up the story. And on it went. By plane and snowmobile, sightseers and the curious headed to Husky Lakes.

An organization was formed to protect the whales and to try and save them. Funds were raised, especially in the South. Custodians took turns around the hole and kept watch day and night. How did the whales come to be there? They had become lost in the maze of channels at Husky Lakes and couldn't find their way out. The custodians decided that the whales didn't seem to be in very good health and must be hungry. They were sent food from Vancouver, all by airplane of course – fish, shrimp, and even some meat. Where would it all end? There were discussions and

Beluga whales stranded at Husky Lakes, date unknown. (Inuvialuit Communications Society)

debates. The Inuvialuit, who knew about such things, said that they had no chance of survival and should be killed right away, to put them out of their misery. But the campaign continued. A generator was brought onto the ice, and there was electric lighting for the whales. Tuktoyaktuk, which didn't have electric lighting yet, also began to get upset and protest. How is it that you can move heaven and earth for whales, but for us, you can't lift a finger to improve our lot? The question was brought up by the local newspapers, but the party continued for the whales. The custodians took turns breaking the ice and maintaining the hole, which, in spite of their efforts, was getting smaller, because the cold was intense. Then along came a storm and there was nothing but ice. Goodbye whales. They died and would remain at the bottom of the lake and rot. Who was right? The specialists? Or the Inuvialuit who could have benefitted? Of course I sided with the Inuvialuit, and I strongly encouraged them to protest.

At that time, Max Ferguson, a well-known comedian who had a daily program on CBC Radio, came to visit. He talked a bit about the trapped whales when he did his radio program from Inuvik. It was done in a humorous way. He also described how a special squad that had been trained right in Tuktoyaktuk fought petroleum pollution in the sea. As soon as an oil spill was detected, the anti-pollution squad was called out. They pushed their kayaks into the water, he said, and armed themselves with big ladles and empty barrels. Once at the site of the disaster they collected the oil, filled the barrels, and then went and resold it. It made us laugh, in any case.

At present, there is a lot of talk about ecology and conservation. The Inuvialuit kill only as many whales as they need. They aren't very pleased when they hear about – or see for themselves – whale meat or carcasses carelessly left on the coastal beaches or in bays. Each year in summer, at their meetings, this question is raised and penalties demanded for those who are guilty of wastefulness. Two or three years ago not a single whale was seen or taken around Tuktoyaktuk, or in the bay at the western mouth of the Mackenzie River. The elders talked to me about it. In their memory, and as far back as they could recall, it was the only summer without whales. There was an obvious

114

explanation. Permits for seismic operations had been granted to an oil company. We had asked that the operations be postponed until late August, after the whales had come and gone, but they were begun in July and the whales, which are very sensitive to noise, didn't appear at all that summer. I don't need to tell you how the people felt. Only one whale, a dead one, made it to Tuktoyaktuk that summer. Reports were sent to the authorities – our representatives in Parliament, the game warden, representatives of the territorial government – and I spoke about it on local radio, too. How could the whales possibly have stayed in the bay when even on land we could hear and feel the detonations? In the water, when the operations were under way, huge geysers of water shot into the air. They could be seen from the town. That wasn't the only complaint that we brought to the authorities. Since fish were rather scarce at a time when they were usually plentiful, we investigated and discovered quite a number of blocked creeks. In late spring, the oil companies had made earthen bridges to get across some of the creeks, and they hadn't taken the trouble to open them up again. Another company carried out seismic operations right in the port at Tuktoyaktuk. Some people who went fishing and hunting at the far end of the bay noticed a large number of gulls there. That wasn't normal at all. Usually when they act that way, it indicates whales, a dead body, or a wounded animal in the water. To find out what happened, the two hunters went to have a look and found themselves in the middle of a school of dead fish, floating belly up. Right away, they turned around and went back to tell the police all about it. The police wasted no time. They went to the other side of the bay by boat and asked that the operations be stopped immediately. The companies coming to work in the Arctic unfortunately showed a lack of tact and courtesy towards the people who lived there. But once they had been warned, they fortunately changed their ways. Now there are consultations, and meetings and assemblies are held to keep the people informed of what is happening, and to obtain permits.[1]

Chapter 10 Note

1   Concerned with oil and gas exploration activities the late 1960s and early 1970s, the Inuvialuit began to demand a role in approving development on their traditional lands. This led to the Government enacting the Territorial Land Use Regulations, and local Hunters and Trappers Committees were given authority to approve or disapprove development activities.

11

Getting Together

Visiting time with Father Robert Le Meur. Tuktoyaktuk, date unknown. (Provincial Archives of Alberta/ OB 22068)

I f I had to count the cups of tea and coffee I've had to drink while visiting Inuvialuit in all the years I spent in the Great North I think they would fill some fairly good-sized barrels. Sometimes, if I'd already visited many homes, I've had to refuse another cup because my stomach was flooded. Each time that happened I was asked, "What, you're leaving without having anything?" They understood my reason well enough, but it was a sign of the hospitality of these people, my family. No matter when I arrived at their homes, if they were at the table – so to speak, since often there wasn't one – they would say, "We're eating" or "We're drinking", which was an invitation to join in. I appreciated that sense of hospitality and sharing, and I hope they'll keep it for a long time yet.

Solitude weighs heavily in the North, and any reason is good enough for a visit. People talk about the day's activities, catch up on the news, and often play cards. There is always a cup of coffee or tea and something to eat. But there are important gathering times that are almost a necessity up here. As in the past, the most important are Christmas and Easter, and I have many memories of those times from my early years in the North.

The week before Christmas you would see trappers and their families who had been alone for several months, isolated from others except for a few brief visits to town for supplies, coming from every direction. What wonderful days those were, and what joy everyone felt, those who stayed in town as well as those who arrived after two, three or more days of travel. They had so many things to say to each other, news and things that might seem insignificant to people in the South but that seem vital to us Northerners – the health of the dogs, the number of foxes caught, the ice conditions, the weather, the hunting, and who knows what else. After several cups of tea and a chunk of bread, tongues were loosened and everyone had something to say, some news to tell. You have to experience those times to understand what that atmosphere meant, the joy of being together again. The concept of time as Southerners know it disappeared, and the hour of the day meant nothing. I joined in like everyone else – after all, I am here for them. As for the children, they participated wholeheartedly. So much of the time when they were away from town they have had to amuse themselves, with only their

Children playing at the Paulatuk Mission, circa 1946-1950. (Le Meur Family Collection)

brothers and sisters for companions. It's good to have other boys and girls to play with, to make slides on the snow and ice, have dogsled races, and do other things together.

Everyone, from children to grandparents, generally wore new clothing at Christmas, and the women were kept busy making boots and parkas. But not everyday ones. After all, it's Christmas, and the women made an effort to find or invent embroidery patterns that were different from the

Left to right: *Carrie Goose (sewing), Simone Goose, Father Tardy, (Tom) Kangoak Goose (with drum) and Molly Goose. Holman (Ulukhaktok), circa 1940s. (Holman Photohistorical and Oral History Research Committee/NWT Archives/N-1990-004: 0258)*

117

others, or parka trims with borders cut and sewn in geometric shapes. It was like a competition, without calling it that. On my visits I took a mischievous pleasure in teasing the women and girls who had no time to stop, even for a cup of tea. They spent night and day at their sewing machines, the kind without legs, which they knew how to run so well and so quickly. The young girls were also involved. Often they would, in a way, adopt one of the boys in the family to make his clothing. The best of the hunters, the best trapper, or at least the one who had better luck than the others – for example, by taking a wolf or a wolverine – had the advantage in this competition. How proud they were to have a new *itirvik*, the trim on a parka hood, made from that fur!

As for the men, selling furs at the store and buying provisions took up most of their time. The trading post or store was a meeting place, *the* meeting place, even for me. I went by every day, and was sure to find a few elders or other people I was looking for. It was the place for discussing the price of furs, talking about the fairness of the trader, and sharing news of upcoming ceremonies, races and prizes that would be offered, dances and other events. It was a genuinely pleasant atmosphere that I missed when, in 1956, I spent my first Christmas back in France. I felt melancholy and couldn't stop thinking about the North. It was a green Christmas for me, and I missed all those activities and the companionship. I couldn't stay still, and walked from one place to another, from one house to another, looking in vain for what was missing.

I took advantage of those days to see and teach, both the children and the adults. The instruction that I provided was the kind known in France as *Exercices de la mission*, mission exercises. Everyone participated. You feel very small in our land, faced with that white desert that seems endless, without limit, and the fury of those elements that surround you without mercy. Maybe the fact that people were isolated for much of the time played a part in those acts of faith. Everything was in Inuvialuktun – songs and sermons and instruction. Discussions after the services went on late into the night, or into the early morning.

Father Le Meur conducting a service in the chapel of one of the missions, location and date unknown.
(Le Meur Family Collection)

How could a person sleep anyway? The children coming and going at any hour to say hello – just as likely at three or four o'clock in the morning – didn't really leave much choice. In those days we always had visitors camping at the Mission, and the mission house was always open. The women took care of the meals, which were often very simple. Some raw fish, frozen, or some caribou or moose meat boiled or in a soup did the trick. But for Christmas, out came the wild geese that had been kept in the ice cellar for that occasion. Cakes were also an essential item on the menu. I would make a large quantity, and bread as well. We missionary Fathers and Brothers were also bakers, since there was no bakery on the coast in the early days.

Father Le Meur holding a child beside a Christmas nativity scene, Tuktoyaktuk, circa 1960s. (Le Meur Family Collection)

On Christmas Eve the chapel, which often was in the same building as our house, was decorated with makeshift decorations. There was no end to the comings and goings. Well before the evening Mass the house filled up with people. Everyone wanted a place. Protestants and Catholics alike crowded around the altar. I don't know if it matched the Masses in a cathedral, but the atmosphere of piety and reverence, and the participation in the songs, could certainly withstand comparison with any church. Songs and Christmas carols followed each other in Inuvialuktun and in English, and after the ceremony everyone shook hands and wished each other Merry Christmas. Then there was a *réveillon*, a Christmas Eve party. Candy and toys were given to the children. One benefactor in the United States sent us balls every year. Everyone had fun throwing them all over the place, so a lot of lamps in the house were damaged. After that it was time for bed.

When we woke up, late of course, the dog sled races – the most popular game – began. God knows the people had been talking about them, openly or between partners. It's a serious matter, and bets were made. The track had been known for a few days already, and some had already tried it. Others had taken their dogs and, far out of sight of everyone, trained them. Everyone was ready. The dogs were affected by the excitement, and they barked and howled as they were being hitched. Some hadn't had much to eat the night before, to make sure that they don't stop too often on the trail. I've known some practical jokers who, during the night, would feed seal oil to another dog team. The unfortunate driver is sure to have many stops, as well as black stuff under the sled,

A dog sled race at Tuktoyaktuk, 1987. (Inuvialuit Communications Society)

which isn't ideal for gliding on. It was the event of the year, and the whole population was on the ice, no matter what the weather. When everyone was lined up ready to start, the signal was given, a rifle shot, and the race began. In an instant, dogs and drivers were out of sight. There were some unexpected incidents, of course. Some of the leaders, feeling excited with so many commands being given around them, turned back towards home or run off the track. All those things have their charm and added to the general enjoyment. The spectators stayed and had fun on the ice, or would go to the nearest neighbour's house for a cup of tea. They knew approximately when the teams would start to re-appear on the horizon. Then it was time to go back out on the ice to watch the finish. Sometimes it was head to head, until the best leader gained the victory. The spectators rushed to lift the winner's sled, with him in it, chanting three or four hurrahs and cheers to celebrate the win. Those who came first and second were given dog food as prizes, and the last driver to come in received a can of molasses as a consolation prize.

Other races were held as well, even though there isn't much light at that time of year. There was a race for the men, with only one dog, where they had to stay in the sled. Another was a dollar race, where posts were set up here and there with one, two or three dollars randomly attached, and the drivers didn't know which were pay posts. That race showed which dogs were the good leaders. The driver couldn't step out of the sled to grab the money, so it required a good dog, one that was able to obey and go round the posts, passing close enough to them for the driver to reach the prize. Other times, they had to run in one direction or the other around empty barrels on the ice. There was a lot of talk afterward, and the whole race was recounted in detail by one person then another, all in an atmosphere of relaxation and camaraderie. Children also got to show their skill at handling dogs, with more fun, laughter and teasing.

Then it was time for a meal. In the past, food was provided in the past by the Hudson's Bay Company. It wasn't every day the famous Company gave gifts. It has received a lot of criticism, but it was one of the first companies to employ the local people many years ago, and it's important to remember that. Volunteers prepared the meal, and the people all brought their own cutlery and helped themselves.

Christmas in the Aklavik community hall, circa 1950. (F.S. Farrar/Inuvialuit Cultural Resource Centre)

In the evening, everyone gathered at the school or the community hall. Children and parents were there, waiting impatiently for the drummers. In they came, moving at a dignified pace, sitting down and taking out the drums, which were carefully wrapped in a canvas bag. The frame was made from wood that was steamed or soaked in hot water and then bent to shape. The drum skin was a piece of caribou skin which the women had worked, scraping and scraping again repeatedly until it was very, very thin, almost transparent. The skin was then soaked in water and stretched over the frame. Before it is used the drum skin is wetted again, an operation that is repeated several times during the dance session. The drumsticks are made from wood and are a little longer than the circumference of the drum, because they don't hit the skin directly, but the edge of the frame.

Singers lined up beside or behind the drummers. Everything was ready for the first songs, just a few notes and fairly short songs to make sure the instruments and singers are in tune, "A... a... ya yanga... a... ayanga ya ya... ay ya..." Then the dancers would come forward and stand in front of the drummers, the men in front of the women. Everyone starts to move, the men swinging their arms, with their gloves held tight in their hands, between their fingers, and the women staying in one spot, their bodies swaying left and right, calling out from time to time for others to join the group – a kind of strident, throaty call. Then the song begins. The drums beat a fairly slow rhythm to start with. The drummers are hidden, with only part of their faces showing, from the eyes up. The men dancers move their arms and legs, their feet marking the beat here and there as they strike the floor, their bodies first erect, then bent towards the ground, while their partners, the women, stay in the same place, on the tips of their toes, making their bodies sway and moving their arms, first towards then away from their faces, as if they want to push something away from them.

The songs are composed by Inuvialuit elders, and are prompted by their inspiration. They relate a feat of some kind, a hunt, an encounter with a bear, an event they took part in, or who knows what else. Although not originally from this area, probably introduced from Alaska, the songs

A drum dance in the Aklavik community hall during Christmas celebration, circa 1950. (F.S. Farrar/ Inuvialuit Cultural Resource Centre)

and dances I like best are the descriptive ones, the *sayun*, such as ice fishing. In that dance all the actions of fishers are imitated, starting with cutting a hole in the ice, removing the broken ice from the hole, a fisher's actions and movements of handling the line in the water, pulling the fish out of the hole, putting the fish on a string and carrying it on his back, walking home. Because this song comes from Alaska, the drummers sometimes have to be begged to play it – there is national pride at stake here also. Two or three hours are devoted to this art, giving the older people an opportunity to express their joy and their feelings in song and dance. Their faces may not show much, but the movements and poses, the movements of their hands, arms and body can be calm or lively, humble or impassioned.

There is also a hint of melancholy. Memories from the past are associated with the dance, and with the drum. At one time the oldest drum in Tuktoyaktuk was one that had belonged to the founder of the village, Mangilaluk. Naturally, its skin had been changed many times, but the frame was still the same. But where is it now? Felix Nuyaviak, the son-in-law of Mangilaluk, who was in charge of it, greatly regrets having sold it, against his will. Someone came to see him and noticed the drum, examined it and asked about its history, and finally asked to buy it. The old man said, "No. There are too many memories attached to that drum. It's a question of family." The visitor insisted. "Finally," Felix Nuyaviak told me, "to avoid offending him, I told him it's too expensive, the price I had to ask was far too high. I just wanted to make him understand that I valued it. I was tired of fighting, so I told him a price that seemed exorbitant to me – $50 – and the visitor produced the cash. I was caught in my own trap. Since I'd given my word, I couldn't go back on it. So I saw that drum that was dear to me and to Tuktoyaktuk change hands. It will be hanging somewhere in Canada or the United States." Laughing, he added, "I'm not so clever after all, eh?"

When the traditional dancing was over and the drums were gathered up a fiddler and one or two guitarists would take their place, and the square dances began. They would go on late into the night or into early morning.

Mabel Stefansson and Kenneth Peeloo|ook square dancing at a Christmas celebration, Aklavik, circa 1950. (F.S. Farrar/Inuvialuit Cultural Resource Centre)

The celebrations continued the day after Christmas, this time with dog sled races for women. The dogs were well aware the women weren't their bosses, and wholeheartedly gave themselves over to delighting and pleasing the spectators. Some of the women drivers found themselves on the trail only to be promptly taken back home. Others were taken on a tour of the village. But some, who were accustomed to handling dogs, headed in the right direction. There are a few more games on the ice, and foot races, weather permitting, and in the evening another dance, or some traditional games with teams, sometimes made up of people from different camps, competing against each other. They didn't play so much for the prizes as much as for the honour, and for the audience's enjoyment.

Everyone – from youngest to oldest, and even visitors from outside – enjoyed the holiday. Nearly every year, a good friend of mine, an Englishman who had worked on the Distant Early Warning Line and is now in England after spending nearly three years at Tuktoyaktuk, reminds me how much he'd loved those Christmases in the North. They were the best of his life, he says. There was a special atmosphere in those days, unique to the North. Friendship, fraternity and joy were shared by all, like one big family, all in the greatest simplicity. One incident from those Christmases, which I won't forget either, shows how people all wanted to participate. At Holman Island, in 1950 I think it was, a woman had her baby at around six o'clock in the evening on December 24. At Midnight Mass, when I turned around for the first "*Dominus vobiscum*" – we were still saying Mass in Latin – who did I see in the middle of the assembled crowd, packed tight as a tin of sardines, but the same woman, smiling at me. Yes, the same woman, with her baby on her back. The next day she shocked and made me shudder again, when I saw her outside in temperatures of minus 35 to 40 degrees with the baby on her back under her parka. The baby was nice and warm perhaps, but she had an axe in her hand and was chopping frozen seal blubber. I went over and gently told her to go inside and rest. That was her husband's work, at least for a few days.

*Mona Thrasher (**seated**) ice fishing at Husky Lakes, circa 1955. (Bern Will Brown/NWT Archives/N-2001-002-6217)*

On New Year's Day the community ceremonies and recreation followed the same routine as Christmas – religious services ending at midnight, then best wishes to everyone and visiting until very late. The next day, there were the usual races. After a week of that, when the Mission was often a gathering place and camp site, it's not surprising that we missionaries felt the need for silence, meditation and a little peace. The best thing was to go away, like everyone else. The people went to their trap lines, and we would set off to visit a fellow priest at another Mission. Ah, that first night alone in the tent in the vast silence, how restful! After all the comings and goings, the excitement, the early mornings, it's difficult to express what I felt that night – peace and quiet, no problems for a few days, a rest for the nerves as well.

Easter was another important time for getting together, with the same proceedings and the same games, plus a few others because the days are longer. There often was a shooting competition, and God knows what good shots the Inuvialuit are. In the army, they would be snipers or sharpshooters. There were foot races for all age groups, from youngest to oldest, sack races, needle threading, a woman being pulled and then taking her turn pulling a man. But the days of rejoicing don't last very long at Easter. Hunting quickly takes its rightful place, and there are traps that have to be retrieved and put away for next winter.

After Easter, at the end of April or the beginning of May, it is the time for spring fishing at places like Husky Lakes, east of Tuktoyaktuk. This could also be described as an outdoor holiday. It's one of the times of the year enjoyed by everyone who doesn't have a regular job. There at the lake, under the midnight sun now, fishing is at its peak. It doesn't matter much to people if they catch a fish or not; it's so good to be far away from the village, in a peaceful setting with no clocks. Men, women and children head for the fishing holes, at any hour, and drop their hooks into the water hoping the trout will bite. And what trout! They are big, up to 18 kilograms or more. Spring fishing at the lake lasts two to three weeks. In past years, practically no children remained in

First Winter Carnival with Queen Florence Hagen, East Three (Inuvik), April 23, 1957. The winter carnival was later known as Muskrat Jamboree. (Robert C. Knights/NWT Archives/N-1993-002: 0005)

school – a trip to the lake was just too tempting. But school days have now been changed so that children can accompany their parents out on the land in spring.

I should also mention some of the other holidays and activities that have been added to the calendar. There is Labour Day, when everyone rests; Thanksgiving, the day when we are supposed to officially give thanks to God and the Holy Spirit; Halloween, a day of ghosts and phantoms; Remembrance Day; etc. These were all unknown not so long ago. How could they be known? And, to be honest, it was something we priests and brothers knew nothing about at first in our life in the Great North. These were just some of the things accompanied advancing bureaucracy. Then came the carnivals – the Beluga Jamboree in Tuktoyaktuk, Muskrat Jamboree in Inuvik, White Fox Carnival in Sachs Harbour, Buffalo Frolic in Fort Smith. What's next, I wonder?

One of the new events that has caught on and truly touched the Inuvialuit soul is the Northern Games.[1] There are three or four full days of traditional games and competitions, such as the arm pull, one- and two-legged jumps, jumping while supporting themselves only on their fists and knees, and activities such as muskrat skinning and tea boiling. These games and competitions require physical endurance, and strength of spirit. There are also songs and dances every evening. The Northern Games give all the indigenous people in the North, who are united by their desire to keep traditional languages and identities alive, the opportunity to meet. I encouraged these efforts to revive and maintain their heritage, but I have just one regret, which I expressed to those in charge of the games – it's too bad we can't use those opportunities to bring together for a general assembly to make political, social and cultural decisions for the North as a whole. It's a chance in a thousand, and this would carry a lot of weight in dealings with the Government of Canada and the Canadian nation. It breaks my heart to see some of the best of the North gathered in one spot and not take advantage of it.

Traditional Northern Games. **Left:** *Leonard Harry teaches the one-arm pull, date unknown.* **Right:** *John Elanik performing the one-foot high kick, Tuktoyaktuk, 1980. (Inuvialuit Communications Society)*

Chapter 11 Note

1   The Northern Games continue today as the Traditional Circumpolar Northern Games.

Tuktoyaktuk – The Early Days

Aerial view of Tuktoyaktuk in 1946, the year Father Le Meur first arrived in the settlement. The harbour where legend tells of swimming caribou turning to stone, giving Tuktoyaktuk its name, can be seen. (Kirk Family fonds/NWT Archives/N-2005-001: 0136)

Tuktoyaktuk, as it's now known, or Tuk for short – *Tuktuyaaqtuq* is the true Inuvialuit name – is the village I know best, and is where I have spent almost one quarter of my life.[1] Tuktoyaktuk has existed since the beginning of time, the elders say, perhaps not as a true settlement, but as a stopping place, a fishing and hunting place. The proof is in the many discoveries of old, very old, bones and hunting and fishing items. Before modern houses appeared there were also many sod houses, *igluryuaryuit*, made from driftwood carried by the Mackenzie River in spring. Felix Nuyaviak told me how the name 'Tuktoyaktuk' came about:

~ *The Legend of How Tuktoyaktuk Got Its Name* ~

Felix Nuyaviak, Tuktoyaktuk, 1969. (Herbert Schwarz/NWT Archives N-1979-007)

"Once, long ago, there were two families living in tents on the island opposite the present village of Tuktoyaktuk at the mouth of the harbour. The men went off to visit their fish nets, taking the children with them, leaving the women at home. While one of the women was sewing, she heard a noise like someone falling into the water, and then swimming. Not a man, certainly, it made too much noise. It could only be a caribou. But according to a taboo she wasn't supposed to look at or touch caribou at that time. She kept on sewing for a minute or two. The temptation to go outside and see what was happening was very strong. She resisted for a little while, but curiosity was eating at her and she really wanted to know what was happening not very far from

An artist's interpretation of the story, 'How Tuktoyaktuk Got Its Name', based on a story told by Felix Nuyaviak. (Autumn Downey/Prince of Wales Northern Heritage Centre)

her tent. From time to time she stopped sewing and listened. The noise continued, she could still hear it, but it was moving away, although not very quickly."

"Then the needle was flying in her hands, fast and even faster, but her imagination was running wild too, and tormenting her. She stopped again, took a step towards the door of the tent, hesitated for a moment, and suddenly had a clever and brilliant idea – why not look without going outside? No one would know, no one would see her. She walked slowly to the back of the tent, where there was a tiny hole in the tent wall. She made it bigger, just a little, as big as her little finger. She hesitated again, but couldn't resist. Even without trying she could see the daylight. It wouldn't matter much if she got closer and put her eye to the hole, which she did, and she saw three caribou that were swimming away from the spit at the harbour entrance. They were heading for the opposite shore when, before her astonished eyes, they stopped in their tracks, stopped swimming and stood dead still. They turned into stone, and the boulders are still there for everyone to see when the water is very low, looking like the backs of caribou. *Tuktuyaaqtuq* – it looks like a caribou."

The citizens of Tuktoyaktuk had to fight to keep this traditional name. When a post office was established in 1948 the name was officially changed to Port Brabant, but the people of the village refused to let the name be changed, no matter how famous that person might have been.[2] The way they saw it, this was their land and it was their name. They continued to put Tuktoyaktuk on letters, and petition after petition was sent to Ottawa. They won their case, and Tuktoyaktuk became the first community in the Northwest Territories to reclaim its traditional name.

Ah, if only those boulders that gave Tuktoyaktuk its name could talk, and relate everything they have seen and heard since the founding of the village. They would have some stories to tell! Many things have happened, and what giant steps forward have been taken! William Mangilaluk, the founder, and his companions wouldn't believe their eyes. A school named Mangilaluk School, and oil wells and television? Actually, Lisiuk, an elder, had predicted it. Although he'd never gone to school and never left the area around Tuk, Lisiuk predicted a brilliant future for the small colony of Inuvialuit who settled there. "In a few years," he said, "there will be other men, white men, who will come and settle here with us. There will be many houses, and they will push the dirt up like pieces of ice piled up by the force of the current and the storms along the crevasses on the sea." Ah, yes, that is indeed how it is nowadays.

The history of Tuktoyaktuk gives an idea of what is happening in nearly all the villages and hamlets on the Arctic coast. We have to go back to 1905 to see its beginnings as a year-round

"People at Tuktoyaktuk, 1925." (William Mangilaluk is standing at left with his hand in his pocket.) (L. Hanson/Danish National Museum/Fifth Thule Expedition/Neg. 2425)

settlement. It began with just a few families that came together. Some of the men, past middle age and perhaps tired of living a hard life and travelling around from Herschel Island to Baillie Island, decided to settle down in a place that had plenty of fish, good shelter in summer, was close to where the white whales passed, and had a fairly good supply of wood – not growing trees, of course, but driftwood.

William Mangilaluk – or just Mangilaluk, as he was often called – the founder and for many years the traditional leader of present-day Tuktoyaktuk, lives on in the people's memories, a legendary man, loved and respected by all. A quick look at one of his photographs reveals a man of high stature – both moral and physical – 6 feet tall, with square, broad shoulders and a dignified appearance, holding himself very erect, his eyes looking intently at the person he was speaking to, or at the horizon. He was known to all the whaling-boat crews and was considered the best athlete in racing or weight lifting and other competitions on Herschel Island and Baillie Island. He had experienced all the adventures of hunters on land and on the pack ice, as well as all the dangers, and had emerged from them victorious and crowned with the glory and honour of a man who knows extraordinary success in all his endeavours. He truly was his own master, and in a sense he felt himself responsible for the village of Tuktoyaktuk. He built the first log house, which he sold and then built another one, big enough to accommodate friends and visitors. He liked to offer hospitality to one and all. His house was always open to everyone, and there was room for everyone at his table. There was no lack of fish, or *maktak*, or whale oil. He took pride in treating well those who came to see him. His many stories added to the pleasure of the evenings when people got together.

William Mangilaluk, Tuktoyaktuk, 1925. (L. Hanson/Danish National Museum/Fifth Thule Expedition/Neg. 2020)

Boys and (mammoth) tusk, Stanton. (Missionary Oblates, Grandin Archives at the Provincial Archives of Alberta/OB. 32250)

Mangilaluk liked to tell the story of how, before his birth, he had travelled amongst animals, and even inside animals, going here and there, and from a distance studying and noting the actions, behaviour and way of life of people. He had set out from the east and had gradually moved west. He travelled on the pack ice and followed a leader. Which one? He couldn't identify it now. "Animals don't think like men," he said. They saw men who chased strange, large animals, mammoths, which they killed on land where there was grass and willows all around. But those people paid no attention to him and his animal companions, and they continued on their way, with Mangilaluk looking for a mother. They stopped at a number of other places, the names of which he's forgotten and which he couldn't even clearly describe. Wherever he went the people paid no attention to anyone but themselves. Finally, they caught sight of the pingos near Tuktoyaktuk, and continuing on they saw some human beings. There, he said, they stopped again, with him still looking for a mother. He could see inside a woman, and he thought that was what he needed, and he went in, into a very small place. But there something changed in him. He was already starting to think. It wasn't like when he was travelling in the guise of an animal. Animals don't think, but can only see, and based on what they see, they act. This woman that he had chosen, and that he was now inside, became pregnant with him. And since he found it cramped in his mother's womb, he came out. One of the elders wasn't very happy when he saw him, and was also a bit afraid. That child, he said, already knows too much. So he called the child and, using his charms and spirits, pricked him a few times on the buttocks after throwing him to the ground. The child immediately lost all his knowledge and became like the other children, who know nothing, understand nothing, so soon after their birth. Later he started learning again like all children do. As he grew up he recovered his lost knowledge, he said, and realized that life as a human is much more beautiful and more interesting than life as an animal.

~ *Adrift on the Ice*[3] ~

Mangilaluk had many adventures. He liked to relate the story of what had happened to him many years before at Baillie Island while travelling on the frozen ocean. That day, looking at the weather and inspecting the horizon, he saw in front of him, not too far away, some dark clouds over the ice. That is an indication that underneath the clouds there is water – open water we call it in the North. That would be a good place to hunt seals. The wind was from the right direction, so it seemed there was no danger. The preparations were quickly completed – a small *arrinaq*, or pack, with a piece of fish and a little bannock; his rifle; his *manaq*, a grappling hook for retrieving seals after they were shot, which he'd made himself, carving it from a piece of wood, and to which was attached a long line of strong cord; and his walking stick, which he used on the ice from time to time to test the thickness and strength. And then he was on his way, travelling on foot. He was alone, but not for long. Shortly after his departure, as he was walking on the ice, he heard behind him the crunching sound of footsteps on the frozen snow. He knew someone was following him, but given to teasing as he was, he didn't turn around, and began walking a little faster. Since he was a tall man and had long legs, it wasn't difficult for him to pull away from his partner. Then he stopped and tested his rifle. This gave his pursuer time to catch up. It was his friend Kaobviak, who, to pay him back, teased him about his shooting. Then two others – Sitorana and Chiksak[4] – also arrived. They continued on their way to the open water, while checking all around, especially behind them, to make sure that the ice wasn't moving away from land. Everything was fine, and in front of them the dark cloud was still there too.

But suddenly and without warning, as often happens in the Great North, the wind shifted and began blowing hard, a strong east wind, and immediately everything began to move. All around them the noise of ice breaking and grinding and piling up could be heard. *Quick, turn around, go back!* But it was too late. The wind became a storm, and the snow began to fly. A moving white shroud wrapped around them, covered them, until they could no longer see in the blizzard of swirling snow. Now, completely enveloped in whiteness – white under their feet, white above them, in front of them and behind them, nothing but white everywhere – they kept walking, in a group, and staying close together, forming a living, moving wall, trying to use each other to shelter themselves from the wind that was blinding them. The only thing that mattered now was finding pieces of ice large and strong enough to prevent them from being crushed by icebergs that crossed in front of them. They jumped from the piece of ice they were on to another, and then onto another that seemed stronger and more resistant, going with the wind now, since it was pointless to try to walk. Where on earth could they go? There was nothing but broken ice everywhere. They knew it, even without being able to see. Still, they had hope. With Mangilaluk, there was always hope, and that wasn't the first time he'd been adrift. They huddled together. It was essential now. If a hunter becomes separated from his companions in that blinding, blowing snow he is lost to them forever. Mangilaluk, remaining true to form, tried to see through the whiteness, to see what was happening. Suddenly he nudged the person closest to him and gestured with his hand. There was no point in talking, the wind was too strong. There, in front of him, he had seen something that looked like a high white hill, probably a large piece of old ice.

Now Mangilaluk was on the lookout, all his senses directed towards the large piece of ice. His muscles were tensed and ready for the effort he would ask them to make. With his whole body he leaned towards the mountain of ice that came closer and then, with the current, moved a bit farther away. But it came back, and came closer again, travelling against the wind. Mangilaluk stood tensed and poised. As soon as the ice mass came close, he threw his rifle onto the ice across from him – having the rifle over his shoulder or his back would have interfered with his movements – and with one leap, he jumped over the gap and the cold water, and landed on the ice, on the side of the ice mountain. While his companions looked on fascinated, he gripped the ridges of ice and climbed all the way to the top, where he found himself on a flat area, like a platform. Without wasting any time, he took his grappling hook out of his backpack and threw it over to the other piece of ice, which was beginning to move away. The hooks bit into the ice and, in no time, his three companions joined him on the floating, drifting iceberg. At least they could breathe easily there, where there was no danger that they would be crushed and torn apart by the pack ice and without warning. After resting in an ice shelter they continued their journey. Where to? They had no idea. They went wherever the current and the wind took them, while their thoughts turned to land, to their home back on Baillie Island.

Back at the camp everyone was despairing. The hunters hadn't returned, and they were afraid that in the blizzard conditions the hunters wouldn't be able to save themselves this time. After all, what had they taken with them for a trip that was supposed to last no more than a few hours? Not very much really – a little bit of food, but no sleeping bags or canvas for a shelter, nothing but the clothes on their backs. Oh yes, of course, these were good and warm, double caribou parkas, but in the storm, without shelter and exposed to the wind, that wasn't enough. The snow penetrates everywhere. Sitorana's father, Alarpana, feared for them. How did Mangilaluk come to leave without taking his amulets? He knew that the three other companions were depending on Mangilaluk's skill and resourcefulness. Ularpana didn't hesitate a second longer. He took off his own charm and, putting it in his hand, let it fly away on the sea wind and told it to go to Mangilaluk and rescue him. Kaopkrun, Mangilaluk's mother, remained calm even though she was anxious. She didn't want to show it. She tried to encourage everyone, and offer some courage and hope – "Mangilaluk will come out of it all right again, he'll manage all right." In keeping with custom, she also turned for help to her protective spirits. She took a pair of Mangilaluk's boots and hung them from the ceiling of the snow house, after first putting in some wood shavings. That done, she continued with her chores, without much enthusiasm, but to keep busy and pass the time. Evening came, as it had the day before, but Kaopkrun couldn't sleep – she was thinking about her boy out there on the ice. Suddenly she heard what sounded like a footstep. She knew what that meant. She was familiar with the traditions and knew that the boots were moving all by themselves. They were rocking slowly back and forth like someone walking, and were rubbing against each other while moving. Kaopkrun had received the answer she had asked and begged for – her son Mangilaluk was still alive and was walking somewhere on the ice. The next morning she took the boots and inspected their contents. Yes, the chips had moved and they were higher in the boot. She left the house immediately and went to visit the neighbours, telling them not to worry, the signs said that Mangilaluk was alive and that they would be coming back soon.

The four hunters, Robinson Crusoes of the ice, were indeed alive, but they weren't enjoying the miserable adventure they were having in the pack ice. They were in darkness, with the noise of waves attacking the ice, not knowing where they were, cold, hungry and thirsty, huddled together, shivering, teeth chattering, moaning, afraid of what tomorrow might bring. At daybreak, with the light they saw a large ice field, but how to get there was the question. The stretch of open water between it and their small floating island was too wide to jump across. Even Mangilaluk, good athlete though he was, knew he couldn't make it. They hoped that the current would bring them to closer, but time passed and nothing happened. Mangilaluk, always full of practical and clever ideas, saw only one possible solution – to build a bridge. Without wasting any time he got down to work. It was risky, but their situation was precarious. He put his walking stick across the open water and began cementing small pieces of ice that were drifting past to the stick, using snow mixed with water. He used both hands, bare, in the cold sea. First, he went as far as he could while lying stretched out to his full length, and then, still on his stomach, he ventured out onto the bridge he was building, collecting little bits of ice and attaching them to the stick. And he kept going like that on the miracle bridge that he was building until he reached the other side. The others followed, and now there they all were on a sheet of ice that stretched far into the distance. They began to walk. They were all feeling the weight of fatigue and didn't walk very fast, but Mangilaluk continued on his way, out in front, offering an example, while the others followed, but half-heartedly. Sitorana accompanied Mangilaluk and kept pace with him. Chiksak and Kaobviak slowed down and lagged far behind the leaders. The progress that Mangilaluk and Sitorana made didn't help them very much, because, once again, a wide stretch of open water appeared in front of them, and this one was far too wide to build a bridge across. When the laggards arrived they sat down, discouraged and dispirited. "Where are we going," they asked. "Is it the right direction?" The only thing they could do then was wait. But wait for what? No one said very much. Each man kept his thoughts – often rather sad and gloomy – to himself. The less said, the better, to avoid adding to the weight of his own disappointment. All four men were sitting and thinking about their tragic situation like that when a strange and noise coming from the water made them look up and pulled them out of their musings – a noise as if a seal was about to surface. There was a movement in the water, and from the depths of the ocean a slab of ice covered in small pebbles appeared before their startled and amazed eyes. It positioned itself crosswise between the ice field they were on and the one across from them.

It was truly providential. The Robinson Crusoes stood up. Mangilaluk checked to see if the ice could bear his weight, and then they quickly crossed over to the other side. But they weren't saved yet. Nothing was visible on the horizon, no hill or high point of land, nothing but ice and more ice. They walked and walked. Exhausted, they decided to call a halt. They sat down in the shelter of an old piece of iceberg and talked. Not everybody agreed on the direction to take, and the hunters split up. Sitorana stayed with Mangilaluk, while Chiksak and Kaobviak went off in a different direction. After a few miles of walking, Mangilaluk and his companion stopped and built a shelter to protect them from the wind. In their polar bear pants they didn't feel the wetness of the ice, and almost immediately they gave in to sleep, a half-sleep at least. And both of them seemed to hear a voice that came and breathed in their ears, "Sitorana, don't stop, keep walking. Otherwise you'll freeze your feet. Walk, walk, and get warm, then keep going towards the east." It was strange. They both wondered who on earth had been speaking, and looked all around them. There was no one. They shook their heads and exchanged surprised looks, then stood up and set off towards the east. They had renewed courage and seemed to have renewed strength as well. Land appeared in the distance, a small black speck, flush with the horizon. But it grew bigger, and longer and rose up towards the sky. As they got closer, they recognized the headland of Baillie Island.

They felt stronger now – gone was the paralyzing fatigue they had felt just a few hours ago. Their stomachs painfully empty, their limbs cold, their faces half-frozen, but in a confident frame of mind they kept going, heading towards home. As they came closer to the hills they made out a woman on land, on the edge of the frozen shoreline. She was tanning a skin, and from time to time she stopped and looked towards the open sea, towards the dark clouds. The two men knew what she was thinking and what she was trying to see on the pack ice. So great was her concern, and so absorbed was she in her work, that she didn't notice Mangilaluk and Sitorana were standing next to her. She could only say these few words expressing her joy and her surprise, *"Akrale!* Where on earth did you come from?" And the two men pointed in the direction they'd come. "From over there," they said. Their camp was nearby, and someone had seen them and went to give the news to Kaopkrun. She rushed towards the arriving hunters and threw herself into Mangilaluk's arms, hugging him tightly and welcoming him back. The other two men also made it to the camp. After they'd had something to eat the whole trip and all the adventures were related down to the last detail over many cups of tea and coffee.

The next day, the weather cleared and Mangilaluk felt full of energy. It wasn't a day for staying in camp and resting. After a hearty breakfast, he set out again on the pack ice, with his rifle, grappling hook and his backpack. Maybe he would have more luck this time. The dangers and miseries of the previous days were already forgotten. The camp needed blubber and meat. He set off alone, but no, after him again came his faithful friend, his companion in good times and bad, good old Kaobviak. That day was uneventful. All was calm, and the hunt was successful. Both men returned to the camp proudly, each dragging a seal.

That was the story, a first-hand experience that many others also had. The Inuvialuit took such things as they came, without bragging about them. It's just something that happens, something that is a normal part of life as a trapper and hunter.

Hunting beluga whales from a whaleboat, 1936. **Left to right**: *Bertram Pokiak, Gerard Siksigaaluk, Roy Kikoak. (Richard N. Hourde/Hudson's Bay Company Archives/1987/363-E-341-034)*

134

Bessie Raddi with a dog team hauling ice for drinking water. Late fall or early spring, 1940s(?). (Gruben Family Fonds/NWT Archives/N-2003-038: 0057)

William Mangilaluk clearly was marked and well served by Providence, and by his parents, and by his own experience and industry. He was a born leader, and had a lot of influence and authority in Tuktoyaktuk. He was the judge and the magistrate of that place. It is said that, on at least one occasion when the police were afraid to apprehend some wrongdoers, he, Mangilaluk, went to find and pick up the guilty parties, and when he delivered them to the police he told them that the sentence, the penalty, was to be an absence of two months from the village and the surrounding area. Another time, a young man was causing some trouble and misbehaving in the village. Mangilaluk went to find him and told him to harness his dogs, take what he needed for fishing and hunting, and leave. The punishment he gave him was one month outside of Tuk. No one questioned his decisions, there was no appeal, and everyone respected him. Like all the others, he liked the quiet, peaceful life of the Great North. He could afford that, although even in his semi-retirement he still had to cope with life and continue to work and hunt and fish, because there was no pension yet in those days. His life continued as before, with less spontaneity perhaps, and not quite as many activities, but always showing the way through his advice and his leadership.

In the early days of the village Mangilaluk and other people who lived there followed a yearly cycle of travel, hunting and fishing not too different from the way Felix Nuyaviak told about in his 'Memories of the Past', but with some new tactics and methods because they had tools and equipment that they got from the trading posts. In July and early August people from Tuktoyaktuk moved to Nalruriaq – Whitefish Station – some 30 kilometres west of Tuk, close to the mouth of the Mackenzie River to hunt beluga whales. Then it was back to Tuktoyaktuk to lay in a stock of dried and smoked fish, as well as putting some into ice cellars. Fishnets were set in the harbour, sheltered from the waves and breakers. In late September, the waters around Tuk itself fill up with herring that are caught using the "sweeping" net, a long and deep net that is thrown into the water and pulled back onto land. This operation calls for a cooperative effort, with a number of people working together and sharing the spoils. Several canoes and men work together. After one end has been attached on land, the net is put into a canoe and the two or three men in the canoe gradually spread the seine, create the circumference of a circle, and bring the rope back to land. Then those on shore begin pulling it, closing the circle and imprisoning the fish caught in the trap. Once the net is on shore, the canoes are placed along its length and the fish are thrown into them. With good hauls of fish, the canoes are filled to the brim after just a few operations. A number of times I've seen full canoes coming back, and from shore it can look as if the man in the canoe is sitting in the water, the canoe is so low in the water.

Fishing went on for a couple of weeks until the ice started forming. A few days of calm followed, a time to prepare the dog harnesses and the sleds for the trapping season. At the end of September the men waited impatiently for snow, as did the dogs, who were tired of being chained. As soon as ice had formed in the harbour, and if the weather was cold enough, even for just for a day or two, everyone was busy on the young ice setting nets. Then fishing through the ice continued all winter. In October people would go to a small lake just outside Tuktoyaktuk and begin cutting ice, their water supply for the winter. And trips by dogsled on the land close to the village also took place. The willow ptarmigan are in good condition that time of year, and hunters armed with a .22 rifle or a shotgun could bring back a large quantity. But while these ptarmigan are good, they don't have much nutritional value, so very often they are prepared as a soup – ptarmigan meat, and a broth thickened with rice or macaroni. Those who went out hunting also took advantage of the opportunity to bring back a good load of the driftwood that litters the beaches. Attentive to their environment, people would know if foxes would be plentiful that winter. Their tracks are visible in the snow, as are those of lemmings that the fox feed on. (Lemmings are present in very large numbers some years. I have followed one of their trails at Paulatuk – about 30 centimetres wide, the width of my toboggan. They had crossed the bay, climbed the hill, then disappeared, falling over a precipice on the other side. If there are a lot of lemming tracks the Inuit predict a good year for foxes.)

Peter Esau on his trap line, Banks Island, circa 1960s. (Photo credit: Peter Usher)

Enoch Pokiak with trapped muskrats, Peel Channel, 1914. (Royal Canadian Mounted Police/Library and Archives Canada)

In November it was time to prepare the trap lines. Some men would head to Warren Point, *Igluuk*, a place some 40 kilometres from Tuk, where they would set traps and hunt seals in the open water. They would just take only as much meat as they needed to continue their journey along the coast and cache the rest for later trips. For the rest of the winter trapping would be the major occupation. From November until April everything revolved around trapping fox, both white and coloured varieties. A few years ago, coloured fox had little value, and in fact fur merchants didn't even want to buy them, but Inuvialuit would use them to make clothes, mittens, hood trims, and small craft items. Trapping was interrupted by community gatherings at Christmas, the New Year and at Easter.

As soon as the fox-trapping season was over, 'ratting' – trapping and hunting muskrats, began. Sometimes it was worthwhile, when the prices for muskrat furs were good and weather conditions were favourable, while other times it was disappointing. Trapping and hunting muskrats is a hard, tiring job. It requires long days harvesting the 'rats', as they are known, then afterwards they have to be skinned, their fur stretched and dried, and the price negotiated at the trading posts. 'Ratting' was mainly done in the inner part of the Delta, around Aklavik.

In spring there would be visits to Husky Lakes where fish and migratory birds – snow geese, Canada geese, and ducks – were plentiful. The Inuvialuit made the most of that windfall, and everyone ate well.

When the weather warmed up about the middle of May, before the white blanket of snow had left the ground, the hunters and fishers returned to Tuktoyaktuk. Tents were set up until the snow around the houses had melted. Once the ground was free of snow and had dried out, they cleaned up around their houses and then moved back in.

"Natives at the fish camp east of Kittigazuit (Kitigaaryuit), repairing nets and tools, July 1927." (A.E. Porsild/Library and Archives Canada/PA-101960)

Then it was time to go to the trading post, taking their furs and buying supplies – gun powder, sugar, tea, salt, molasses, and needles and beads for the women. In those days, they didn't burden themselves with too much. At first they went to Fort McPherson, but in 1912 the Hudson's Bay Company built a trading post closer by, at Kitigaaryuit. The annual cycle of activities then began over again.

It was in that relative calm that Tuktoyaktuk began to develop, no faster than the weather or the wind. A few families joined those that had already settled there, the Mangilaluks, the Yitaoriuks, the Mangilanas, the Sapotaituks, the Siksigaaluks, the Angisinaoks, and the Arnarenaks. From around Warren Point, 40 kilometres north, came the Unalenas, the Ilavineks, the Kraterariuks, the Ivitkunas and the Koiksaks. In addition, people from Atkinson Point and locations farther east settled in the vicinity of Tuk, in what we might nowadays call satellite villages or camps, such as Krernersek, Naparutalik and Nalruriaq. People moved so often from place to place that it is quite difficult to determine who is who, and who was where, but what made Tuktoyaktuk stable was that some people like William Mangilaluk, and his son-in-law Felix Nuyaviak who settled there in 1916 or 1917, stayed in the same place. So, year after year, the number of people at Tuk increased.

That was the general attitude until the 1930s. The Hudson's Bay Company was looking for a port to serve its trading posts on the Arctic coast to replace its base at Herschel Island. They wanted a place that offered good shelter for ocean-going cargo ships and that wasn't too far from the Mackenzie River, the shipping route for goods from the south. Tuktoyaktuk seemed ideal. The HBC closed its post at Kitigaaryuit in 1933 and opened a post in Tuk in 1934. In 1937 the HBC built a warehouse in Tuk to store freight brought down the river before it was loaded onto ships that carried it on to coastal trading locations.

138

"The Hudson's Bay Company trading post at Kittigazuit (Kitigaaryuit)", 1928. (Hudson's Bay Company Archives/ 1987/363-K-20-2)

That was the real start of the development of Tuktoyaktuk, and it hasn't stopped since that time, although it's had ups and downs, as happens everywhere. People from surrounding areas came to the Hudson's Bay Company store to sell their furs and buy what they needed. Other merchants also came, but didn't stay long as the small population couldn't support more than one store. People were also attracted by the seasonal work that the HBC offered them – freight had to be loaded and unloaded, and a few residents were also employed on their boats. In other places the population went down. The price of fox dropped, and the HBC closed its posts at Baillie Island, then at Maitland Point and Pearce Point. The Royal Canadian Mounted Police also closed its detachments in those locations. In area that had been a centre of activity for nearly two decades it was as if the sea had engulfed everything and wiped it off the map. Some of the people from there moved to Tuk, and others emigrated to the Delta, and the area around Aklavik in particular. Life was certainly easier there – wood is plentiful and there is quite a lot of game. People from Tuk still travelled to the Delta in the spring to hunt muskrats. Some come back richer, others poorer – there are many temptations in Aklavik, and poker games are easy to find once the hunt is over and the money pocketed. The most far-sighted bought provisions in the better-stocked stores and took them back to Tuk with them, or to their camps. In years when the price of muskrat furs was high, in two months of work a good hunter could collect two or three thousand dollars. Later, in the 1950s, the Delta would be completely closed to muskrat hunters and trappers from Tuktoyaktuk, the lands having been divided among the inhabitants of the Delta. Instead of the whole territory belonging to everyone, each family was allocated its own territory, and no one else could venture into that territory to hunt or trap muskrats. This didn't contribute any to improving friendships between the Delta and the coast, and from time to time, relations between the trappers in the two areas were somewhat strained. This is certainly understandable – the people of Tuk saw themselves deprived of several thousand dollars of their annual income. But this also left them free in May and early June to go to Husky Lakes to fish and hunt. In bad years, this lake was to become a place of refuge and salvation for some families, if not most of the people, by providing

Tuktoyaktuk harbour in the 1940s, showing schooners and the Hudson's Bay Company buildings. (A.L Fleming Collection/NWT Archives/1979-050-1224)

them with enough fish and game to prevent them from starving. Many times, in such years, a number of families lived on only a little tea, some fish, ptarmigan, muskrats and geese. When they returned to Tuk the HBC and the Northern Transportation Company provided seasonal work, which was more than welcome. Maybe it wasn't very much, and the work didn't last very long — after all, the quantity of goods was still quite limited and there weren't as many trading posts as before — but it allowed them to buy the necessities, especially nets for summer fishing. Some also made money by making dried fish for customers such as the Royal Canadian Mounted Police, who used a lot of it to feed the dogs when they went out on patrol.

How did William Mangilaluk face all these changes and this increase in the population of Tuktoyaktuk? He certainly didn't get upset. He'd known much worse, and had seen and experienced constant changes in life since the days of the whalers, when he worked for them. After the decline of bowhead whale hunting, he, like the others, had been a trapper, one of the best. Calmly and quietly, he went about his everyday life, and he could also count on his children and grandchildren. Until his death in 1940 he was still the village leader and advisor, still just as generous, and just as hospitable, especially at the evening gatherings, during which he liked to relate his experiences and his travels. This served two purposes — to pass on the traditional knowledge and tactics that were necessary for survival, and to acquaint the young people with the history and folklore of this North that he loved so much.

Both the Anglican and Catholic churches established permanent missions at Tuktoyaktuk in the 1930s. For us, the Roman Catholics, Tuk seemed to be an ideal location. There were plenty of fish, drinking water wasn't too much of a problem, and there was lots of driftwood. When William Mangilaluk was approached, he had no objections to our presence in his village. He told us that we could use a piece of ground in the centre of the village, on the point of land on which the Hudson's Bay Company buildings stood. The first of our mission buildings was brought from

140

The Roman Catholic mission at Tuktoyaktuk, circa 1950(?). The building at the left with the bell tower is "Our Lady of Grace" church. The larger building in the centre of the photograph is the mission house where Father Le Meur lived while stationed in Tuktoyaktuk. (Le Meur Family Collection).

Herschel Island in 1938 on *Our Lady of Lourdes*. Some touch-ups were needed, and these were begun the same year and eventually completed the following summer. The fishing was poor that fall, as we had yet to learn where the good fishing spots were and what kind of nets to use, and so in September Father Franche, the first resident missionary, and his companion, Brother Guerin, went to Aklavik for the winter. Still, the work had begun, and it would continue in the years to come. The Church would live with the people, taking part in all the activities. In 1944, a new house was built for the missionaries to live in. In 1945, our tugboat, the *Sant' Anna*, came to Tuk for the first time, bringing the cargo and provisions for the coastal missions that would then be transported from Tuk by our mission schooner, *Our Lady of Lourdes*.

The earliest entries in the journals of the Tuktoyaktuk mission show that it took some time for the church to become accepted. In 1940 the missionary wrote: *"I'm spending Christmas alone, and New Year's Day."* On April 14, 1941 he wrote: *"For the first time this winter, I have a few people at Mass."* In 1942, there was a slight increase: seven people attended Midnight Mass at Christmas. In 1944 another increase is noted, although no numbers are given. In 1945 we read: *"A lot of visitors this February evening at the Mission. We showed some slides. The weather turned stormy and everyone spent the evening and the night at the Mission. No one could go back home, except for the neighbour, who set off alone at first and then came back after stringing a rope from the corner of his house to ours... the children held hands and went back home holding on to the rope*

The Sant' Anna arriving in Tuktoyaktuk with supplies for the coastal missions, circa 1950(?). (Le Meur Family Collection).

and following it... 3 or 4 days of bad weather... on the one hand it's good, it gives me a chance to sit for a while... otherwise, when the wind is from the right direction, or when there is no wind, it's coal or wood duty, or visits to the nets, or a trip, or a hunt."

The weather was faithfully noted in the journals, and how it affected people. An entry in September 1944 reads: *"Huge storm, the sandbank at the harbour entrance is completely submerged... 30 dogs drowned, at least 200 barrels of gasoline and oil were carried away by the water... the water rose by at least 10 feet, and there is a lot of damage... the Company's store and warehouse are flooded... at Tapqaq, 5 or 6 miles from Tuk, the people would have drowned if Dick's house hadn't been built so high on the shore... a boat sank with all those on board, crew and cargo lost."*[5] And in 1945: *"The Hudson's Bay Company was flooded again, and the manager came to take refuge with us and spent the night in our house."* Similarly that year, there was a big storm in December: *"A part of the wharf was picked up by the wind and blown onto the ice, and at the police detachment the heavy door of their shed was carried away and is now lying on the sandbank... the police officers had to get up and put bags of cement on the roof to prevent the wind carrying it off... After the storm, we went to look for those who were missing from the village... everyone was found. A man was lost on the lake some 30 miles from here. His boy made it to the camp, but not the father... an expedition was organized and it followed the places where the hunter had camped, a few small igloos were found where he had camped, but no trace of him or his dogs."*

Another thing often mentioned in the journals was people's health, the illnesses and epidemics. For a long time we had to be the doctors and nurses. It wasn't easy, and it gave us a lot of concern, especially in isolated places, and with no radio and no means of communicating with the outside except by dogsleds. Many times we wondered what to do – especially for the babies. In the end, we did what we could, sometimes under the most unimaginable circumstances. From time to time, epidemics broke out and ravaged the population – for example, epidemics of influenza in 1947, and again in 1950 and 1955. In Tuktoyaktuk the school and the mission house were transformed into hospitals. It wasn't until later in the 1950s that a nurse was stationed in Tuk, and that the Department of Health would make a significant effort to come at least once a year to more isolated places such as Stanton and Paulatuk. Between visits, we had to manage on our own to provide health care. I could give a number of examples, but here is just one. A man who was sick with cancer was flown from a hospital in Edmonton to Aklavik, since there was nothing more that could be done for him. After he'd been in Aklavik for a while, the medical authorities decided to send him back home, to Stanton, but without consulting or notifying anyone. One fine day he arrived at the Mission. There was almost nobody around – just two families with a lot of children, so they had no room for him and couldn't care for him. I was getting ready to leave for Tuk to pick up the mail, and then go to Paulatuk to take the mail to the priests and the people who lived there. There I was, trapped at Stanton. I took the sick old man in, and tried to care for him and help ease his pain and end his days in some kind of peace. But how was I to do it? I hadn't even been given any painkillers. I also had to come up with a way of giving him food and drink through some rubber tubing. Don't ask me how I got through those days or what I was feeling – pity for the patient and resentment against the doctors. Anyway, I stayed at Stanton for a month and a half to care for him, and then to bury him. Then I set off for Tuk, and from there I carried on to Aklavik, where I tore a strip off those in charge. Their response? "We wanted him to die at home." Did he even have a home? And where was his family at that time, in the middle of winter? We had more or less the same problems and the same difficulties when I moved to Tuk, but morale was good, and, after all, if everything always went really well, life would be a bit monotonous and would lose its charm.

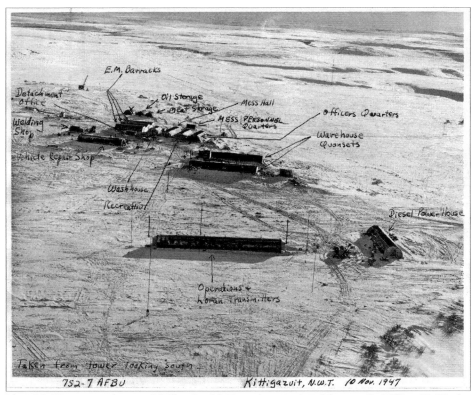

The LORAN station code-named 'Yellow Beetle', November 10, 1947. (Photo credit: William H. West)

In 1946, there was a development 40 kilometres from Tuktoyaktuk that would also begin to change the lives of some people in the village. The Canadian and American militaries had joined forces to test a Long Range Navigation (LORAN) system for aircraft flying in the north. This radio navigation system relied on signals from two stations – one near Tuk, the other at Cambridge Bay.[6] So there the armed forces were, right on our doorstep. Military personnel often came to Tuk on holiday. Some Inuvialuit got jobs at the LORAN station, and began putting their mechanical and driving skills to use. The base was in operation for just two years, but Inuvialuit who worked there had got a taste of a different lifestyle, that of the wage-based consumer economy. In a way, the construction of the LORAN station was a blessing for some people, because the winter of 1947 was very severe. There were few furs and prices were low, and any wage employment was most welcome. Very often in the North things go from one extreme to the other. It's poverty, dire need and hunger or just the opposite: prosperity, abundance and plenty. There is no happy medium it seems.

Little by little, the population of Tuktoyaktuk grew and the people started to become settled. New houses, made of driftwood, were built in the village and on the island opposite Tuk. Until 1947, other than missionaries the only whites in the place had been the Hudson's Bay Company manager, and sometimes a member of the crew of the HBC boat. But then other organizations began appearing on the scene. In 1947, the Anglican Church established a day school at Tuk. There was just one teacher and six or seven children the first year. The federal government then bought the school, but for some years there were only a few children attending it. The parents had known the schools in Aklavik – boarding schools run by the Anglican and Catholic churches, Anglican and Catholic – and for a time preferred to send their children there. The school in Tuk

"Western Arctic homes made from driftwood piled up along the Arctic shore, Tuktoyaktuk, 1950". **Left to right**: Lucy Raddi, Ivy Raddi, Susie Sydney, Raddi Koiksak, Moses Raddi, Willie Raddi, (boy) Raddi, Sarah Raddi, Marjorie Raddi. (S.J. Bailey/Library and Archives Canada/A-167666)

operated with just one teacher until 1956. Then another teacher was added, and still others, as the number of students enrolled grew.

For several years, Tuk had no permanent police services. The Aklavik Royal Canadian Mounted Police detachment came to patrol the area from time to time, and to deal with emergencies as necessary. Since the population of the place was growing, the RCMP opened a detachment in Tuk in 1949. The police would not be full-time residents that year, but starting the following year there would be one or two officers or constables constantly present in the village.

Dorothy Robinson, the first teacher at the Federal Day School in Tuktoyaktuk, with several students, circa 1947-1956. (Norman MacPherson, 'Dreams and Visions', 1991, p. 80)

In 1951 it seemed that Inuit had moved up a rung on the country's social ladder. They had been issued identification numbers and discs[7] in 1947, the same year they began receiving family allowances, and now here they were, being recognized as citizens, being given the right to vote, to cast their ballots to elect Councilors for the Mackenzie District.[8] But this process was not without its problems and challenges.

Left: *"Eskimo Identification" Disc #W3-803, issued to Emma Gruben Fitztinger of Tuktoyaktuk. (Prince of Wales Northern Heritage Centre/Accession #2004.5.072)* **Right:** *"Peter Kamingoak voting." Coppermine/Kugluktuk, date unknown. (J.H. Webster, Hudson's Bay Company Archives 1987/363-E-130/22)*

Weather is a factor, especially since the ballots and ballot boxes are transported by plane. I know that at Tuk there was at least one time the plane with the ballots couldn't come because of bad weather. And imagine trying to explain to a nice elderly woman that she has the right to choose whichever one of two candidates she wants. She asks who she is to vote for, whose name she is to mark with her X, but gets no answer. Despite all the explanations she is given and the freedom she has, she decides to leave without doing her duty. "How am I supposed to vote, if nobody tells me anything or who I should vote for?" she wonders.

As for the Mission itself, it continued to live with the people and to serve them. Father Franche and the others, each according to their availability, continued to help in every possible way. Different projects were attempted to improve the well being of everyone. Commercial fisheries were tried in the winter, as well as boat building – not pleasure boats, but boats that could be useful in the North. All of this without any profit to us in the missions, of course, that goes without saying. In every way, we tried to listen to the people and be aware of situations that arose.

"Tootsie", a boat owned by Eddie Gruben. The builders were Father Franche and Raymond Mangelana. (NWT Archives/Northwest Territories. Dept. of Information fonds/G-1979-023: 1196)

Chapter 12 Notes

1   Father Le Meur served at the Tuktoyaktuk mission from 1951 until 1953, and from 1955 until his death in 1985.

2   Angus Brabant was a long-time employee of the Hudson's Bay Company.

3   This story was told to Father Le Meur by Felix Nuyaviak, a son-in-law of Mangilaluk.

4   'Chiksak' may be a misspelling of the name 'Sisksigaaluk', one of the people who lived at Baillie Island in the early 1900s.

5   A schooner owned by a reindeer herder, Rufus Kalialuk, sank in 1944 during a storm while crossing from Cape Dalhousie to Baillie Island. Eleven people, including some children, lost their lives.

6   The Long Range Navigation (LORAN) experiment was a secret operation, code-named 'Operation Beetle'. The test station in the Mackenzie Region was called 'Yellow Beetle'.

7   Starting in the 1940s, the government began to issue 'Eskimo Identification Numbers' to Inuit. In the western Canadian Arctic these numbers were preceded with a "W", and in the east they were preceded with an "E", followed by a number that represented a region or community, and then the number assigned to the individual. Each person received a disc with his or her number stamped on it. Some people added their names to their disc. The use of these identification numbers was discontinued in 1970.

8   Prior to 1951 the 'Council of the Northwest Territories' consisted entirely of appointed members. In 1951 three elected members from the Mackenzie District joined five appointed members on the Council. Inuit were granted the right to vote in federal elections in 1950, but the next election date was not until 1953.

13

A Turning Point for Tuktoyaktuk

Tuktoyaktuk in 1956, with the newly constructed Distant Early Warning (DEW) Line site in the background. (Photo courtesy of Parks Canada).

1955 was a turning point, bringing changes to the Inuvialuit and their way of life, with ramifications not just for those alive then, but for their children and for future generations as well. Many of these changes were brought about by the construction of the Distant Early Warning, or DEW Line, a defense system using radar and telephone communication that stretched from the Aleutian Islands and across the Arctic to Labrador and Greenland.

I was living at Stanton in the spring of 1955, and I decided to go to Tuktoyaktuk to visit the resident priest, Father Franche, make my Easter confession, and, as always, pick up any mail that might have accumulated there. During my stay at Tuk, a plane arrived. We knew the pilot, Ernie Boffa, very well. He was one of those "bush pilots", as they are called up here in the North. He could fly in any weather, knew the whole country like the back of his hand, was ready for any emergency, and was always very pleasant and obliging. After greeting me, he introduced me to his passenger, a Mr. Wilson, and asked if they could stay at the Mission house for the evening. I took them there by dogsled, and Father Franche of course offered them his hospitality. During supper they told us about the DEW Line, and what was going to take place in the coming days and months as the DEW Line sites were built all along the coast. They told us to expect some big changes. Since he knew we were familiar with the region, Ernie Boffa asked us about ground conditions at Tuk, where it was possible to arrive by boat, and where a landing strip for airplanes could be built.

Sure enough, before I went back to Stanton the first tractor train arrived at Tuk. It would later be followed by many others, including the one we called the Monster, which was a formidable sight – a train of huts strung out one behind the other, pulled by a large tractor with two big diesel engines. The Monster had been manufactured in Texas, and then taken apart and brought in by plane to Alaska, where it was reassembled. It came to a strange end while making its way back to

147

Tractor train hauling supplies along the Babbage River to DEW Line sites on the Arctic Coast, circa 1955. (Shulist Collection/Yukon Archives).

Alaska, when the brakes failed and the whole train was lost. Other tractor trains would also come to Tuk, but were just passing through, and continued on their way to the east to other locations selected for DEW Line sites, each about 100 kilometres apart.

As for airplanes, we would see them too, dozens in a single day, and all different sizes, including the big ones, huge Globemasters that could transport large trucks, tractors and cranes to the interior. The first time, like everyone else I went out onto the ice to meet the plane, but another was already landing before I got back to the Mission and we soon stopped going to see them. Back at Stanton I would sometimes hear airplanes flying low over the Mission. When I went to the DEW Line camp at Nicholson 20 kilometres away I was told that when the weather was bad the mission house was used as a landmark for the pilots. Seeing it from the air, they knew where they were. On my visits to the camp at Nicholson the dogs had no problems finding their own way, as the cooks treated them royally, a good beefsteak and a pound of butter for each.

But Stanton's days were numbered. The place was emptying of people, and for several years there had been some question whether we should continue to have a resident priest. Many families had moved to the Delta, and now, in 1955, more people headed for Tuktoyaktuk, where construction was booming. Construction camps were being built, as well as homes, garages, warehouses, a gas station, towers, fuel tanks, and who knows what else. At Tuk, everyone, with few exceptions, had work. The pay was good, and the work wasn't too hard. It was a time of plenty. The Hudson's Bay Company store was empty by June, and when the first boat of the year landed the provisions weren't bought by the pound, but by the box – a box of oranges, a box of eggs, a large box of potatoes. Outboard motors were purchased even before they were put in the store. I even had many offers for my dog team, unreasonably high offers. I couldn't sell them, of course, but, as they say, there's no harm in trying.

This promotional photograph for the DEW Line, titled "Inuit family in a variety of gear" with a United States Air Force Globemaster aircraft in the background, was taken at Iqaluit in 1956. (Department of National Defense/CPU PL 103322)

Sometimes the people were puzzled when they had to do certain kinds of work, such as removing rocks from an airstrip that was under construction, or when they had to just wait, and pretend to be working – but the money was welcome. Many worked right in Tuk, while others went just about anywhere, as needed. Those who were most successful and benefitted most were those who had already had experience working with tractors and trucks, so the former employees of the LORAN camp had an advantage. This would continue for two years, winter and summer. Construction moved ahead, cement was poured, buildings were erected, and the work was continuous. The food was as good as that on the outside, probably even better. For us on the coast, it was an amazing time and a period of transition too. The people came together in centres like Tuktoyaktuk, where the population soared, quickly reaching more than 400, not counting the workers from outside. We tasted many fruits and vegetables that we hadn't seen for a very, very long time – carrots, lettuce, raspberries, radishes, even cauliflower and bananas – not to mention fresh milk. What treats, and what excess! Some suspected this period wouldn't last too long and so they stocked up on equipment while they could – boats, motors, and everything else they would need.

There were other changes as well. The people now stayed all year in places with schools, nursing clinics, and stores. The women and girls adopted the fashions of the south, something practically unheard of on the coast before then. Perfume, lipstick, all the various items used for make-up, could be found in the store. Meals took more preparation and meal times became more regular, and visiting among the people less frequent, because the workers had to be on the job early in the morning. Attitudes changed a bit, and the people became more independent of others. In 1957, just as the construction was coming to an end, there was a crime wave involving some young people. They could be seen doing next to nothing, living off others, playing poker, drinking a lot and bullying some people. Fortunately, that crisis didn't last very long, and everything would return to normal, although not without fatalities, some regrettable deaths and accidents – for example, five people died of poisoning after drinking pure alcohol.

(At this time I must respond to those who thought the DEW Line was the salvation of the Inuvialuit, bringing them wealth. They were forgetting that many people had been making much more money by trapping white fox. Some trapped as many as 600-900 foxes in a season, and this gave them a small fortune in good years when the price for fur was high. Once the DEW Line was completed, it wouldn't employ very many northerners and most of the people would have to go back to their old way of life.)

What was happening in the village during this time? Houses were being built, as well as shacks made from discarded materials such as plywood and shipping containers. Starting in 1956 a nurse was stationed in Tuktoyaktuk on a permanent basis. In 1957 Northern Transportation Company Ltd., a government-owned company, and Arctic Shipping, a private company that would operate for only a few years, came to Tuk. Arctic Shipping initiated a new shipping method, using a huge steel barge and a tugboat that ventured out into the open sea. They had some problems, though. There were times when they couldn't deliver their goods, and they lost some barges that drifted off and weren't recovered until the following summer. But the idea gained ground, and now it's not unusual to see these big barges being pushed or pulled by tugboats or other boats. There is even a dry dock at Tuk, where damage to ships and barges can be repaired.

The DEW Line completed the airstrip at Tuktoyaktuk, but only after having to raise the level because of high water when the west wind blew. They had been warned, by us priests and by Inuvialuit. *But they had maps!* Maps that had been made when an east wind was blowing off the land and the water was low. The first time there was a storm with a wind from the west the airplanes at the airstrip had to take off as fast as they could to avoid being inundated. That airstrip, and the DEW Line property itself, was the object of much criticism from us, and would cause a lot of ink to be spilled. We were on Canadian soil, but to land on the strip we had to have permission from Paramus, in New Jersey, where the headquarters of the DEW Line was located. This situation wouldn't be remedied until 1973. We had been visited by the federal Minister of Transport, Don Jamieson, and complained strongly about this difficulty, this aberration, and that summer the Department of Transport took over management of the airport and the landing strip.

The construction of the DEW Line required so much material, with barges and boats coming and going, that facilities to handle them were built in the inner part of the harbour. A pier was built, made of log posts and squared timbers, extending quite far out into the water. We were curious to see what would happen the following winter. Because of the pressure of the ice we were fully expecting to see the posts and platforms lifted, and that's exactly what happened. Before the following winter, pipes were installed all around the pier and steam was passed through them. They called this the Bubbling System.

For a while after William Mangilaluk's death in 1940 his grandson took his place as Tuktoyaktuk's leader. Some called him Chief, but it was really just an honorary title. In 1957 a government Area Administrator arrived in Tuktoyaktuk, who would act as a kind of town secretary, looking after those who were destitute, government-related matters, statistics, Family Allowance problems, and admission to the boarding school in Inuvik.[1] Once it took root, the bureaucracy would continue to increase, and would grow everywhere on the coast, to such an extent that we didn't know who was who. There were so many people working for the government that it became ridiculous, almost a joke.

The inner harbour at Tuktoyaktuk in 1982. Port facilities in this location were first built in the 1950s for the construction of the DEW Line. They were later expanded during the oil boom in the 1970s and 1980s. (Photo credit: Harry Palmer)

With the arrival of government administrators a change in the attitude of some people was starting to emerge, with less self-respect, less personal initiative, and more dependence on the State. Previously, each person was responsible for his or her own life and subsistence, and mutual help was something normal and expected. Later, the Hudson's Bay Company, the police, and the missionaries also provided assistance to some of those who were destitute and needed help, but it was always done in accordance with people's connections to the land. The help didn't amount to very much — mainly ammunition, nets, a little food, enough to help the hunter and the trapper to get started and to work. In addition, they were asked to do something in exchange for this help. When the government arrived, all that changed. Thinking that what had been done before had no value, the first administrators ignored the experience acquired by those who had lived in the North for years, who knew the land well, who could fend for themselves when travelling, fishing or hunting, who knew the local language, and knew its people, and who, in general, also had the people's trust. In 1957, outwardly at least — I'm not judging intentions, but simply looking at the external evidence — a kind of government paternalism appeared. They were trying to buy the people. That's how most Inuvialuit described the government's method. That winter the weather had been bad, and trapping brought in only a few furs. Some people stayed at home and received financial assistance from the government, which led to some resentment. Others came to see me asking to lend them or advance them a little tea and sugar and oil, just what was necessary, because, they said, they didn't want to be bought by anyone. A different policy could have been followed — that of providing work and paying the workers — but it was impossible to convince the officials of this. Many times in the years that followed we tried — in vain, unfortunately — to have that policy changed and to recommend a more humane system, where the people could have kept their pride, but there has been no way to change that way of thinking. There is — and I've heard it many times from my people — something absurd and illogical about helping only those who were in need. Many times I pointed out the problems that resulted from this way of doing things, of neglecting those who were trying to do something by themselves without accepting handouts from the good offices of the government. The Church's efforts to help those in need created problems for the government, and were criticized, but we didn't worry. After all, we'd been in the land for quite a number of years and would be staying there for a long time yet. We saw the damage that the government's policy could do. Our position was governed by and directed towards the people's well being and their independence.

In response to the growing government bureaucracy, the people of Tuktoyaktuk established the Hunters and Trappers Committee to protect their interests. The HTC was the link between the government administrators and the people of Tuk, and it would become increasingly important in the years to follow. Officially, it was through the HTC that the people let the government administrators know what they wanted with regard to hunting and fishing issues. In fact, the elected members of the HTC looked after just about everything when the need arose. It was the organization to contact with regard to festivities in the village, or if someone lost his belongings in a fire, and who knows what else. Various other committees also were established, such as the Community Association and the Advisory Council, but the HTC was the nucleus. It wasn't until 1970, when the village acquired the status of Hamlet, that a definitive solution was found with regard to local responsibilities, although some time earlier, when the last Area Administrator came to Tuktoyaktuk he adopted a policy of allowing and encouraging the elected members of the Advisory Council to make the decisions, which he then simply endorsed. Tuktoyaktuk is greatly indebted to him for its status as the first Hamlet on the Arctic coast, achieved through his humane methods and his sense of leadership that he shared with the people.[2] But here I'm anticipating events that would come later, only after several years of frustration, delays, dissatisfaction, empty words, and decisions made with no prior consultation.

So it could be said that, for the Inuvialuit, those years immediately following the construction of the DEW Line were a period of adjustment to a new lifestyle, and greater involvement in the affairs of the village. With regard to church work, our activities continued as in the past, and even increased as Tuktoyaktuk took shape. Our lifestyle, following that of the local people, also underwent changes. Because almost everyone now lived in the village we had fewer trips to make out on the land, and when we did visit camps we used a snowmobile, a Bombardier, purchased by Father Franche. What adventures we had with that machine! On those trips here and there, over hundreds of kilometres, we really had to believe that Providence was giving us special guidance and protection. Many times we broke skis and springs, but we always managed to reach our destination. Just once, there was a forced march of a few dozen kilometres before reaching Inuvik, and that was because we ran out of gas.

The ecumenical movement being talked about so much now has existed in the North for a long time, and rivalry between churches has been exaggerated and misunderstood.[3] Obviously, we weren't about to change the doctrine in which we firmly believe in order to attract people, or try to convert them. Our personal and spiritual relations with the people were frequent, but without any of that proselytizing of which the northern missions have often been accused. Faith can't be bought, and it can't be sold. From the beginning, the Roman Catholic priest has travelled with the Protestant minister and they have helped each other, in spite of a fear that doing so might

Father Le Meur on the mission's snowmobile, Tuktoyaktuk, circa 1960. The log building behind him is St. John's Anglican Church. (Le Meur Family Collection)

not be understood by the church authorities. But the authorities were quite a distance away, so with no means to communicate by radio or by correspondence – with mail only twice a year, it would take at least six months to receive a reply – we simply went ahead. Besides, not knowing the environment or the circumstances, who could have condemned us, and – as we would say to each other when we met – where and to what harsher place could we be exiled? Siberia, our neighbouring land? As early as 1939, the priest said prayers in place of the minister when he was absent. He helped those who were ill to get to the Anglican hospital at Aklavik, and later on, at Tuktoyaktuk, I myself presided over Protestant burials and conducted ecumenical services. I invited the Protestant minister, who was chaplain on the DEW Line, to come and preach at the church on Sundays, after first consulting my parishioners. He, in turn, invited me to preside and preach when he went on visits to DEW Line camps. Unfortunately, several times circumstances led us to conduct common burials, with prayers in common at the gravesite, and the whole village present to pay their respects.

I also added a civil marriage to my experience. A few years ago some friends wanted to get married, and asked me to be their justice of the peace for the occasion. So, having received the necessary permission from my Bishop, one Saturday morning I waited for the appointed time. As usual, I was starting to get the church ready for Sunday services. This meant sawing and splitting some driftwood, bringing it into the church and storing it near the stoves. Wood had to be put into the stoves in the morning in order to raise the temperature from some 30 or 40 degrees below zero to a decent enough temperature that my parishioners wouldn't freeze during Mass. While I was working, an airplane arrived with the bride and groom. The woman was a dentist, and the man was an employee of the government who worked in Ottawa. It was time to go back inside and dress as a clergyman, and arrange a table with some flowers – artificial, and quite old, but flowers all the same. That added a little something to the ceremony, which, to us in the North, who are used to a good audience – almost the whole village turns out – seemed sad for want of people. Before proceeding I asked the bride and groom if they had witnesses for the ceremony. The pilot would be one of them, they told me, and as for the other, anyone would do. As it happened, I had a visitor who had followed me to the Mission, and I asked him if he would mind being of service by making this marriage valid by his presence as a witness. He said he was honoured to be present. I explained to him, in Inuvialuktun, the ceremony that was about to take place, and assured him that it would brief. And then I proceeded. Brief it was, especially for the witness, who, when it was time to sign, asked me when the ceremony was going to take place. It was incomprehensible to him that two people could get married in private, and so quickly, without the presence of friends, and I had to explain that kind of ceremony and compare it with the church ceremonies. On other occasions, whether a marriage or a death, the whole population took part, no matter in which church the ceremony was held. When the married couple left the church they were inundated with rice, and in the evening there was a dance that everyone attended. So my friend's surprise at such a ceremony, so quickly performed, is easy to understand. For burials, the presence of all the people of the village is also almost guaranteed, with the children following or preceding the funeral procession, curious to see the end of the ceremony at the cemetery, collecting stones along the way to put in the grave.

The cemetery caused some dispute with the government. The Administrator wanted the site for other purposes, and had contacted some people in that regard, including me of course. My answer was that although the site was at the Mission, it really belonged to the people, and that I wouldn't do anything without their consent and without hearing their opinion. First, it was a matter of choosing another burial site – not a serious or complicated question, and the people came to ask for my opinion in that regard. Next, it was a matter of not simply taking part of the site, but taking the whole thing and digging up all the bodies that were buried there. The people didn't like that idea at all. The thing was that the people were starting to get fed up with being told what they should do, and what should be where in the village, without having much say. At a first meeting, they seemed to be more or less in favour, but a few days later, when the Administrator wanted a definite answer, they simply said that they would leave the dead where they were and that the government should find a site somewhere else. The people of Tuk responded the same way to another headache that the government was dealing with. The school that had just been built was in danger, because the site where it stood was being eroded by ocean waves, and the people were asked for their thoughts on the problem. They answered that this wasn't their problem. They had been given no opportunity to speak when the school was being built, and what's more, the people who already had a house on that site had been required to move. Yes, of course, they had received compensation, but the principle behind all this was the question of ownership. Did they really own the land on which their houses stood, and where they had lived for so many years?

Along the shore where the school was located the government built a sloping wall of rocks, one on top of the other, to try to stop it from washing away. For added safety a vertical wooden wall was also built along the shore. As if such a piece of straw could stop the tides and the waves! The wooden wall was almost totally destroyed the first year, and then rebuilt the same way. Engineers would come from Ottawa and study the project to try to improve it – making it longer was one idea, using bags of sand and stones all along the shore!!! Would this be possible, and would it be economical and realistic? They would come see me and asked what I thought. I told them that it needed something sloped and continuous. Why not use the driftwood available on the beach and make a barrier with that? Trees are stuck in the sand and lying on the shore, so the material is there, as is the manpower. The material wouldn't rot very quickly in this land that remains frozen for nine months of the year. As well, with a slope the pressure of the water wouldn't be as great – the water would wash over top instead of hitting against a straight, vertical surface. But try to tell that to specialists!

People were asked if they wanted to move the village away from the eroding shore. It was a disease, an epidemic of moves. It began with Aklavik, which was moved to Inuvik in 1955.[4] There was also talk of moving the village of Coppermine, and now we were also being asked what we thought of moving Tuk to the other side of the bay. Was it because the village was too close to the DEW Line site? We were promised an ideal place, with a good harbour and other things we would need. The people told me they didn't want to move. Tuk's location is much more sheltered, it was easy to fish there and they could leave the harbour more easily from where they now were. On the other side they would be farther away from the sea. We were promised that a harbour would be created especially for us. But how? And where? The Northern Transportation Company Ltd. camp that was on that side was facing quite a number of problems – there was no gravel and so trucks and tractors were getting bogged down in the mud, and the water in the surrounding lakes wasn't very good. When the people said what they thought, the government representative didn't much like the response. He resorted to childish arguments that weren't very flattering to us – we were acting like children, we were never satisfied, what was it we wanted? My response was the people are old enough and responsible enough to know what they want and what is best for them. I wasn't really interested in continuing the discussion, but he kept repeating that it was going to happen. Well, what else could I say but that I was with the people, and that there would be two villages, with the whites on one side and the rest of us where the village still stands. (I don't consider myself to be from the south. Many times I have been told, "You are one of us, you belong to us", and as for the children, they find it hard to believe that I was born in France or anywhere else. Probably hearing me speak their language has something to do with the way they see me.) Instead of us moving there, a few years later, in 1966, NTCL moved over to the side of the bay where the village is. It now has easier access to the airport, and it is also easier for the Inuvialuit who work there. Before, it was a problem getting to the other side of the bay by boat when the weather was bad.

For many of us, the seasons were determined by NTCL. It started opening up the camp in spring, and shut down in fall, once the ice was solid and had taken possession of the sea, and the boats couldn't move any more. For me, it is a joy to see the sailors arrive each year. Some come every year, and all were very good to me. There was always a place for me at their table, and the change in diet and cooking did me good. The friends we make in the North are for life, and occasionally we will meet them on our trips to the South. For a number of them, it's not just a short stay at Tuk – they keep in touch with the village and to some extent serve as its representatives and promoters in the South, and look for different ways to interest southerners in the North. I know some who have done something for the village almost every year. Once, they managed to get a piano for

Playing soccer on the ice in the harbour, Tuktoyaktuk, date unknown. Father Le Meur is in the centre of the photograph, facing the player with the ball. (Le Meur Family Collection)

Tuk. Another year, they collected ice skates to give to all the school children, and the sailors made swings and toys. I can say that each time I needed special help of some kind, the people at NTCL, and at the DEW Line – and now the oil companies – were very kind and did the impossible to meet our requests. It was their way of showing that they belonged to the village and wanted to be part of Tuktoyaktuk's community life.

After my arrival at Tuktoyaktuk I had introduced the game of soccer, played on the ice in winter and to some extent on land in summer, although the ground wasn't really suitable. This gave us the opportunity to bring the young people together with the DEW Line employees, who also liked to participate. With their help we set up goal posts, with old fish nets strung between them. Matches were played on the ice. Even minus 30 degree temperatures didn't scare us. It was not unlike one of the traditional Inuvialuit games, and quickly became very popular. It didn't have all the rules there are now, and believe me, you had to be fit and in good condition to play it. Picture a wide-open field. The boundaries are the two sides of the bay, and between those boundaries the players could go anywhere. The young people would play for hours on end in that cold, without getting tired. Their life trained them to be fit.

A few years ago a missionary friend in the Yukon, Father Mouchet, began to introduce young boys and girls to the sport of cross-country skiing.[5] He was also asked to help set up a skiing program for the students in the school hostels in Inuvik. The aim was to develop a sport that was suited to the local environment, and that taught discipline and effort. The program was successful, and skiers went to competitions in Canada and other parts of the world, including the Winter Olympics. The Canadian government was delighted with this project, and on the way back from the Arctic Winter Games in Quebec in 1976 the team was received in Ottawa by the Prime Minister, Pierre Trudeau. That is what I call using the local resources, human and natural. With snow practically eight months out of the year, they can do a lot of training.

Skiers in Inuvik, 1984. (Dept. of Public Works and Services/NWT Archives/G-1995-001: 5625).

In 1962 Ernest Latour, who worked for the Vocational Education Branch of the Federal Government, came to Tuktoyaktuk to set up a Fur Garment Shop, a place where women in the village who were skilled in preparing and sewing skins were hired to make parkas, boots, gloves and mittens, stoles and other things made from furs that visitors to Tuk and stores in the South might want to sell. A workshop was first set up in a part of the school, and when a new school was built it moved to another part of the old school. This undertaking flourished from the outset, so much so that there were far more orders than could be filled. The Tuk Fur Garment Shop became known throughout Canada, and even further abroad. Ernie was a professional furrier, and he was a good teacher. The women who worked at the fur shop felt quite at ease with him, and very quickly became familiar with the modern equipment and working with commercially tanned furs and skins.

The Fur Garment Shop had its ups and downs, crises, and battles with the bureaucracy. Many times it had to close its doors for lack of tanned furs. Many times unfortunate cases of government interference angered the employees, and made them ready to quit. Each government official who visited from Ottawa felt compelled to give their opinion on the way the books were kept and on the way the sewing was done. Many times I was called to the workshop to hear the women's and the manager's complaints, and many times I intervened to ensure they would be

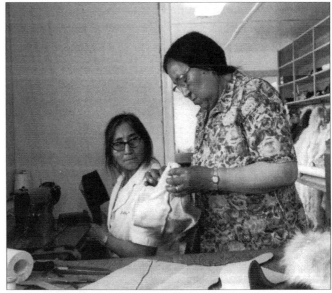

*Pearl Pingo (**sitting**) and Bessie Wolki (**standing**) in the Fur Garment Shop, Tuktoyaktuk, circa 1962. (Le Meur Family Collection)*

157

Employees of the Fur Garment shop in Tuktoyaktuk. **Seated, left to right**: *Hester Adam, Alice Gruben, Ivy Anikina, Bessie Amos, Laura Raymond.* **Standing, middle row, left to right**: *Sam Jacobson, Billy Panaktalok (Panaktaloak?), Ernie LaTour (Manager), Sarah Gruben (McKay), Agnes Klengenberg, Pearl Pingo, Christina Klengenberg, Suzanne Ettagiak or Mary Avik, Mary Kotokak.* **Standing, back row, left to right**: *Cora Kimiksana, Bessie Wolki, Hester Cockney(?), circa 1962. (Le Meur Family Collection)*

left in peace. I remember one time in particular that the employees asked for me. An inspector had arrived, and according to him there were no skins available in Canada. He also wanted to give some advice to the seamstresses. I went to meet with the visiting inspector and very politely asked him, on behalf of the seamstresses, if he could really help them, and in what way. He gave me lengthy explanations concerning his visit and the problems with finding furs and money to maintain this project. My response came immediately – I told him that the employees were tired of seeing so many inspectors, and a good way to save money was to refrain from coming all this way, since such trips cost quite a bit. Add in his wages, and the total amount could have bought quite a number of furs.

Another time the bureaucracy created a problem for the Fur Garment Shop occurred when Stuart Hodgson, the Commissioner of the Northwest Territories,[6] came to visit the community and to meet with the Hamlet Councilors, of which I was one at the time. On such occasions visitors usually went to the Fur Garment Shop. However, the women at the shop had almost no furs to make anything with, and almost nothing to show or sell. Some government personnel from Inuvik, rather than helping them acquire skins so that they could make things themselves, instead brought items from the Inuvik cooperative and placed them in the shop at Tuk to show off to the Commissioner. The employees of the Tuk Fur Garment Shop were very unhappy with this, and their morale was low. I promised them that I would come to the shop with the Commissioner and make him aware of the situation, on one condition: that they wouldn't be afraid to speak out too, and would state their grievances and say what they wanted. On the day of the visit, before the meeting with the Hamlet Council started, I took the Commissioner aside and whispered to him what was going on and asked him to visit the Fur Garment Shop. As soon as they saw him, the women began to chant, "We want work. We want work." Mr. Hodgson, the Commissioner, was

158

amazed and couldn't believe his ears. He turned to me and told me that he would take care of it right away. After listening to the workers' grievances, he asked the staff members accompanying him who was responsible for that situation. And he told them frankly what he thought of it. I received some unpleasant looks from several members of the group. As for the Commissioner, he got on the telephone immediately and began dictating the steps to be taken to his assistant in Yellowknife. "And right away," he said, "because all the women are on my back." The driver of the Tuk bus, an Inuvialuk, said to me, "You're harsh, and I feel sorry for the poor guys who'll be hearing about this from the

Sarah Gruben [Mackay] in the Fur Garment Shop, Tuktoyaktuk, date unknown. (Inuvialuit Communications Society)

Commissioner." I answered that his wife had no work, and that a quick decision had to be made to resolve the situation. I didn't feel sorry for those who were responsible for that mistake. They paid the price for their lack of honesty. Then he said, "I understand. It's a good thing that you're here and that you're not afraid to speak out." The Commissioner reassured the workers and said that supplies would arrive within the week. Sure enough, hundreds of pounds of skins and furs arrived by airplane. That evening, when I led the group back to their plane, several members of the group didn't say goodbye to me. That didn't matter to me.

We could have had many markets opened to the Fur Garment Shop. One of the District Managers of the Hudson's Bay Company was ready to buy all the products and then take responsibility for selling and distributing them in the south, but the bureaucrats simply laughed at him and stopped any chance of development. We also had to fight to prevent that workshop from being turned into a branch of the welfare office and employing women who had no resources. To us, it had to be a factory that would employ the best workers, and that should be able to make its own way and make a profit as well. How they managed to block business! One time, it was someone from Ottawa that had to look after sales and purchases. Other times, they were short of money, and the shop was full of manufactured products. It's in that kind of environment that our presence is useful to lend encouragement and to assert the rights of the workers, loudly and without fear. A few years ago, when the government wanted to wash its hands of it, the employees asked me if I could help them, and asked me to take charge of the project. I assured them of my support and my advice, and even my presence – not continual, but more than occasional. But before this could take shape, someone from the south was asked to come and take charge of the business as administrator. The Fur Garment Shop is now a cooperative, and makes and sells parkas, boots, mittens, souvenirs made from fur, just about everything.

In my opinion, to really flourish, local undertakings such as the Fur Garment Shop should be out of reach of the government. Do I have a conflict of interest there? Probably. Practically the only projects that work well are those that were originated in or by the Church and have the missionaries behind them. They are also the ones that started up without any financial assistance or ties to anyone. Might there also be a kind of underlying jealousy? No matter what the motives and reasons, we missionaries think we should help in the beginning and then step aside and be simply advisers, and then only if and when we are asked. I've initiated and participated in many projects at the beginning, then withdrawn from them, staying in the background and only lending a hand if asked. As the villages develop, we also make any effort that the needs and circumstances require. For this, all we had to do to be useful was simply be available each time, be willing, and show a little imagination.

I have so many happy memories of Inuvialuit children! They were the first to help me to learn the language, repeating words and phrases for me without losing patience. They followed me everywhere, asking and posing questions that, at the time, I couldn't answer, because I couldn't communicate. I always wondered about that, the children's attitude towards me, an experience that I had and that gives me a feeling of humility and of respect for them. Each time we meet on the street, and even from a distance, the children will call out, "Hello Father", and they'll keep it up until I answer. At the school as well, going out or coming in, they'll greet me, something they don't do to others. Many times when I'm visiting their homes and am ready to leave, the children will rush to the door and block it, saying, "You don't have to go. You can stay here. There's a place for you. We'll give you a room." They often come to the Mission house just to say hello or to see what is going on, and they are always ready to help with any small chores, such as doing dishes. Do they see the presence of the divine in us missionaries? Someone different from the others? Whatever the reason, others have also noticed this openness of the young people towards us, and their respect. One little thing that happened – funny maybe, but significant – will prove this. Having accidentally bumped into me while walking and playing in the street, one child apologized, and the others told him, "You don't need to say that. See, it's the Father." Such a remark indicates that I was like one of them, like a member of the family.

Children at the Paulatuk mission, circa late 1940s. (Le Meur Family Collection)

The school in Tuk is named Mangilaluk, after the founder of the community. But his son-in-law, Felix Nuyaviak, told me, "When we were asked to choose a name for the school at Tuk, I put my piece of paper in the box, too, and I had written Lisiuk's name. When I see the children disappear every day into the school, I have the impression that the school, that big building, is swallowing them like food into its stomach." I understood exactly what Nuyaviak meant. He was playing on the meaning of Lisiuk's name, the elder who had prophesized the future of Tuktoyaktuk. In English 'Lisiuk' means 'the one who tries to swallow'. Felix was expressing his opinion of the education provided to children today, the changes that were taking shape,

160

Rosie Albert teaching an Inuvialuktun language class at Sir Alexander Mackenzie School in Inuvik, circa 1980. (Inuvialuit Communications Society).

some of which he had adopted, was benefitting from, and was grateful for, but he also had some criticism and resentment. It would be closer to reality, and to his state of mind, if I said he was more worried about the way of life, the traditions of the past and the Inuvialuit culture.

It used to be that the parents themselves did all the educating. For example, a boy went hunting and fishing with his father, and accompanied him on all his trips. That way, he acquired experience and learned about the history and the geography of the land, and about the animals and their habits. As for the girls, they learned from their mothers how to prepare skins for clothing, sewing, cooking and other jobs around the home.

The children don't speak Inuvialuktun much now. After pressure to introduce it in the schools it is now being taught there, although not for enough hours, in my opinion. There are many other gaps to be filled as well. For example, why not teach the history of the North, and its geography? The children learn what is happening elsewhere, in China, Japan and Europe, but they don't know what is happening in their own neighbourhood, such as at Paulatuk or Sachs Harbour. Several years ago, I started a program bringing some elders to the school in Tuktoyaktuk where they related their experiences and the traditions of the past. The parents are beginning to realize that there are these gaps, and parent advisory groups are putting pressure on the school administration to do something about it. All these things won't change overnight, but the most important thing is that positive steps are being taken.

When the school was in full operation we had to use our ingenuity to find a way to ensure that the students came to school fit and awake. Up here there are 24 hours of daylight starting at the end of April. There is no night, and in the evening the temperature is not too cold, so it's a great time for playing, or going for a walk, or going hunting around the village. Many times I've seen children of all ages still outside and playing very early in the morning. Often children would go to school and would barely have sat down before they fell asleep at their desk. What could be done to get the children to go home at a suitable hour? The parents wanted a curfew. I proposed ringing the church bell at 10 pm and seeing how that went. This proposal was approved, and each evening the bell was rung. I don't know which made more noise, the bell or the dogs, which, I think, couldn't stand the sound of the bell, and each time it rang they would howl one after the other throughout the village. Sometimes I happened to be at the DEW Line or at the Northern Transportation Company camp and was a bit late with the bell. When the children saw me running and hurrying on the ice, I heard them saying and shouting, "Here's the Father going to ring the bell. We'd better hurry, it's time we went home." I don't know exactly how to evaluate the curfew, but it helped a bit.

There is a rift growing between the old people and the young. Everything has changed. The parents can't help their children very much in their studies, and when the children come home from school, what is there for them to do to help out at home? No longer does wood have to be to be chopped – the houses all have oil furnaces – and no ice to be cut and brought in, as water is now delivered. There are no dogs at the house, so there is no need to have as many nets under the ice. What is there left for parents to teach their children? Just a bit of fishing and hunting, more as a sport than a necessity. Clothes are now bought in stores, ready-made and manufactured, and in school the girls are also taught home economics. The relationship between children and parents has certainly become a lot weaker in recent years, and that poses a great risk to Inuvialuit society, which used to be so family-centred. As elsewhere, a lot of parents feel overwhelmed by events, and by the new methods of teaching. They – especially the oldest among them – wonder what they can give the young people now. The younger parents, who, for their part, have all gone through the school and the system, see the need for their children to attend school and are really interested in providing them with an education, but one that is better suited to the North.

It isn't easy for the people to keep their cultural identity, yet not remain isolated from the world. No one can live on an island, alone, in today's world. And we can see all the means of communication penetrating the North – first radio, and now television – putting them in touch with the whole world. There are advantages and disadvantages. Life is becoming more complicated in the North, and the problems are not that easy to solve. The older people can live off the land and rely on their earlier training, and may be able to live in very harsh conditions and with little, but can the young people? Are they prepared for such a life? It doesn't seem so. For the majority at least, life is easier and softer. The consumer society is coming to the North, and has already arrived. A lot of needs are being created, and the young people wonder what they will do with the education received. In the minds of the people, this major question is always present: What will it be like tomorrow? How many jobs will there be? What will become of the land? What will the children do? I must admit that we can't answer that question.

Some time ago, I was called a dreamer by Arthur Laing, the Minister of Indian Affairs and Northern Development, because during one of his visits to Tuk I had put forward some ideas that seemed to me, I wouldn't say revolutionary, but practical. We were less interested in his vision of the North – what might happen in 25 years – than we were in what the Government had planned to meet the needs of the people of the North now, particularly for education, training and employment. Since we received no specific answers I pointed out that the Russians had a five-year

Imperial Oil Ltd.'s drill site at Atkinson Point, 1970. (Glenbow Museum and Archives/IP-7a-1)

plan and were developing their North much better than the Department of Northern Affairs, and that they, the people in Ottawa, were thinking only of continuing an arbitrary and imperialistic regime, without letting us know anything. If I was a dreamer and an idealist, at least my dreams and my projects were in the North, not far away in Ottawa. Too often, the people in charge depended on reports prepared by people who simply passed through the North and immediately thought they were experts. The worst of it was that, at that time, they were believed. And we who lived in the North were given extra work and ridiculous orders. Little by little, though, the people gained the upper hand and would no longer let others step on their toes or push them around.

Petroleum companies started to get interested in the Delta and in the area around Tuktoyaktuk in the late 1960s. Soon there was feverish activity with seismic explorations all around us – boats on the ocean, skidoos and all kinds of tracked vehicles in winter, and detonations everywhere. This extensive exploration led to the discovery of oil and gas a few kilometres from Tuk, both on land and in the ocean.

It wasn't necessary to look very far for workers for the oil and gas boom. There were people right here at Tuk; all that was needed was to provide some training. But it is not always easy to reconcile this employment with local

Drilling for oil at Atkinson Point, 1969. The Imperial Oil Ltd. employee on the left is Jimmy Joe Esagok. (Glenbow Museum and Archives/IP-14d-69-57)

163

lifestyles. At certain times of the year there is a kind of spring fever – the weather is nice, the days are long, the migratory birds arrive, or the white whales are there – and there is a desire to be independent, to answer the call of nature. So let them go back to hunting or fishing full time, people have sometimes said to me. A number of times I responded to those criticisms by inviting one of those big talkers to take my dog team and to set off from his place, where he is so comfortable, with just a little tea and a little hard-tack, to go and experience for himself the things he was talking about. Or to put a net under the ice, ice more than a metre thick, and try to pull a few miserable fish from the water. The argument usually ended there.

I could add that many of the government workers and other employees from the South have job security and high wages, as well as benefits such as isolation pay because they are in the North. None of which the Inuvialuit have. The people's criticisms of this situation are understandable. When they travel by plane, for example, or buy their food or anything else at the store, they have to pay a lot more than people in the South, because the distances are enormous. They don't like this very much, and they are not afraid to say so to those in authority.

Someone reading this or hearing me speak might think that I had my hand in quite a few things. Oh yes, certainly, but then it wasn't always me speaking officially, far from it, but the people themselves, to whom I'd perhaps given advice and guidance, and with whom I'd held discussions. They were and are capable of standing up for themselves and expressing their opinions to any audience, although it was hard sometimes for them to do this. They listen, but don't always like to make suggestions, or offer their own opinions. When Charlie Gruben was chosen to be a delegate at one of the first international meetings of circumpolar countries, he met with me and a few other people to talk about what he should say. I promised him I would write the text for his presentation, but when I gave him the text he told me it wouldn't help him much, because he didn't know how to read. I explained it all to him in Inuvialuktun, then in English. The meeting was held in Edmonton, Alberta, and delegations had come from Russia, Finland, Sweden, and other Northern countries – experts on just about every area of activity and science. It was a good group, about 150-200 scholars and representatives from those countries. Before he gave his presentation Charlie met with one of the delegates from the Nordic Association, who read the text to him again and added an appeal to the specialists not to forget the burning question of Aboriginal rights.

~ Charlie Gruben's Presentation ~

"My name is Charlie Gruben and I come from Tuktoyaktuk, Northwest Territories. I'm very pleased to be here in Edmonton for this meeting, and I greatly appreciate the fact that I'm representing the Inuit. These problems you are discussing are not unfamiliar to us. They concern us, and are of vital importance to us. After all, we live up there, we have lived up there, and we will spend our lives – we and our children – up there in the North, our homeland, our territory. Aren't we the true inhabitants and indigenous peoples of this region? All the others come and go, most of them in any case, with a few exceptions. That's why I think that we shouldn't be just observers, but should be active participants and share equally in the responsibilities, and have the right to discuss and vote on resolutions. Why? Because we are involved and included in all these problems, whether you like it or not, and we don't want to be just spectators on the sidelines. All these changes, all these concerns, concern us. These changes, these developments in all areas,

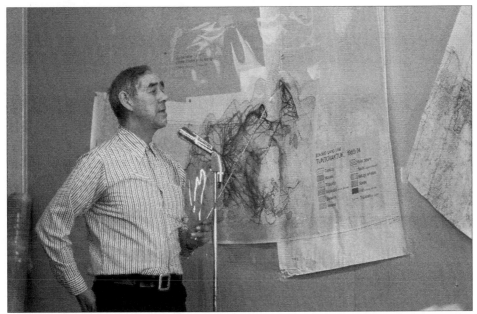

Charlie Gruben making a presentation to the Berger Commission, Tuktoyaktuk, 1976. (Photo courtesy of Michael Jackson)[7]

such as the economy, community life, industry, education, ecology, trade, politics, all of that and more concerns us too, and all of this will affect our life and our ways, our lifestyle and our whole economy. In short, everything is going to change in the North, and is already beginning to change and to move. What will our future be? We are interested parties, and we want to be part of this future development of the Arctic regions. We also want to receive the information requested, and know about the action plans, and be consulted so that our opinion and our point of view will be known. Too often in the past decisions were made and actions taken without us being consulted, and we found ourselves faced with *faits accomplis* and situations for which we hadn't been prepared or received notice. Now we believe that such policies and procedures can and must be corrected and replaced, or even discarded and replaced by more communication and exchange of information among all groups. Southern civilization is coming farther and farther North and invading and penetrating deep into our country, the Arctic, on land, on water, and in the Arctic sea. A lot of ideas and questions, as well as issues, points, must be clarified and clearly explained, because they are all very important, crucial and urgent these days. Here are some examples:"

"*The question of land*: Several times in the recent past, in the North, in the villages, such as Tuktoyaktuk, some people, their homes, have been moved here or there, without them having any say. I've even had that experience myself. In 1955, coming back from Banks Island, I found my house somewhere else, on a lot I hadn't chosen. Or, to make room for a school, those who were on the selected piece of land were asked to move somewhere else, and the same happened when a new house was built for the Royal Canadian Mounted Police. Compensation and damages were paid to the people affected, which makes us think that, after all, we must have some rights to our lands, but what are they really? We'd like to know what our legal rights are, our rights to the lots we live on, where we've built our houses, and to the areas where we hunt and trap. Until now, we've considered these territories as ours, the land where we've harvested our furs. Where are the rights of the first occupants? Where are the rights of the indigenous peoples? What compensation will we receive? These are just some of the questions we'd like to have answered quite soon. And how can our Prime Minister say that these rights won't be recognized, when right next door to us, the Inupiat of Alaska are in the process of negotiating a treaty with the American government?"

"The question of trapping grounds: Development is moving ahead quickly where we are, and the consequences are right there in front of us, for all to see: intensive searching, exploration, on land, on water, on the ice, which, for us who are living in the midst of all these changes, gives rise to a number of questions and problems. In our region, the territory of Tuktoyaktuk, since 1955, the date construction of the radar line began, trapping has been getting poorer and poorer. It's now become impossible to live by trapping alone. Why this reduction in animal life? What impact, effect and consequences do all these things have on our territory – for example, planes and helicopters in the air, tractors, tractor trains and big trucks on land, and explosions from seismic operations on land and in the sea? Take the airplane from Inuvik to Tuktoyaktuk and you'll see lines and marks everywhere on the ground. Last year, we had to strongly protest to the Government and the oil companies, because some small rivers had been blocked up and the dams hadn't been removed after the machines had gone by. As a result, the people at Tuk didn't catch any fish in their nets. That summer, no white whales were caught by the people of Tuk in our waters. Is this due to the seismic operations? We may not be experts, but all of us at Tuk believe that these operations drove away the whales, who are very sensitive to noise. And our patriarch told us that, in our memory, this had never been seen before at Tuk, or in the surrounding area. From Tuk itself, we could also see the water geysers shooting up from the sea each time there was an explosion and, what's more, the houses themselves felt the explosions.[8] Are we going to simply accept such a situation without protest? We still have to live in the winter once the companies leave. That is why, on behalf of all the people I'm representing here today, I ask all interested and responsible people to first think about our problems, and then make decisions and study our interests and concerns, look out for our well being, and seriously consider our request and our appeals."

"What can be done for our territory? It seems that this territory is damaged and is becoming poorer in wildlife and harvests. What are our rights? What will happen if minerals and resources are found under our soil? Will we be able to benefit from these discoveries? We are in a different situation than the Indians, in the sense that we have never wanted to accept treaties with the English or with the Canadian government. Bob Cockney, Nuligak, relates that, in 1929, when we gathered again at Aklavik after the muskrat hunt, an important man, a representative of the Government, also came to Aklavik. His name was O.J. Finnie. He called a meeting, and a lot of Inuvialuit were present at that meeting. He then told us that the Government was interested in us and wanted to sign a treaty with the people of the coast, the Inuvialuit. Through our contact with the Indians, we knew what such a treaty meant. When he was asked what we'd receive for the 12 months of the year, he answered that we would receive $5.00. Then Bob Cockney responded on behalf of the people present at the meeting, "Keep your $5.00 and your money. What help would $5.00 be to us in this land, our land, where everything is already so expensive. Here's what we want – no treaty, but that those who are in need receive material assistance, that widows and widowers, and those who are blind, disabled, or sick also receive food assistance." Mr. Finnie responded that those were very fair and reasonable words, and that there would be no treaty, that what we had asked him for would be taken into consideration and would be followed as a policy in the future.

But now where are we? What is our situation? We don't even own the land our houses are on, and more and more it seems that it will be very difficult to live just from trapping."

"So we have no choice any more, no choice but to submit, like everyone else, to the labour and employment economy, to find jobs as workers, part time or even full time. For us to be able to adapt successfully to such a life, we recommend a number of measures:

1. That there be more communication between the companies that employ us and the workers, the employees, and at the same time, more extensive education and training.

2. Practical training given, if possible, in our environment, in the North, and even at Tuktoyaktuk itself. Here at Tuktoyaktuk, there are a number of ships in the harbour. Why not give some people education and training on board these ships? (This is being done in other provinces, such as Newfoundland.) The oil companies are also working at Tuk and in the surrounding area. Education and training could be done on site. And the same applies to other industries in the North.

3. Why wouldn't we see factories in the North? Manufacturing – such as Tuk's factory for making fur clothing – is already doing well. Wouldn't it be possible to have others? A fish cannery, for example? All these possibilities should be considered and weighed."

"Gentlemen, you are very interested in and concerned about the tundra, the environment. But we who have lived here for a very long time and who still live in the North are, more than ever before, concerned about and interested in conserving and protecting the land itself and its inhabitants, our culture, our way of life, and I appeal to all people of goodwill and especially to you, the delegates, to help us in our fight and in our efforts."

When he got back from the conference Charlie told me it wasn't that easy to speak to so many people, and that his legs seemed a weak when he had to appear before such an audience. But once started, his speech went very well and was warmly received by all the delegates, who adopted it and asked that the text be given to the Minister of Northern Affairs, Jean Chrétien. Then they also passed a resolution asking that the rights of the indigenous peoples of the North be clarified and precisely established. So it was a job well done, and while the results weren't immediately apparent, people in the South were beginning to understand that this was a serious matter and that, in future, these problems would have to be taken care of.

Charlie knew what he was talking about. He had been hired to monitor seismic operations at Husky Lakes. He'd seen large numbers of dead fish, belly up, following explosions in the water. Under pressure from Inuvialuit, the government established regulations that had to be followed for various operations. Before permits were granted, companies had to appear before the Hamlet Council and explain the operations they wanted to carry out, the locations, and the methods they would use. The regulations also required the companies to make extensive studies on the flora and fauna. These concerns may seem exaggerated to some, but those that know the land know it really doesn't take very much to destroy the balance of nature and do irreparable damage.

To cope with all the changes that were occurring nearly everywhere in the North, people realized that they must have a certain unity of thought and action, and present a united front. Local advantages must not make them forget the common good, and that other places that could soon be suffering the same shock and facing the same difficulties and problems. Sometimes actions taken by the communities had been going in opposite directions. This has created the impression of differences of opinion amongst the Inuvialuit. This of course gives the companies and all those who wish to profit from the North's resources an advantage. They judge the people wrongly, saying they don't know what they want, since the decisions and the resolutions made have been contradictory. To remedy this situation, and to help communities that might be unaware of the procedures to be followed, or the people to contact for help and advice, an association, the Committee for Original People's Entitlement (known as COPE) took shape.[9] This association brought together all the indigenous people of the Northwest Territories – Dene, Inuvialuit and other Inuit and Métis. Complaints were reported to this organization's centre in Inuvik, and opinions, recommendations and advice were provided by the centre. Essentially, it was an information centre with a dual purpose: to receive information and to provide information. This was a big help to the various groups. But in spite of the results obtained, the moral support and the help that COPE provided seemed to be inadequate for some of the problems facing the North. What was needed was unity of action for the North as a whole. So another association began to take shape, bringing together all the Inuit from Tuktoyaktuk to Labrador. As a result, in February 1971, Inuit Tapirisat ('Inuit Brotherhood') of Canada was formed.[10] Its aim was to bring all the Inuit together to preserve their culture and their traditions and, at the same time, to determine what their tactics and policy would be concerning development in the North. They wanted to assert themselves and play a dominant role in the events taking place in their land, and to be able

Left to right: *Freddy Greenland, Billy Day and Tony Green, Committee for Original Peoples' Entitlement (COPE), date unknown. (Photo courtesy of Inuvialuit Communications Society)*

to make decisions and assume more responsibility. Such an organization would therefore make it possible to give the young people a new sense of pride in being Inuit, to save the environment, and to determine how to combine the two ways of life, the old and the new. In short, it would make it possible for them to control their life and to survive as Inuit. How? By helping, in every possible way, to preserve Inuit languages and traditions; by promoting dignity and pride in their heritage; by uniting all Canada's Inuit; by protecting the rights of hunters and trappers; by fostering communication among all those living along the coast; by obtaining all the help and assistance possible to publicize and make known the general and specific problems of the Inuit, and at the same time, notify them and make them aware of the situations and problems concerning Inuit rights, government plans, legal assistance available to them, education and training, politics, and the future; and by providing the necessary assistance to allow the Inuit to find their place and take their full place in Canadian society today, as full, first-class citizens; and, lastly, by making the situation and problems of the North known to everyone in the South.

Looking back, in the time since I arrived in Tuktoyaktuk, there have been many changes in who speaks for the people, and makes decisions. People may wonder what my role was and still is in all this. It's certainly a relevant question. As I've said several times already – and even though I'm repeating myself, I'll say it again – I lived and continue to live with the people, for the people and like the people, as much as possible being one of them. I have been a supporter, advisor, and spokesman as necessary. I didn't go looking for this work, but did what the people thought I could do for them. I have no regrets. The experiences I've had were wonderful and very rewarding. These various occupations gave me the opportunity to meet a great many people who have taught me a lot, from every point of view.

Father Le Meur standing in front of a map of Tuktoyaktuk outside the Hamlet Office, date unknown. (Photo courtesy of Dennis Lowing)

Chapter 13 Notes

1   The 'Area Administrators' were employees of the federal Department of Indian Affairs and Northern Development. In 1969 the Government of the Northwest Territories (GNWT) took over responsibilities for communities from the Federal Government, and the position title was changed to Settlement Manager. The Settlement Manager administered all the GNWT programs in the community: Public Works, Welfare, Housing, Municipal Services, Power Generation, Economic Development, Finance and general administration.

2   In the Northwest Territories, 'Hamlet' is a type of municipal corporation with the authority to provide services identified in legislation. Hamlets have an elected council and mayor. The Area Administrator Father Le Meur regarded so highly was Dennis Lowing, who arrived in 1968 and stayed until 1971. By that time, he was the Tuktoyaktuk Hamlet Council's Settlement Manager.

3   Ecumenism is the idea of Christian unity among differing branches of the religious community and that there should be a single Church structure sharing a common set of beliefs.

4   Aklavik is often flooded by the Mackenzie River during spring break-up when water levels are high. In the mid-1950s the Federal Government encouraged residents of Aklavik to move to the new town of Inuvik that was built on higher ground on the east side of the Delta. Many refused to move, inspiring Aklavik's motto: "Never Say Die".

5   This was the Territorial Experimental Ski Training (TEST) program. During the winter of 1967-1968 TEST skiers skied more than 35,000 kilometres in training and competed in 45 races. Significant cross country races for the TEST skiers were in the 1968 Canadian Championships, the 1969 American Championships, the 1970, 1974, 1978, and 1982 World Ski Championships and the 1972, 1976, 1980 and 1984 Winter Olympics, A comparable program operated out of Old Crow and Whitehorse.

6   Stuart Hodgson, the Commissioner of the Northwest Territories from 1967-1979, was the Government of Canada's representative in the Northwest Territories.

7   The Berger Commission was a government inquiry held in the mid-1970s to examine the social, economic and environmental impacts of a proposed pipeline connecting the Beaufort Sea-Mackenzie Delta area with the south.

8   The 'geysers' and 'explosions' refer to seismic activity in the water and on the land.

9   The Committee for Original Peoples' Entitlement (COPE) was formed in 1970 by Inuvialuit together with other Aboriginal groups in the Northwest Territories. The Dene and Metis later withdrew to pursue their own land claims. In its earliest years COPE worked with Inuit Tapirisat of Canada to develop the Nunavut Proposal, a land claim for a new Inuit territory in Canada, but within a few years COPE decided to focus on a regional land claim for the Inuvialuit. COPE disbanded in 1984, following the successful negotiation of the Western Arctic Land Claim – Inuvialuit Final Agreement (IFA). The responsibility for implementing the IFA was assumed by the Inuvialuit Regional Corporation.

10   Inuit Tapirisat of Canada is now named Inuit Tapiriit Kanatami ('Inuit United with Canada').

Royalty, Politicians and Other Visitors

Greeting the Royal Family at the airport Tuktoyaktuk, 1970. **Left to right**: *Prince Phillip, Queen Elizabeth II, John Steen (Chair, Tuktoyaktuk Hamlet Council), Father Le Meur, Margaret Lowing, Dennis Lowing (Settlement Manager). (Le Meur Family Collection)*

The Distance Early Warning Line and oil exploration brought an increase in airplane traffic, and since 1961 scheduled airline services have connected Tuktoyaktuk to Inuvik, carrying mail, cargo and passengers. We received a growing number of visitors, not only from Canada but also from all over the world. Where we were once so isolated, suddenly we were at the centre of activity.

Northern airplane pilots are a special breed, often having to deal with bad weather and poor visibility. To give one example, on one of my trips I boarded an airplane at Inuvik to go to Tuk. It was a twin-engine Otter, carrying a full load of passengers and freight. As we approached Tuk we encountered clouds of snow and freezing drizzle and the airplane began to ice up. We could hear bits of ice breaking off the propellers and wings and striking the airplane as if they were machine gun bullets. Through the mist we vaguely saw the pingos south of Tuk as the pilot began the approach. From the window I could see a few buildings, but since the airplane wasn't lined up properly we climbed back up into the clouds until we could see the sun. We circled around, and I thought we were going back to Inuvik, but the pilot told me he was going to try the descent

The Ibyuk pingos serve as landmarks for airplanes and boats approaching Tuktoyaktuk.

Father Le Meur, Tuktoyaktuk, July 1952. (Le Meur Family Collection)

again. No one spoke; the only sound was from pieces of ice hitting against the plane, and the engines. Looking into the cockpit I saw that the whole windshield was completely covered with fog and ice. The pilot certainly couldn't see anything in front of him, and he was looking out the side at the land. He put the plane down on the strip and we got off. As simple as that. Before taking off again for Inuvik, he had to melt the ice on the windshield.

In 1961 a representative from the Vatican came to visit us at Tuk. Every six years church officials would come to check on our activities. I must say that their thoughts and opinions of us didn't always seem very flattering. Too often the impression we gave on the coast was that we were mavericks. We must not have appeared anything like the traditional missionary, or the perfect priest. I think it's the country that demanded that. How could they judge us in just a few hours and in the context of the life we led – a battle for survival? The fact that we didn't wear the cassock very often or for very long, or that we weren't at the chapel at a particular time, may have given the impression that we felt we were special. We were far away, and such visits were rare. We did what we could, which isn't to say that the judgments didn't bother us – we are human after all. But this time, it was VIPs – Very Important People – coming to visit us: our Superior General, our Bishop, our Provincial, and another Bishop who was very highly placed in the Church, close to the Pope. Father Leising, a pilot who flew the Vicariate's airplane, picked them up at Fort Smith. Before arriving at Tuk they'd had an adventure that could have taken a tragic turn. While flying from Hay River to Fort Providence the engine stopped. Father Leising tried to start it up again, but in vain. He switched fuel tanks. Still nothing. Apparently the silence was very impressive up there in the clouds. There was only one thing that Father Leising could do – he had to find a place within gliding distance on which to land. As the airplane began to descend he spotted a lake that seemed long enough, and turned towards it. No one spoke. Everyone was deep in thought, praying for a good landing. The airplane skimmed past trees, almost seeming to touch them, and then set down on the lake. Father Leising sent a message over the radio, and a helicopter soon came to pick up the passengers and take them back to Hay River while he stayed behind to clean the tanks and carburetor and fuel up with gasoline brought by the helicopter. He then took off for Hay River, collected his passengers, and flew them along the Mackenzie River and over the coast to Tuktoyaktuk.

Almost every summer ambassadors of different nations in the world came to take a tour of the North that was offered to them by the Canadian government. Since I'd been on the coast for so many years, I was asked to meet them when they arrived at the airport, welcome them, give them a tour of the village, and give them an idea of the land, the people, the economic situation and other information, acting as a kind of guide and public relations man. There were some days I hardly had time to eat or sit down. On some of those tours I had to use both English and French, and sometimes even just French.

One time the English High Commissioner and his wife spent the night at Tuk. I was asked to prepare something special for that visit. I showed him some of my photographs, spoke about projects we were doing to preserve the traditions and folklore of the North, and we took him on a tour of the village. But we were caught unprepared, and had only one English flag, so we carried it from one place to the next as needed. The next day we gave him a tour of the harbour in one of the hovercrafts that were operating around Tuktoyaktuk. We had first become acquainted with this means of transportation – a machine riding on air cushions – in 1966. That spring, some engineers from England decided to test this equipment at Tuk to see how it would handle in the cold. After it was brought here in pieces on board a Hercules airplane it was reassembled and the tests began. In the spring, it travelled up the Mackenzie River but ran into some trouble on the way, and both machine and passengers had to seek shelter while the break-up of the ice began on the river. Fortunately, they were able to park in a small river, a tributary of the Mackenzie, above the ramparts near Fort Good Hope. Last year, again at Tuk, another machine, much larger, was tested and showed that it could be used to cross the river or the bays and could serve as a ferry. It is strange how the older people described that machine. They already had a word for it, and I understood right away what they were talking about – *pamroliak*, something that crawls on the ground. As for the children, some said to me, "Hey, Father, have you seen the holy craft?" That's what they were calling it, the holy craft.

I also had the opportunity to meet a Soviet delegation at Tuk, some engineers who had come to visit the oil company camps and see the development that was taking place in the North. The head

Northern Transportation Company Ltd.'s hovercraft at Tununik Point, circa 1970s. (Glenbow Museum and Archives/IP-14d-74-470)

173

of the group gave me a medal, a souvenir of the Russian revolution. I would really have liked to give them one in return, but I didn't have any with me. I wonder how they would have reacted.

1967 was Canada's centennial year, and quite a number of visitors came to Tuk, including people from the media. They tried our patience, but I knew that just one word, one article published in a newspaper or magazine, could give a bad impression and be a black mark against the village, so I had to be available all the time, to be gracious to everyone, and submit to endless interviews several times a day. So it was that I came into contact with teams of filmmakers from Japan, Germany, England, Switzerland, Austria and even Italy. The latter perhaps didn't appreciate my sense of humour. I was pointed out to their director as the man to see. He introduced himself and gave me some details about their project, and asked me when the best time would be to shoot the films. Then he asked me if I was really a priest. I had been working outside, and was wearing overalls. I replied that, yes, of course, I was a priest. He didn't seem to believe me, and he asked me again. I quickly enlightened him, explaining our situation in the North, where the priest is a jack-of-all-trades. The cassock and Roman collar don't help us very much in our work of fishing or hunting, feeding the dogs, cooking or cleaning the house, or painting. I don't know if he understood, but I didn't lose any sleep over it.

First among the important people I had the opportunity to receive were the Queen of England, Elizabeth II, and her husband, Prince Phillip, as well as their children, Prince Charles and Princess Anne. That was on July 6, 1970, the centennial year of the Northwest Territories. They arrived at Tuk around seven o'clock in the evening. The purpose of the trip was to see Tuk and the midnight sun on the Arctic coast. A platform had been erected outside, near the school, where, if the sun appeared, the Royal Family would be able to admire the midnight sun and the land around us. All this had been prepared down to the last detail. Anyway, I went to the airport with the Chairman of the Hamlet Council, John Steen and the Settlement Manager, Dennis Lowing, and his wife, Margaret Lowing. It was cold, with a wind blowing from the north, so after a word of welcome to the Queen and a handshake with Prince Phillip we quickly departed for town. The royal visitors rode in a black Cadillac that had arrived here by barge a few days earlier. The RCMP provided security, and all the officers wore their dress uniforms with red serge tunics.

We went first to the Fur Garment Shop, where the Royal Family admired the work of the local seamstresses. They were presented with gifts, which their attendants accepted on their behalf. That was protocol. Then the Queen officially opened a sod house, the kind that Inuvialuit in this area used long ago, which we had built as a 1970 Northwest Territories Centennial project. From there we went to the school gymnasium. There were a few introductory

1970 visit of the Royal Family to Tuktoyaktuk. Princess Anne is shown wearing a parka with the hood up; on her left is Queen Elizabeth II, and in front is Prince Phillip. (Photo credit: David Cairns/ London Daily Express)

words by the Commissioner, followed by a demonstration of drumming and dancing. A little girl presented the Queen with a bouquet of flowers that had been picked in Tuk. The girl curtseyed, and responding to the Queen's thanks, she said, "I even took a bath this morning." Then there was an informal walkabout in the gymnasium. The two princes, Charles and Phillip, impressed everyone with their charm and mingled with the crowd, while Princess Anne was rather reserved. The Queen didn't make a speech. That was a disappointment, for the people were expecting to hear her voice. Perhaps it was too cold. Since the weather was getting worse, the group left almost as soon as the visit to the

A driftwood and sod house in Tuktoyaktuk built in 1970 as a Northwest Territories Centennial Project. **Left to right**: *Mike Lowing, unidentified person, Father Le Meur, unidentified person. (Le Meur Family Collection).*

school was over. But the airplane the reporters were travelling on had mechanical problems, and they had to spend the night on the floor in the gymnasium. They told me it was quite a long night.

Another visitor that we haven't forgotten was Pierre Elliott Trudeau, the Prime Minister of Canada.[1] The people weren't expecting such simplicity. He arrived at Tuktoyaktuk without too much fanfare with a group of politicians and assistants. I was at the airport with John Steen to receive him, and as we were going towards the door of the airplane who should came out first, and jump down before the stair were in place, if not the Prime Minister? He even secured the stairs for the others before turning around to greet us. There was the same tour – after all, Tuk isn't that big – and then a gathering at the school, in the gymnasium, where, after some preliminary words of welcome, Mr. Trudeau made a speech, speaking in English and in French. In English he said that he had come to see the Arctic and to meet with the people of the North, but he wasn't coming as a saviour or with paternalistic ideas. He told the people that if they needed help, he and his government were prepared to help and collaborate, but not to give everything for nothing. "I'll give you this example of a Chinese saying," he said. "What good does it do to give you fish today and again tomorrow. I prefer to give you a net and teach you to catch fish." And he continued in the same vein. Then he spoke in French, because, he said, "It's one of Canada's languages and there are some French and French-Canadian people here." During his visit to the Fur Shop, a Northern Transportation Company Ltd. employee who knew the Prime Minister came to the shop with a package that he wanted to give to him. The RCMP questioned him, and called over one of Mr. Trudeau's assistants, examined the package, and only then informed the Prime Minister of the request. This goes to show that, even in the Arctic, security isn't ignored. The day before, at Inuvik, it seemed for a moment that the Prime Minister had disappeared. But he was just outside the door of the hotel taking a break, smoking a cigarette and talking to some priests. He had a habit of mixing with everyone, without protocol. So I wasn't surprised to hear that one time when he visited Moscow he took possession of a police motorcycle and set off on a tour of Red Square, much to the despair of his escort and the police.

Another politician who plays a significant role in the North is Jean Chrétien, the Minister of Indian Affairs and Northern Development.[2] It's not an easy position. It requires a lot of travelling and meetings, and a lot of diplomacy. More and more resources – oil, gas, and minerals – are being discovered in the North. He is caught between those who want immediate, large-scale development, and the wishes of indigenous people who are demanding respect for their rights, revisions to their treaties, land claims, protection of the environment, and to participate in the development and the industrialization of the North. Mr. Chrétien is therefore the man of the moment. He doesn't just stay in Ottawa, but travels a lot and receives a lot of delegations. It seems to me that he has opened the doors to dialogue and discussion. Of course, he must put up with quite a lot of criticism from all sides, but he knows how to deal with it, and he knows how to listen. I've had the opportunity to speak with him many times and to tell him how people feel about various problems in the North, and he has responded quite a few of the people's demands. How long he'll be able to withstand the pressure from the large companies is another question.

What does the future hold? We don't know. We'll soon see how things turn out. One thing is certain: from now on politicians can't ignore the North, or its people. The people here have something to say, and they have no trouble saying it, and saying it often.

Chapter 14 Notes

1   Pierre Elliot Trudeau was Canada's Prime Minister from 1968-1979 and from 1980-1984.

2   Jean Chrétien was the Minister of Indian Affairs and Northern Development in the Government of Canada from 1969-1974. He also served as Prime Minister of Canada from 1993-2003.

Ambassadors from Tuktoyaktuk

*Naudia Lennie (**left**), Sammy Lennie (**centre**, in fur parka), Father Le Meur (wearing baseball cap), Christian Brincourt (looking at a newspaper). France, 1973. (Le Meur Family Collection)*

The Inuvialuit knew about France – after all, how many missionaries came from there? But to actually go there, that is another story. It is a long way to travel, and expensive. Yet I dreamed about taking some people there, so that they could see for themselves what it's like. In 1973 that dream came true. The year before a French television station, *Office de Radiodiffusion-Télévision Française* (ORTF), had come north to do a program on me, an Oblate missionary living among the Inuvialuit.[1] When we finished filming I expressed my wish that some Inuvialuit children could visit France. I had no idea at the time that anything would come of this. What a pleasant surprise it was when I got a phone call from Christian Brincourt at ORTF, saying that they would like to do a program about two children in Tuktoyaktuk, including a trip to France, and asking for my assistance. I was in Fort Smith at the time, supervising students at Grandin College,[2] but my bishop, Monseigneur Piché, offered to pay my way to France. I went to Inuvik to meet the television team, and we set off together for Tuktoyaktuk. As soon as we got there we began making arrangements. Naudia (age 18) and Sammy (age 14) Lennie were selected for the program, which would be called 'Inglangasak', after the name of their grandfather, Lennie Inglangasuk. I have been asked how I made my

*Filming 'Inglangasak' in Tuktoyaktuk, 1973. Father Le Meur (**left**) and Sammy Lennie (**front**). (Le Meur Family Collection)*

choice. I must admit, it wasn't very easy. We needed someone who would be good in front of the camera, someone lively and straightforward. They were to be ambassadors of the Inuvialuit, their representatives in France. My choice was accepted by both the people in Tuktoyaktuk and by the media. We worked together every day, and Naudia and Sammy did well in front of the camera. Their parents, Sam and Margaret Lennie, were very happy to learn that their two children were going to France with me. They told me they had no worries at all about leaving both their children in my care. "Keep them as long as you want," they said, "we know they're in good hands."

Margaret Lennie is a dignified, hard-working woman who was concerned for her family and the education of her children. Much could be said about her dedication to various organizations, such as the school board, and about all the work she does at home, because she has a large family with nine children. This is what she wrote to Sammy the day we left Tuktoyaktuk, in a letter that she slipped into his hands and told him not to read until he was on the airplane: "*Dear Sammy, be good and listen closely to Father. Don't stray too far in case you get lost. Watch out for your sister Naudia, and above all, don't you two fight. We'll be thinking about you the whole time you're gone. Don't forget to send us postcards of all the places you visit, and to collect postcards too. Be sure that nothing you do dishonours your family, your people or your country, so that we don't get a bad name. We love you a lot, your Dad and I. Take good care of yourself. Love, Mom.*" That is what a woman of the North, without much formal education, wrote to her son before the great adventure. But I wasn't surprised, having known these people for so long. The first time I met her, it was quite funny. Sam, her husband, came to say hello. He was accompanied by an elegantly dressed woman, very reserved, who I hadn't met before. I started speaking to Sam in Inuvialuktun, talking about this and that, and finally curiosity got the better of me and I asked him, still in Inuvialuktun, who the beautiful woman there in the corner was. They both started laughing, and he said to me, quite simply, "well, that's Margaret, my wife." She was smiling, because she'd been in on the little game and understood everything I had said. After that, I saw them quite often, even though they weren't my parishioners, and I got to know all their children from a young age. I never visited them without coming away with something – some bread, smoked fish, and who knows what else.

The children's passports weren't ready yet – delays, misunderstandings and errors had slowed things down. Since time was running short, I went to see the Royal Canadian Mounted Police and asked them to help contact the Department of Immigration in Ottawa. When we got the secretary on the telephone I asked to speak to the boss, whoever was in charge of the office. Everything would be taken care of, I was told, he would give instructions to the Edmonton office, because we had to go to Edmonton to catch the plane for Montreal. Even Saturday or Sunday, someone would be at the office to do what had to be done. It was like that for the whole trip, it seemed. Everyone was ready to do anything for us.

Naudia Lennie in the Mirror Gallery at Versailles Castle, 1973. (Le Meur Family Collection)

That visit was full of joy for me, and for Naudia and Sammy. It was a chance for them to discover another culture, another way of life, another way of thinking – and they took in so much in such a short time. It is likely that no one they met would ever forget them, and my only regret is that we weren't able to respond to all the requests from schools and institutions that wanted to see us and talk to us. Our schedule was packed and we barely had time to catch our breath. Suffice to say that a number of times while we were in Paris, as soon as we got back to our rooms we went straight to bed and to sleep, without supper. It was the air

in the city, I suppose, that just did us in, and often in the car that drove us around they slept on my shoulder. I let them sleep, and young Sammy returned the favour. When he saw me asleep on a chair or in an armchair, he warned the visitors, telling them to let me sleep, just for a minute. I don't remember him refusing any requests while he was France. He must have drawn and given away dozens of pictures of dogs, dog teams and igloos. Everywhere he went, he exuded freshness and youth, and he was happy, always smiling. And what energy! He took in everything with his eyes, met everyone with a simple hello and a smile. What joy he got out of meeting and sitting with the pilots of the jumbo jet, mixing with the passengers, and helping the stewardesses hand out candies and matches. And all the questions he asked me! There were nights when my head was so full I could

An illustration of a caribou drawn by Sammy Lennie for a school class in St. Jean du Doigt, 1973. (Le Meur Family Collection)

179

Sammy and Naudia Lennie in a horse-drawn cart, St. Jean du Doigt, 1973. (Le Meur Family Collection)

barely speak coherently. I couldn't think clearly any more, switching from French to English and back again. Still, I managed to survive it all.

Paris made a huge impression on Naudia and Sammy. We'd just come from the land of snow and cold, and to see rain, grass and flowers in November was something quite extraordinary. Then there was the food, although sauces made with wine didn't go down well at all with either of them. There was that witty remark at dinner on a pleasure boat, when the waiter

Father Robert Le Meur visiting graves of family members, St. Jean du Doigt, 1973. (Le Meur Family Collection)

brought a cake and flambéed it with alcohol. Sammy nudged me and said, "They're not very smart, your countrymen. Look, now they're burning the cake and melting the icing." But after a few days Paris to them was simply a line of houses and crowded streets, everyone in a hurry and looking sad. As for Brittany, they fell in love with it. I can still picture Sammy saying to me one morning in St. Jean du Doigt, "Father, I'm going to say hello to your parents. I know where they are." And it was true. After I had come back from visiting the village cemetery he asked the film crew what I was doing there. They told him, and afterwards he went alone to visit the graves of my family and friends.

*At the school in St. Jean du Doigt, 1973. Naudia Lennie (**left**) is showing students fur for making clothing, Father Le Meur (**centre**) is pointing to a map and Sammy Lennie (**right**) is demonstrating how to jig for fish. (Le Meur Family Collection)*

Our visits to the schools were always a success. Sammy became the centre of attention among the youngest children, with whom he played frequently, and he was a real ambassador. On the day we were to leave they told me, "You must be crazy. Why do you want to go back to the North? It's nothing like here. As for us, we've found moms and dads and families." The spirit they found amongst members of the television crew that followed us about and the other people that they met really impressed them. As Naudia told them, "I don't need any Christmas presents from you, everything is written here in our hearts." But for Naudia and Sammy, and for me as well, there was something missing – snow and ice. A green Christmas didn't really feel like Christmas.

When Naudia and Sammy returned home they immediately got down to work at school. Their mother wrote to me, saying that she didn't understand how they had applied themselves so quickly and so diligently to their schoolwork. I think that seeing the young people they'd been with in France working seriously at their books and studies had a lot to do with their attitude. They have just one wish, and I think they'll get it one day – to go back to France and Brittany on their own. That's what they have told me many times since they got back to Tuk. And who knows? The world is much smaller now, and I know they will be welcome in many homes.

Chapter 15 Notes

1   The program produced by *Office de Radiodiffusion-Télévision Française* in 1972 was "Okrayyoaaluk, celui qui parle bien" ("Okrayyaaluk, the one who speaks well")."Okrayyaaluk", or "Uqayuyualuk" as it is spelled today, means "The one who speaks well" in English.

2   Grandin College was a Roman Catholic residential school that focused on training aboriginal students who were recognized as having leadership potential.

16

Tuk Radio

Father Le Meur standing outside the CFCT radio station, Tuktoyaktuk, 1981. (Canadian Broadcasting Corporation)

So how on earth did a little place like Tuktoyaktuk come to have its own radio station? It's quite a story. It began in the winter of 1969, when Richard Rohmer, a lawyer from Toronto, came to Tuk. He was the driving force behind the Mid-Canada Development Corridor Foundation, an organization that was examining ways to improve economic development and communication in the middle and northern regions of Canada. (He was also engaged in an attempt to get a university or college for the North. Later on, I would also be involved in those meetings.) Dennis Lowing, at that time the government's Area Administrator, and I met with him first, and that evening we held a community meeting. He told people at the meeting that he had heard about Tuk, about the spirit to be found there, and that he'd come to ask us if we would like to have a radio station. He thought he could get us one. All those who were at the meeting were in favour of the idea, and the arrangements went forward. CHUM, a major Toronto radio station, helped us get this project off the ground. They bore all the costs for the broadcasting equipment and radio tower. All they asked us to do was to provide a building for the radio studio.[1]

We needed a license for the station, and Richard Rohmer helped us there as well. I went with a delegation to Calgary to make sure that it would be accepted, and the members of the Canadian Radio and Television Commission approved it without any objections. On the contrary, they were moved by the application, apparently quite a rare occurrence in that department. Applications usually were made by presenting figures and dollar amounts. In our case the radio station wasn't a commercial undertaking, but simply a way to communicate news and what was happening in the community. For example, so-and-so is back from his trap line and he killed a wolf or caught so many foxes, or the weather conditions. What's more, the station would be operated by local people, with training provided by CHUM. We also had assurance from the Distant Early Warning Line that their technicians would help maintain the equipment. The first license required us to provide four hours of operation a day, and we chose one hour in the morning, from 8:00 to 9:00 am, when everyone, including the children, would be up, and three hours in the evening, from 7:00 to 10:00 pm. The station would be bilingual – English and Inuvialuktun. Our official radio station name was CFCT – CF means a Canadian radio station, and we chose C for CHUM and T for Tuktoyaktuk, but we usually called it 'Tuk Radio' or 'Radio Tuktoyaktuk'.

A building for the radio station was erected beside the Mission, and in the summer, the tower, a transformer and equipment purchased by CHUM arrived. But when the workers came to put up the tower, it was discovered that there was not enough room to attach the cables that would secure the tower to the ground, so we moved the building to another location a bit farther out from the village. An engineer from CHUM radio came to Tuktoyaktuk to install and test all the equipment. It was like a dream, a fairy tale for us at Tuk.

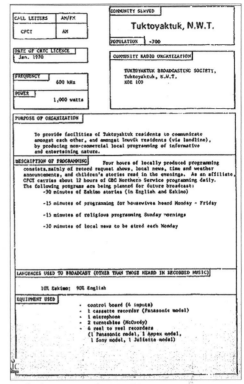

Radio license issued to CFCT, January 1970.

The send-off ceremony for the CFCT radio tower, Toronto, 1970, with Richard Rohmer standing second from left. (From 'Generally Speaking', by Richard Rohmer, 2004. Used by permission from Richard Rohmer.)

CFCT Radio station with the first sunrise of the year on the horizon, Tuktoyaktuk, January 1971. (University of Saskatchewan, Archives & Special Collections, Institute for Northern Studies fonds, Slide 3883)

When I first got involved in this project I didn't realize I was going to end up as the program director, in addition to preparing programs and being one of the radio announcers. We had only got three or four days instruction time from CHUM, and in that time we had to learn how to operate all of the equipment – the turntables, microphones and tape recorders – and how to coordinate everything. The day after the station opened we were left on our own, and we had to operate four hours a day by ourselves. Fortunately CHAK, the Canadian Broadcasting Corporation station in Inuvik, helped by supplying us with records and tapes of some of their programs. Every evening at 7:00 pm we had a program for the children, a story and some songs, and there were two 45-minute programs in Inuvialuktun each week, some stories and legends that I gathered from the people in town, and local news and announcements. We also had permission from another radio station to tape their morning and evening news on the radio at the Mission and then replay them at the radio station. I put in a lot of hours preparing those programs for CFCT. I got up before 6:00 am every day to record the news on the radio that we would broadcast later. I also visited elders and recorded them on tape telling their stories in Inuvialuktun, and then I translated what they said into English, and added introductions and music. I didn't have much time to rest any more.

Billy Emaghok in the CFCT radio station, circa 1981. (Canadian Broadcasting Corporation)

After a few months we went from four hours to eight hours a day, and then from 7:45 am until midnight. At that point the workload really

184

increased. Fortunately, we were now affiliated with the Inuvik CBC station, and had a direct telephone line that allowed us to take some programs directly from them.[2] Often I had to prepare a program every day and, believe me, that's hard work. I continued the Inuvialuktun program with legends and peoples' experiences, and I also prepared a program of local, regional and national news for Wednesday evenings and a daily 15-minute program that covered the history of Tuk and the surrounding area. This program very quickly grew in popularity and became a hit. One contractor even asked me to move it to another time slot because, he said, his employees didn't get much work done when the program was on.

During the years that I worked for the radio, I gained a better understanding of both the people and the traditions, and expanded my Inuvialuit studies and writings. Years before I had started gathering making notes on conversations I'd had with people, their experiences and their legends, and all of that was valuable in my radio work. Those papers are invaluable – they are the memories and stories of the people themselves, which they wanted to pass on to others. I don't know how to express my appreciation to all the elders who shared their experiences and lives with me, and took the time to share their feelings so extensively.[3] Then there were the technicians at the DEW Line who volunteered their time, and helped me out so many times when there were technical problems in the studio. No one ever refused to help out when it came to the radio. It wasn't a professional operation, but it was the people's station, and it operated for them and with them.

I smile when I remember the first commercial that I broadcast on CFCT, an advertisement for Skidoo snowmobiles. I'd been given the text to read, something with technical terms more suitable for the South. I decided to adapt it for the North, and added sounds of barking dogs and engine noises in the background. I used my Honda motorbike to simulate the roar of Skidoo engines, starting the engine and revving it at top speed. We had a good laugh later, when people found out it was my motorbike they were hearing.

Father Le Meur on his 'Honda 90' motorbike, Tuktoyaktuk, circa 1970s. (Le Meur Family Collection)

Things didn't always run smoothly. Sometimes I had to fill in for others, having to go to the station to open up in the morning, or taking a turn at the microphone. Sometimes the announcers would fall asleep while a record was playing, and when it ended you could hear the sound of the needle as the record kept turning until I got there to wake up the person who was supposed to be working. In the spring, in late April or early May, I spent a lot of time in the studio, working five to six hours a day, because at that time of year everyone in Tuk who could, headed out to Husky Lakes to hunt and fish and take advantage of the sun and nice weather. I liked the radio work then, because I could keep in touch with people who were away from the village, giving them the news about what was going on in Tuk, the comings and goings, and other information. Everyone listened to the radio, even when they were at their camps. Wherever the people went, they took their transistor radios, and we were sure to be able to reach them when someone wanted to give them a message. As well, messages were very often sent via our station to other communities in the area – requests for fish or meat, messages of thanks for packages received, birthday wishes accompanied by a song, and many other things.

I became an interview hound. Many times I spent a morning or afternoon with a tape recorder on my back, interviewing people – Inuvialuit for my program on local history and legends, and visitors as well. Anyone who came to Tuktoyaktuk could expect to be interviewed for CFCT.

Father Le Meur recording Felix Nuyaviak telling a story to be broadcast on CFCT, Tuktoyaktuk, circa 1981. (Canadian Broadcasting Corporation)

The people could hear what their representative on the Territorial Council, the Territorial Commissioner, the Minister of Northern Affairs, government ministers visiting Tuk, doctors, scholars, and game wardens had to say. That way, the people of the village knew who the visitors were, and the purpose of their visit. Everything that happened in a village, including meetings, was summarized on the air. News travelled fast. The people could talk about it, and knew what was happening around them. I even received cards from Alaska, informing me that people on the coast there were tuning in to our programs, especially the programs in Inuvialuktun, and they really appreciated them.

CFCT showed the people the power of radio, and what they could obtain through radio by forcing issues, and by making even influential men listen and big companies go about things the right way. For example, when one of the oil companies discovered an oil reserve just a few miles from Tuktoyaktuk we only learned about it through a radio station in the South. I didn't like that attitude very much – we had a station right in Tuk, and the residents were the last ones to find out something that affected them directly. I wrote a protest and read it myself on the air that night. The next day I saw one of the people from Tuk who had been at the company's camp, and he reported their comments to me. "You're wasting your time," he said, "they're laughing about it in the camp." I told him, "Just wait a bit, you'll see some results." I said on the air that the people of Tuk resented the company's way of doing things, and that we were entitled to some respect, because, after all, they were on our doorsteps, and this was the people's land. And yes, I got results.

The next day I got apologetic phone calls from Edmonton and Calgary, where the head offices were, and a few days later the company representatives and their public relations spokesperson were in Tuk and came to see me, to apologize and tell me that it would never happen again. They kept their word, and after that gave us the news of their new discoveries first, even if they had to delay giving the news to other stations in the South.

That is how I helped to bring radio into the life of the people of Tuktoyaktuk.

Chapter 16 Notes

1   Richard Rohmer was legal counsel to CHUM radio in Toronto. CHUM's initial contribution for establishing CFCT was approximately $40,000, and for several years they provided an operating grant. The Tuktoyaktuk Hamlet Council established the 'Tuktoyaktuk Broadcasting Society', and was able to provide CHUM with a tax receipt for their donation.

2   The CHAK programs were sent over the telephone line because the radio signal was weak in Tuktoyaktuk, and a power line that connected Tuktoyaktuk to Inuvik created interference.

3   Following Father Le Meur's death in 1985 the church gathered his research notes, taped recordings and other documents from the Mission in Tuktoyaktuk. They are now preserved at the Provincial Archives of Alberta.

Persis Gruben's First Year on Banks Island

Lennie Inglangasuk and wife Sarah and their children, circa 1930s. Lennie is holding Sam, in front of Sarah is Alberta, Persis is holding Winnie. (Pierre Duchaussois fonds/NWT Archives/N-1990-026: 0002)

Among the first modern pioneers of Banks Island were Lennie Inglangasuk, Adam Inuałuuyaq and David Bernhardt ('Piqtuqan') who, together with their families, spent the winter of 1928-1929 on the island trapping white fox. I invite you now to read a story told by Persis Gruben, Lennie Inglangasuk's stepdaughter, who was there at the very beginning. They are her memories of when she was a young girl, about ten years old, told as an adult nearing her 60th birthday.[1]

~ *My First Winter on Banks Island* ~

I recall that my dad, Lennie Inglangasuk, was a great traveller. After we got our schooner, the *Reindeer*, we visited many places and wintered here and there, never staying too long in one place. Dad liked adventure, trying new places, although the first time we went to Banks Island was more than just a whim. Older people who had heard stories about Banks Island described it as a land of milk and honey, a wonderful place to live. They said that Alaskan Inuit who were with the Canadian Arctic Expedition got good catches of white fox.[2] Those tales were more than enough to excite my dad, making him want to try a new country. He knew the implications very well – the isolation, the unknown, and the uncertainties as far as fox and caribou were concerned – but he resolved to go and find out for himself.

As my dad had set his mind to spend a winter trapping on Banks Island, we went to Herschel Island where he got food and supplies for a year. We loaded everything, including the dogs, aboard the *Reindeer*. When preparations were completed we left Herschel Island for a new land and adventures. We were glad to go, to try a new place. The thought of being isolated didn't bother us. We were used to being on our own and self-sufficient.

And so we began our journey. My dad told us that our trip to Banks Island would be made in easy stages, with stops here and there along the way. The first leg of the journey was to *Tapqaq*, Shingle Point, some 100 kilometres. I do not recall anything special taking place there. It was simply to visit, which Dad enjoyed. Leaving Shingle Point, we sailed to Horton River, favoured by fair

Lennie Inglangasuk's schooner 'Reindeer' with polar bear skins hung out to dry, date and location unknown. (Lennie Family Collection)

weather all the way. For a girl of ten years old, everything at the Horton River trading post was marvellous – full of fun and excitement, meeting people and discovering new things. I must confess that it was frightening at first, as there were so many people there. There were the Levys and the Palayaks on their boat, the Harrisons on their schooner *Bear Lake*, the Kasooks and Billy Thrasher aboard the *Viking*. Bennet Ningasik might have been there as well with his schooner *Shamrock*, and of course the Piqtuqans and Adam Inuałuuyaq and his family on their schooners *Ogpek* and *Okevik*. Both families were uncertain where to go for the coming winter. Learning that Dad intended to go to Banks Island, they immediately expressed their desire to be partners in this adventure. It was not merely words, they meant it, and they began to check their supplies.

We planned to depart the following day, as the weather was fair, and the older people forecast that the good weather would continue. But our departure had to be postponed for several days, as my brother chose that day to come into the world. Dad gave the name, Samuel Aoktalik, to his newly born son. Time for more visiting, more trips to the store and more discussions about what the future held for us on Banks Island. When my mother was back on her feet and in good condition for travelling, it was David Piqtuqan's wife's turn to give birth, to a little girl. As a token of friendship David asked my dad to name the little girl. She would be known as Taliq Emily, he said, after his parents who had died from the flu. Due to this birth there was another delay, and it was only when both mother and baby were well that we took leave from the Horton River.

Persis Lennie with her brother Sam Lennie, circa 1930s. (Inuvialuit Social Development Program/ Bessie Wolki Collection BW-39)

The crossing from Horton River to Booth Island wasn't too far, only about 80 kilometres. There were a few families there, the Sirkroaluks, the Levys and the Palayaqs, who had gone there ahead of us. They had decided to spend the winter on Booth Island and trap in the surrounding country where white fox were abundant. The island offered a good harbour for their boats, and it was a good place for hunting seals and polar bears because nearby there was open water, even in winter. All in all, a good place for a few families. The trading post at Horton River could easily be reached in one or two days by dog team, and there was also a trading post nearby at Letty Harbour. For Silas Palayaq this part of the world was far from new, as he had travelled all around this area when he worked with the Canadian Arctic Expedition. Upon our arrival, I admired Silas' house. To me, then a young girl, it seemed big, like a palace made of driftwood logs, although once inside I found that it was not so big after all. Like everywhere else, Dad enjoyed visiting, and we spent many happy hours there. However, he didn't forget that our final destination was Banks Island, and now time was rather pressing, it being late in the Fall. So after many 'ilaanilu' and 'utirupseptaar', 'goodbye', 'see you when you get back', the *Reindeer* and the other two schooners left the sheltered harbour for the open sea and a new land.

It was a perfect day for a crossing. I must have been sleeping most of the time, but I remember that late in the afternoon, when I awoke and looked out a porthole, and then went on the deck, I was surprised to notice the sea so calm, not even the huge swells usually encountered in these waters, dead calm all over. Nothing to look at but the sea, a sea which a few years ago had been alive with whales and big sailing ships, whaling ships. It seemed unreal as we travelled along. Nobody was visible on the other schooners. They looked like ghost ships, pilotless, only the humming of the engines breaking the silence. Dad, who had been at the helm all night, woke me up from my daydreaming. "*Panik*", ('daughter'), he said, "take a good look ahead. See, we are coming near land now, our land." Although I strained my eyes I couldn't see anything but a white horizon stretching away over the sea, blending with the sky. I didn't realize that Banks Island would already be under

View of Nelson Head, Banks Island from the sea, 1936. (Charles Rowan fonds/NWT Archives/N-1991-068: 0228)

a carpet of snow, and I thought I was seeing clouds. Now, however, my interest was aroused and I tried to see the land. I wasn't the only one on deck; almost all of us voyagers were out there, excited, our eyes trying to pierce the clouds on the horizon. Suddenly, Nelson Head and the high hills around it loomed ahead of us. Land at last, our future home. Our ties to the mainland were cut, and we were on our own for the next ten months.

We approached Nelson Head, and then followed the coast to the west until we reached the Masik River. A house stood there on the top of a hill, although to call it a house was exaggerating. It was an old shack, windowless and doorless, at the mercy of all the elements and wild animals. Everything inside was in a state of shambles. I still wonder today why my dad wanted to camp there. Did he want to use it later in the winter, as a camp on his trap line? No matter his motivation, we all went to work to make it fit for habitation. We spent our first night on Bank Island there. It probably gave Dad some satisfaction to know that on his first day on the Island he slept ashore in an old house built by some trappers like him.[3]

The next day we left Masik River and followed the coast to the northwest in search of a good place for wintering the schooners. This was important for us, as the ships would be the only way to go back to the mainland come next summer. Reaching Cape Kellett, 100 kilometres from the Masik River, we managed to get into a harbour behind a sand spit, not too soon either, as young ice and slush had began to form in the Arctic sea. We were indeed a happy group, landing and taking possession of this place. Our long trip was over with, but not forgotten. The schooners were securely fastened on the shore and we began unloading the supplies and all our belongings. The men took care of the heavy things, and we women and children carried the light items. Time was pressing now, as winter was practically at hand.

On a hill behind the beach stood a small house made from the wheelhouse of a ship.[4] It was well built, and had been banked with sod on the outside. It needed some minor repairs, especially on the inside, but for the time being it would provide us with shelter. Repairs could wait awhile yet, as a safe place for wintering the schooners had to be found immediately, as the ocean had begun to freeze. So during the first days the men spent their time moving the schooners to a small cove three miles east of our camp and preparing them for the winter. The schooners were hauled up on the beach above the waterline, the engines inspected, doors tightly closed – all things that required time and attention. All the men busied themselves with this job, leaving only Adam Inuałuuyaq at the camp with the women and children. I don't think that he could keep up with us children, with so many things to discover in our new surroundings! We spent the time walking around, inspecting the old houses built by the Canadian Arctic Expedition, and playing on a sandy beach with two old engines. Those objects, a mystery to us, provided us with many enjoyable hours.

Coming home from his work at the schooner, Dad spent some time repairing a metal building nearby. Much work had to be done to make it a decent house for the winter. As we were rather crowded in the wheelhouse, as soon as it was fit to live in we moved in. One day my mother sent Winnie, my young sister, and I to fetch some things from a tent where we had piled up all our supplies. Mom often sent us on some errand; this was a way to be of some help to our parents. As we were on our way we could hear pounding at our neighbour's home, where they were building bunks and beds. I chanced to take a look around, and I stopped in my tracks. A huge polar bear

Agnes White standing in the ruins of the house built by her grandfather Lennie Inglangasuk and his family, at Mary Sachs, Banks Island, July 1996. (Murielle Nagy/Inuvialuit Social Development Program-Aulavik—B/W: 8-9)

was going towards their house. My mother also spotted the bear and she called to us to come home quickly, signaling us with her hand through the window. We didn't need any urging, and seizing Winnie's hand I turned and ran for the house. Once inside, behind the protection of the walls, I looked out at the bear. He was moving at a leisurely pace toward our neighbour's house, seemingly unconcerned and unafraid of human voices. Some of the women there heard my mother's shouts and looked through the windows to see what was going on. Adam's wife was asking herself why my mother was so excited. Her daughter Bessie found out when she opened the door to the porch and found herself facing a polar bear. Closing the door and putting her weight on it she said, "There is a bear behind the door." Adam pushed her aside. He opened the door, grabbed his rifle from the porch, and closed it again. The bear turned around and slowly went out. Adam followed, and from the porch fired and killed the bear.

The excitement over, we crowded around the bear and admired its size. What a subject of conversation for us children! The men were working on the schooners and we wanted to surprise them. As we were very excited, talkative and a bit wild, the adults in camp warned us to be quiet and not to say one word about the polar bear. Let the men find out by themselves. A few hours later, the workers came home and supper was ready. The men were very tired and cold, and appreciated a hot meal. So we began to eat, the men telling their stories, what they did, and all the small events of the day. The other adults in the house gave their approval by uttering many "*He... He... He's!*" but remained rather silent, and we waited. Winnie, my younger sister, was very excited, and turned her eyes to our mother and father alternately. I knew it would be only a matter of moments before she spoke, and then she said, "Well, you see, Mom, I kept my promise, and didn't say a word so far." Poor Winnie, the suspense was too much for her. Dad guessed immediately that something was up. For the children's sake he played the game, and addressing Winnie, he asked her, "Well what is it that you didn't want to say to Dad?" Winnie answered, "I have been told to keep a secret, and I'm not supposed to say anything." After a pause and a look around the

Camping on the trap line, winter 1932-1933, Kellett River valley, Banks Island. (Mrs. Peter Sydney Collection/Library and Archives Canada/PA 27689)

house, Dad said, "I know, daughter." Taking a piece of meat with his fork and presenting it to Winnie, he said, "That's it, isn't it? A polar bear? Someone here has killed a polar bear today." We all had a good laugh, everybody talking about the visit by Mr. Nanuk. Such were our ways then, very simple, very human and close to the heart of all, sharing the events and happenings of the days.

Days went by, always filled with excitement and new experiences. Before freeze-up Dad discovered that schools of small fish were travelling in the shallow water along the shore. We spent many hours fishing, using hooks made from safety pins, having fun and at the same time procuring food, as we caught hundreds of them. Doing little things like that made us feel like providers, and built in us some pride for being useful at home.

Fall was behind us now, and winter settled in for good. It was cold, and now and then storms would blow. The men had been waiting impatiently for this period, the opening of the trapping season. All were eager to begin their work. If Banks Island had as many fox as they had been told, it would be a paradise for our trappers. They had high expectations, and much was at stake. In order to come here they were deep in debt to traders on the mainland. Dad wanted to pay one of those traders, Captain Pederson,[5] what he owed for the purchase of our schooner as soon as possible. He had been told by Captain Pederson that furs, any kind of furs were as good as cash. Polar bears and foxes were numerous around our camp, and this seemed to be a good omen for what would be found further inland and out on the sea ice. In fact, so many bears came around the camp that some days we were confined to the house. As everything was covered with snow, it was difficult for us to see them, those marauders and prowlers. I remember one day when we were allowed outside that we saw dead polar bears everywhere. I would say ten at least. I heard the hunters say that when they killed a bear they didn't have time to skin it before another came into our camp.

I still remember with joy, and a pang of nostalgia, that first winter in Banks Island. It was indeed a memorable time and we never felt loneliness, we never had a dull moment. There was so much to be learned, so much to do. However, as is usual in the Arctic, when winter drew to an end we looked forward to spring and summer. As soon as trapping season was over and days began to get longer and warmer, we all moved to the small harbor where we had left our three schooners. It was not the time for rest yet, as much had to be done before breakup. Men and women spent hours every day checking furs, polar bears, white foxes, and seals, cleaning them, a thorough cleaning and scrubbing. Then setting them on a line to be dried by the sun and wind. Mother also spent countless hours sewing sealskins for clothing.

Considering the limited knowledge we had of the island, that first year had been a success. The trappers were satisfied and happy. One needed only to look at all the furs hanging to dry in the sun and swinging in wind to know that it was worth a small fortune.

White fox skins hanging from the boom of Lennie Inglangasuk's schooner, 'Reindeer', circa 1930. The man sitting on the deck may be Herbert Allen. (Archibald Fleming Collection/NWT Archives/N-1979-050: 0293)

Chapter 17 Notes

1 Persis Gruben told this story to Father Le Meur in Inuvialuktun for broadcasting on Tuktoyaktuk's community radio station, CFCT. Father Le Meur re-wrote the story in English and narrated it on the radio after the Inuvialuktun version. It was not included in the original '*Souvenirs de l'Arctique*' manuscript, but from Father Le Meur's notes it seems evident that he intended to add it.

2 The Canadian Arctic Expedition (1913-1918) was a scientific and exploration expedition sponsored by the Government of Canada. From 1914 to 1917 members of the expedition occupied a base camp on the southern coast of Banks Island at a location locally known as 'Mary Sachs', named after one of the expedition's schooners that was abandoned there after suffering damage. Natkusiak ('Billy Banksland'), who was born in Alaska and was employed a guide for the Canadian Arctic Expedition, remained on Banks Island for several years with several other Inuvialuit to trap white fox. Natkusiak eventually settled down on Victoria Island.

3 In 1916 the fur trading company Liebes and Company placed two Inupiat families from Point Hope, Alaska, at the mouth of the Masik River, where they spent two years trapping white fox. The remains of the cabin described by Persis Gruben may have been built and used by those traders.

4 The wheelhouse that the Inglangasuk family lived in during the winter of 1928-1929 was from the Canadian Arctic Expedition's schooner Mary Sachs. It had been brought on land in 1917 to be used as a house for two members of the expedition, although their plans to stay on Banks Island were never carried through. At this location, which came to be known as Mary Sachs, there were also two warehouses that had been built by the Canadian Arctic Expedition, and two engines from the Mary Sachs were abandoned on the beach.

5 Christian T. Pedersen worked as a captain on several whaling and trading ships before becoming a partner in the American-based Northern Whaling and Trading Company, and its Canadian offshoot, the Canalaska Trading Company, in 1923. He established several trading posts along the western Canadian Arctic coast. Many Inuvialuit preferred to trade with 'Captain' Pedersen, as his goods were reputed to be cheaper and of better quality than trade goods offered by the HBC. Although the Canalaska Trading Company was successful in the early years of its operation, by the 1930s its fortunes began to change, and in 1936 it was sold to the Hudson's Bay Company.

18

The Long Crossing

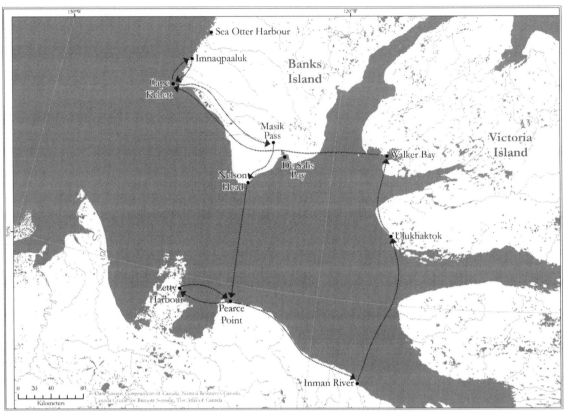

The route travelled by Jim Wolki, Sam Dick Qaatigaaryuk and Raddi Kuiksak during 'The Long Crossing'.

Editor's Note

In 1933 Jim Wolki ('Kakianaan'), his wife Bessie and their children, Adam Inuałuuyaq and his wife Ellie, their son Paul Adam, Sam Dick Qaatigaaryuk and his wife Eileen, and Raddi Kuiksak, his wife Ivy Panigak and their children (Mary, Annie, Sam and Moses), travelled from the mainland in the schooner *Omingmuk* to Sea Otter Harbour on the west coast of Banks Island, intending to spend a single winter there. However, sea ice conditions kept them on Banks Island for a second winter, one for which they were not adequately prepared.

In the 1970s Father Le Meur recorded Jim Wolki telling about the winter of 1934-1935, and a three-month journey by dog team that he, Sam Dick Qaatigaaryuk and Raddi Kuiksak made to a trading post at Letty Harbour on the mainland, and thence to Walker Bay on Victoria Island, before returning to their camp on the west side of Banks Island. This is considered to be a dangerous trip, due to the moving ice in Amundsen Gulf. Father Le Meur also recorded comments by Bessie Wolki, Ivy Panigak and Paul Adam about hardships endured at Sea Otter Harbour while the travellers were gone. Their stories were broadcast on the Tuktoyaktuk community radio station, CFCT, and also used by CBC Inuvik for their series 'A Long Time Ago'. Following is Jim Wolki's account of 'The Long Crossing', and Bessie Wolki's, Ivy Panigak's and Paul Adam's memories of that time, as retold by Father Le Meur.[1]

196

~ *My First Winter on Banks Island* ~

*Jim and Bessie Wolki with their children (**left to right**) Frank, Fred, Sandy and Figures, Aklavik, 1940. (Inuvialuit Social Development Program/Bessie Wolki Collection #18)*

We spent the winter of 1933-1934 at Sea Otter Harbour. We intended to cross to the mainland as soon as there was open water, but the prospects were not very encouraging until late summer, when the ice pack moved a bit. We took a chance, hoping that we would be lucky enough to find an open water lead that we could follow through the ice. Well, our hopes faded away after travelling only about 50 kilometres. We went into another harbour, at Imnakpaaluq, and waited for another opportunity to sail away. Unfortunately, a westerly wind pushed the pack ice to the shore, and the grounded ice sealed us in, preventing us from leaving. We had no other alternative than to spend another winter on Banks Island – and a long one it would be. There was nothing else we could do but face our misfortunes and take the challenge, a very tough one as it turned out.

We had run out of *taniktat*, "white man's food" – tea, flour, sugar – and would have to live off the land. Caribou were scarce, but we hunted seals and trapped every kind of animal for food, even white owls. When winter settled in we had foxes as well. We didn't trap regularly, but they were plentiful and I had one hundred foxes before Christmas. All of us missed *taniktat*, I especially, since in my youth our family had become accustomed to tea, flour, tobacco and other delicacies.[2] By early in the New Year our ammunition was running low, so Paul Adam and I decided to travel to Walker Bay, on the west coast of Victoria Island, where the Hudson's Bay Company had a trading post. We left, but due to our lack of knowledge of that country and because we encountered strong winds and storms, and being short of food as well, we were compelled to give it up and return to our camp empty-handed.

By then, my morale was low and it got the best of me. A plan for another trip began to take hold of me, this time to the trading post at Letty Harbour, on the mainland. I thought about it, and rejected it, but it came back to my mind until finally I couldn't stand it any more. One day I told Bessie, my wife, "I don't like this life, short of everything. I want to try to reach Letty Harbour."

My wife tried to discourage me, and told me "Jim, you know that if you leave you may not come back, there is danger on that ice and you may lose your life." "I have very good dogs now," I said, "and I wish to give it a try, it's now or never." I made up my mind that I didn't care if I lost my life, but I was certain that everything would turn out for the best. I told Bessie not to worry, that we would see each other again. Bessie didn't give up and presented more arguments, but to no avail, and I began preparations for this long crossing.

Having learned of my intentions, Qaatigaaryuk and Raddi told me that they were also interested in taking the trip if it was okay with me. "Of course." I answered, "If you want, come along. Two or three are better than being alone, so you are most welcome, and the sooner we leave the better." We got to work right away, checking our sleds and harnesses. As for food, well, that was not a problem. Since we were short of supplies we would have to trust our luck and rely upon getting seals, polar bears, and foxes that roamed the ice along the way.

We left camp as soon as possible to ease the tension. Everyone was on hand to bid us farewell, the women wary of course, ourselves hiding our feelings, hope mixed with some apprehension, but happy to be on the road. We decided to go by Cape Kellett. Raddi had a trap line there, and on our way he visited his traps and removed some white foxes. As we were eager to keep travelling, Raddi simply threw them into the sled without taking the time to reset his traps. This catch was for us a good omen and lifted out spirits. The furs could be traded at Letty Harbour, and the meat would provide food for us and for our dogs.

We reached the Masik River, and camped there. Unaware of it, I learned later from Raddi that Qaatigaaryuk tried to dissuade Raddi from following me. "You know, Raddi," said Qaatigaaryuk, "I don't much like the idea of going on this journey. It's not too late; let's go back to camp. This is too dangerous, and maybe Jim is doing it for nothing; worse yet, he may lose his life. If we follow him, we may perish as well. It is better for us to turn back." This quiet little discussion didn't shake

Nelson Head, at the southern tip of Banks Island. (Photo credit: Trevor Lucas)

Raddi at all. Refusing to discuss it, he told Qaatigaaryuk "Well, I'm already on the way, and I'm not turning back. I'll follow Jim. If anything happens to him, well, it will happen then to both of us." And that was that on the matter.

For our evening meal we had some rancid seal meat that we had brought along. It smelled bad, but nevertheless we ate it, and fed it to the dogs as well. After a night's rest we continued our journey towards Nelson Head. I had a good dog team, and travelled at a good speed. Being in the lead I ran into three polar bears. I shot the smallest one, letting the other two run away, as we wanted to travel light and fast. That evening, camping at Nelson Head we finished our polar bear meat, one meal for us and a meal for our dogs – we had so many dogs!

Leaving camp the next morning we travelled along the coast looking for a place to get across a shore lead onto the sea ice. I found a safe place to cross and waited for Qaatigaaryuk and Raddi to show up. When they arrived I told them I had reached the point of no return as far as I was concerned, no turning back. "I am on the pack ice now, and intend to keep on going to the mainland. So if you want to be partners, well, come across." So they crossed to the ice and we left Banks Island behind.

It was cold that day, bitterly cold. The temperature had gone down, and a westerly wind blew, increasing as the afternoon went on. Soon it was almost a gale, with drifting and whirling snow, but we kept on going, my dog team in the lead. I checked my course by the wind, travelling straight south. Late in the afternoon the visibility was diminishing, and I stopped the dogs to wait for my companions. Qaatigaaryuk soon arrived, but Raddi was far behind. As Qaatigaaryuk wanted to keep travelling I told him to go ahead and find a good place to camp, a place where the snow would be suitable for a snow house. When Raddi caught up he looked tired and spiritless. I greeted him and asked, "How are you getting along, Raddi?" Coming alongside my sled his dogs dropped to the ice. Raddi didn't answer at all; instead, he fell on the sled, his hands covering his head. "I'm tired," he said. I remained silent, not uttering a word, not even offering a word of comfort, by my silence respecting his sadness and feeling of hopelessness. I felt disheartened myself, knowing what a person feels deep in his heart in such circumstances, and especially having to face someone. Raddi was then in his thirties, a good hunter and successful trapper. After a while he was himself again. He told me, "Jim, I cannot drive my dogs much longer. Two of them are badly frostbitten, so much that I should kill them, and my two other dogs are in poor condition." "Raddi", I said, "don't worry about anything. I have good dogs and we'll travel together. Hitch your two best dogs to my team. As for the other two, unharness them and we'll see later how to deal with them. So don't give up, we'll go through this together." This calmed Raddi, and as we travelled, he was once again himself and happy.

Travelling by dog team on the frozen ocean, Minto Inlet, May 3, 1958. Trail to Sachs Harbour. (Robert C. Knights/Northwest Territories Archives/N-1993-002: 0223)

The dogs followed Qaatigaaryuk's trail, trotting at full speed even though they had to pull a heavier load now, with Raddi's gear added to mine. When we caught up with Qaatigaaryuk, with the cold and the increasing darkness we felt that it was time to camp and call it a day. We found a snowdrift with well-packed snow that we used to build a snow house. We spent a comfortable night there, after a frugal meal, more of the seal meat that we shared with our dogs. We slept well in our comfortable snow house. Maybe what woke us was the slackening of the wind, or perhaps it was the noise of chains as the dogs shook snow off their fur. At any rate, we were early risers. We were eager to get underway, and if all went well we would reach the mainland by evening. Breakfast was taken care of quickly, and we were on our way again.

Everything around us was white, only snow and ice. Some was old ice, but now and then we had to travel on young ice. Fortunately it was strong enough to support the weight of our teams. Our course was south. We didn't have a compass, and had to pay close attention to the wind to keep us heading in the right direction. We journeyed all day, with only brief pauses, Raddi and I taking turns running alongside or ahead of the dogs. This was not because we needed to lead them, my leader was very good, but we wanted the dogs to feel happy. When one of us tired, the other would take a turn.

That afternoon we saw a mirage. Ahead in the distance the coast appeared and remained visible for a while, only to disappear again.[3] Evening found us still travelling, with the moon providing some light. At last, towards dark we were rewarded with a most welcome sight, land ahead, not a mirage this time but a continuous dark line on the horizon. But this was not to be our goal for tonight. In our land of ice and snow, whenever the weather is very clear, visibility is almost unlimited and distant things seem to be very near. We knew it was a long way yet, so we made camp with mixed feelings – happy to know that we were on the right course, but also impatient, knowing that we were within maybe fifty kilometres of the land we wanted to reach. First we built a snow house for shelter, and then we settled in for our supper. All day long the sea ice had been lifeless, no seals or polar bears were spotted. Rummaging in his sled Qaatigaaryuk came upon some seal intestines, and with a smile brought them in and offered to boil them. They were not very clean, but would serve as the night's supper, he told us. Our hunger helped us to swallow them – it was better than having no food at all. Later, Raddi went out. I heard some noise and tried to guess what he was doing. Going out to check I was surprised to see that he was cutting the white foxes he had trapped in half, skin and all. I pointed out that the skins were valuable items with which to trade, good white fox furs. With a grin on his face he answered, "Jim, they are good furs, but the dogs are tired and hungry. I don't want them to be weak. Tomorrow will be another day and they will have to work hard again. How could they with empty stomachs?" So we fed them, giving each dog half a fox.

The following morning our chief concern was to get to land, especially since the wind was blowing from the east and we were afraid that the ice might drift away from the shore. Putting aside our fears and weariness we travelled all day. There was no point in stopping too often, as we were short of food and had only a bit of kerosene for the stove, just enough to melt some snow now and then and have a cup of water. All day long we ran and pushed the dogs to the limit. Darkness fell, but we kept moving, thankful for the moonlight. As we came nearer the land the ice was rough, slowing us down. Nevertheless, we continued on, helping the dogs, pushing and encouraging

*Fred Jacobson with his sons Louie (**left**) and Teddy (**right**), 1936. (Richard Hourde/Hudson's Bay Company Archives/1987/363-E-130/50)*

them. It is difficult to express our feelings as we came on shore after six days travelling on the unfriendly ice. After a journey of some 480 kilometres, we arrived at our destination in good health, our dogs tired but willing to work.

After a brief pause to rest we followed the shoreline, looking for signs of life. We knew there was good trapping in this area, and thought it likely that someone would have a trap line along the shore. Our guess proved to be correct, as we soon discovered fresh tracks of two dog teams. We were comforted and encouraged by this discovery. We were very hungry, and were confident that if we followed the trail we would meet the trappers and could get some food from them for ourselves and our dogs. We agreed on our next move – follow the trail. Although the dogs were tired and hungry, it seemed that they got their second wind and were eager to continue. On their own, not being urged by us at all, they speeded up, sniffing right and left, muzzles always in motion, knowing that soon there would be rest, food and company.

We were favoured with bright moonlight and fair weather on our night journey. We were watching for the camp, but the dogs were the first to detect it. They began galloping, and straight ahead we saw a tiny spark, like a star on the horizon. As we came nearer we saw a bright light shining through a little window, and a small cabin. What a wonderful sight for wanderers, the sort of sign that elates the heart and means so much in the North. It meant food, warmth, shelter, human company, news and directions to our destination. Our fears of having to camp once again in a snow house, with only a few cups of lukewarm water, were dispelled when we saw two men outside near the door. The barking of their dogs had warned of an incoming team. At first sight we identified them, Fred Jacobson's sons, Teddy and Louie.[4] They invited us in and served us tea and food. We sure enjoyed that cup of tea, the first in almost a whole year. It tasted good, very good indeed. So did the bannock. After this we tended to our dogs. Raddi bargained with our hosts, trading a fox skin for a dog pot.[5] This would take care of them for today, giving them a full meal.

201

The Hudson's Bay Company trading post and Royal Canadian Mounted Police detachment at Pearce Point. The Hudson's Bay Company supply ship "Baychimo" and the RCMP schooner "St. Roch" are at anchor, August 1930. (Richard Finne fonds/N-1988-009: 0006)

The next morning at the first streak of light in the sky we left camp headed westward, and the two brothers continued eastward on their trap line. They told us that we should be able to reach Pearce Point in one day's travelling.[6] So we were on our own again, in an unfamiliar land. In the early afternoon a strong easterly wind blew up, causing drifting and whirling snow, blinding us. Unable to see landmarks, our only recourse was to go forward, groping our way. The Jacobson brothers had told about the general lay of the land, but with only vague knowledge of the area we missed Pearce Point. We found ourselves on sea ice, and altered our course toward land. As soon as we reached the shoreline we followed it for a while, still in the dark and the storm. With snow on the ground, snow above the ground and snow all around us there was nothing to be seen. Suddenly, the dogs took off, changing direction and taking us onto the sea ice again. We didn't panic. I simply said to Raddi, "Well, Raddi, it looks like the dogs smelled someone or something, maybe the camp or some game. We will let them go, and maybe they will find the houses."

We let the dogs take the initiative. Their mad rush didn't last very long, and I knew that they had lost the scent. Luckily I had taken notice of their direction as they sped up, and I drove them accordingly. We reached the shoreline, but there were high bluffs, so we stopped and talked about our next move – to camp there without any food, or to keep going? I suggested travelling a little longer, as the bluffs seemed to roll down slowly to a light slope, and maybe Pearce Point was on the other side. According to my observations, it was that way that the dogs had headed. We agreed upon this plan of action and resumed our journey, and were rewarded as we reached the lower part of the bluffs. Straight ahead – a light, Pearce Point. Needless to say, joy overcame us, after so many hours of travelling in the storm and the dark. Yes, this was Pearce Point indeed, only two lonely houses, but how beautiful they looked to us that night. This was the Royal Canadian Mounted Police detachment, one house for the Special Constable and the other for the regular police. We stopped our dogs at the first house. I looked through the window and recognized Bertram Pokiak, who worked for the RCMP. Having spent all day in the open, riding the storm and drifting snow, I assume that our looks were not pleasant – what with frost covering our faces, eyes iced up and our clothes white with snow. No wonder Bertram looked shocked and frightened when he opened the door to greet us. He might have thought he was seeing a ghost. After all, I was supposed to be on Banks Island, not here on the mainland. I extended my hand, wishing to shake hands with him, but he withdrew his, staring at me silently until I said to him, "Hey! Don't your recognize me, Bertram? I'm Jim Wolki." Then I guess he realized that I was really alive and he shook hands with me and smiled, telling us to come in.

"Hunter on the Ice in the Canadian Arctic" - Bertram Pokiak, 1936. (Richard N. Hourde/Hudson's Bay Company Archives/1987/363-E-341/49)

Briefly I told him all the events of the summer and fall, the shortage of food and ammunition and our resolution to go to Letty Harbour to get supplies. I described our trip so far, and said we were out of supplies and hadn't had anything to eat since the morning – no tea, no bannock, no food for the dogs. The only possessions we had left were matches and a bit of kerosene. I expressed our wish to camp there, and to have some food for us and for the dogs. Bertram understood our plea and told me to follow him to the RCMP barracks and talk with Constable Burke, who was in charge of the detachment. Burke was a kind man and very understanding, a true Northerner, and when asked for hospitality, food and lodging, without any hesitation he immediately replied, "Jim, tie up your dogs first and take care of them. Bertram here will help you feed them a good ration, and then you come back here. Don't worry, there is food for all of us and for your dogs." When we were finished outside and came back to the house, what an agreeable surprise. The table was laden with food – bread, meat and fruit, tea and coffee. When we sat at the table, eyeing all that food, I told Burke "My gosh! What a sight, all this food, it has been so long since we have tasted such food, practically one year now. I wonder if we may taste some of everything." Burke urged us to start. "Come on, eat." he said, "you deserve a good meal. Grab whatever you like." We sat down at the table and ate. After the meal, Burke told us, "This table will always be ready for you, any time of the day and night you are hungry. If I am not here Bertram will take care of you and see that you have food as well as tea and coffee." Then turning to Bertram he told him to be available at all times and to take good care of us.

We were told that one of our old friends, Tom Lessard, known to us as *Siuligaluk* – 'Jackfish' –was also here. Tom had spent many years in this part of the Arctic, and previously had trapped in the Hudson's Bay area. This year he had a trap line around Pearce Point and Brook River to the southeast. Entering into his small shelter I said to him, "Hello, Tom, you know me I guess?" Tom looked puzzled and stared at me in total silence, so I spoke again and repeated my words, "Look, Tom, you know me, don't you?" Then I think he recognized my voice, and said "Jim Wolki? How the hell did you come here? I thought you were on Banks Island?" I explained to him that we got

Left to right: *Johnny Ruben, Tom Lessard and Paul Adam, date and location unknown. (Bessie Wolki Collection/Inuvialuit Social Development Program/BW-9)*

stuck there last summer, that we had run out of food, of everything, and we had decided to come this way and get some supplies.

The stormy weather, with wind and drifting snow, continued for four more days; therefore, we had plenty of time to rest, sleep, eat and visit. When I woke up early in the morning on the fifth day it looked as though the weather was finally changing, the storm abating, although it was still blowing and drifting. We pulled out without waking up Bertram. We knew that he would have told us to wait a little longer.

Our goal now was to reach Letty Harbour.[7] There was a long way to go, some 80 kilometres in a straight line, but we followed the coast for a while, camping that night at one of Tom Lessard's cabins. We travelled all the next day. Darkness fell while we were still on the way, but the moonlight was a big help. When we came upon fresh trails we decided to follow them and saw a light near a lake. This was Johnny Green's camp at Fish Lake. We first met his wife, Jessie. It was late, somewhere around midnight. She came outside when she heard noise, and not recognizing us in the dark she asked Qaatigaaryuk who we were. He answered 'Qaatigaaryuk'. She didn't seem to understand, or maybe she didn't hear well enough, so she asked three or four times, a bit puzzled I guess. Anyway she went in and called her husband, Johnny Green, who also asked who we were. Again Qaatigaaryuk said his name, and Raddi for fun answered '*uvugut*', which means 'us'. Johnny recognized

Jessie Green (Uluraq), Paulatuk, date unknown. (Photograph courtesy of Garrett Ruben)

204

The Roman Catholic Mission and Hudson's Bay Company trading post at Letty Harbour, circa 1930s. (Missionary Oblates, Grandin Archives at the Provincial Archives of Alberta/OB.22839)

us then, and of course he invited us to spend the night at his home and they fed us fish. The next day, after a substantial breakfast, we were on the move again. Johnny explained how to reach Letty Harbour, and to make sure we arrived safely Jacob Niparlariuk volunteered to guide us part of the way. When we reached Kamokak, a big bay, he pointed out the direction we had to take and left us, returning to Fish Lake.

On our arrival at Letty Harbour we were met by Jock Kilgour, the manager of the Hudson's Bay Company trading post. I knew him, but he didn't recognize me at first. He kept looking at me, staring as if he had seen me somewhere before. At last, smiling he said, "You are Jim Wolki, aren't you? And how did you come here at this time of year?" I answered, "I'm Jim Wolki, all right, and if I'm here now it's not for the pleasure of travelling, be sure of that, but we've run out of food and ammunition on Banks Island. We hope we can get what we need here." We also wanted some dogs and a sled, and were told that we might be able to purchase those items from the Ruben family, wintered at Tom Cod Bay, on the opposite shore of the peninsula. Qaatigaaryuk and Raddi left for their camp, but I stayed at Jock Kilgour's house for a week, until my companions returned. We purchased a large outfit, a bit of everything, especially ammunition. The supplies made an impressive load when piled upon our three sleds.

As soon as we were ready we left Letty Harbour behind us and headed at last for Banks Island, and home. We were very happy indeed, with hope in our hearts – if not for an easy trip, at least for an uneventful one. We took an east-northeast course the first day. We enjoyed fair weather and travelled all day long without incident. But in the evening misfortune struck. Qaatigaaryuk ran into difficulties and his sled broke, one of his runners crushed to pieces, beyond repair. There was nothing to do but stop and build a snow house. After supper we talked things over, and Qaatigaaryuk decided to return to Fish Lake and ask Johnny Green for another sled. The next morning Qaatigaaryuk left for the mainland and Raddi and I remained at the camp. One day passed, and then another, elapsed, and no Qaatigaaryuk. So, a bit weary we went back to Letty

Harbour, leaving our supplies at the camp, some things in the snow house and some on top of it. We reached Letty Harbour almost at the same time that Qaatigaaryuk arrived there, with another sled. At least one problem was solved.

A southerly wind blew all night, and for us this was not a pleasant sound. We resumed our journey in the morning, following our trail whenever possible, but this was a difficult task because during the night the sea ice had broken all over. Pieces had piled up in ridges and open water in some places forced us to detour until we were again on the trail, a real zigzag now. This lengthened our route considerably as we searched for our snow house, hidden somewhere in the snow and ice ridges. Luckily, we spotted it late in the evening, a tiny black speck on a white background, and arrived at our camp as darkness fell. We were relieved to be there, and to find our outfit untouched, and the snow house still up, although the ice had broken all around with huge pieces piled up nearby. Though the prospects of a quiet and safe night were doubtful, we settled in. But first, anticipating the worst, we loaded all the supplies in the sleds and left the harnesses stretched out in readiness, should the need to escape arise. Thinking about it, I wonder where we could have gone in the dark, with rough ice all around us, and open water leads everywhere. Weary as we were, sleep evaded us, knowing that the ice was breaking up and ice floes were grinding against each other, piling up in ridges. Added to this noise was the howling of the wind. Who could expect to sleep well? We had no other choice than to stay in our snow house, and be ready for any emergency that might have meant going out into the dark and groping our way to safety. Fortunately we didn't have to take such a step.

Morning found us still in our shelter, if not refreshed then at least in a better frame of mind. Daylight restored us in a sense of more control of the situation and ourselves. Going out after breakfast we found that the wind was not as strong, but we were not pleased at the look of our surroundings. During the night the storm had made havoc of the ice, piling it up so that the travelling once again was going to be hard and dangerous. The temperature had dropped and many of the leads had frozen over, but only slightly, compelling us to detour around them – all the while looking ahead, searching for the main ice pack, for a safe road. It didn't matter if the ice pack was moving, as long as it was safe travelling.

All day we proceeded cautiously, travelling east-northeast, and at dark we built another snow house. The following day was a repeat of the day before, and another snow house built for the night. From there we altered our course; it was time to travel straight north, heading for Nelson Head on Banks Island. The weather was fair but cold, with a gentle wind from the west. We encountered many patches of young ice that day, but fortunately it was strong enough to support us. At dusk we came up to a pressure ridge and a crack in the ice, and on the edge we found the tracks of a large polar bear. We looked, but didn't see it. We decided to camp there, as the snow was suitable for building a snow house. We had bought some dog food at Letty Harbour, and it had to be cooked. I made a shelter from blocks of snow to protect the stove. I lit the stove and was getting the dog pot filled with snow when, looking around, I saw a huge polar bear walking leisurely towards us, coming closer and closer. We fired at it, but the bear was only wounded and turned around and fled. The dogs, still in their harnesses, began to bark loudly, and then all hell broke loose. The dogs made a rush toward the bear. Pulling out the anchor, they took off, going straight over the stove and pot. Luckily, being near the sled I jumped in and off we went at full speed. The going was rough, and it took all my agility to hang onto the sled.

While going over one patch rough ice I dropped my rifle, but there was no way to stop my team in order to retrieve it. Looking behind, I saw Raddi following, and when at last I succeeded in stopping my dogs he was at my side. I told him to kill the bear, as I was without a gun. I let some of my dogs loose, and they didn't need any coaxing – they went like arrows toward the bear and stopped it, surrounding it. Raddi gave me his rifle, a .30-.30, and told me that I should shoot it. He would go back and pick up all items we had lost on the trail. So I went up to the bear and shot eight times before killing it. I returned to my sled, the dogs following behind. Raddi was also back, having collected all the items that had been scattered on the ice. We had plenty of meat for ourselves and the dogs that evening. The next day we took along only a little bit of what was left. Our load was already heavy, and there would be game on the ice from now on.

The next day an east wind was blowing, and we knew that the ice pack was drifting westward as we continued our journey in the direction of Nelson Head. The going was slow and fog from nearby leads surrounded us, making visibility almost zero. Around midday the dogs suddenly perked up, and ahead of us we saw a polar bear lying down on the ice. When we got closer it slowly got up and walked away, in no hurry, now and then looking behind. We didn't follow it, what would be the use? We already had some bear meat. Where it had been lying down we found a seal carcass. The bear had eaten only the blubber and had left the meat. This would be good for the dogs, so we took the carcass and went on until evening. We had to detour often, as we met with open water leads. At dark we camped, and slept well, despite the ice grinding and piling up near us.

We spent the next day at our camp. We were surrounded by water, so we decided to go hunting. I went to a lead, taking along our *manaq* – a grappling hook and line – and was lucky in getting three seals. Raddi and Qaatigaaryuk chose another lead and got two seals. Not a bad day, five seals, plenty of meat and blubber. There was a bit of excitement when Raddi fell into the water. He undressed there on the ice, and from his sled he took a set of winter clothing that he had purchased from the RCMP at Pearce Point. This accident could have been a real disaster. Although Raddi took his cold dive into the icy water as a real joke, and laughed about it, if he hadn't had this spare clothing I'm afraid he would have frozen to death.

On the following day conditions were poor for travelling. So we spent another day at our camp. On the third day we resumed our journey, heading in an easterly direction. I had heard from elders that this was the natural course to take when caught on drifting ice, which usually moved west. However, travelling eastward didn't ease our efforts or worries. Often we had to detour when we came to wide leads, and whenever we hit big ice floes grinding and crushing against each other we had to chance crossing on them. Sometimes pressure ridges and piled up ice were so intermingled and uneven, so rugged, that we had to make our own path using our axes. Other times there was no alternative, no other way than going around huge mountains of ice. All day long it was an unknown road, a mixture of good going and then more encounters with heavy ice and open water. All of these of added to the distance we had to travel and hindered our pace. Day after day we went on, travelling as far as we could, but without any change on the horizon, only snow and ice as far as we could see. We camped on ice floes, and hunted seals in open water for dog food. As a rule, we tried to get at least one seal a day before camping. At dusk we would pick a good spot away from the open water and leads, and as much as possible a place free of rough ice. This ordeal lasted ten days and hung heavy on us. We gave up trying to reach Nelson Head, and tried desperately to return the mainland.

We had many adventures on that floating ice. Once we came across a lead that had recently frozen. The ice was all black and very thin, but maybe strong enough to support us and our sleds and us. Qaatigaaryuk had only a light load, so we asked him to try first. Raddi and I anxiously followed his progress. The crossing went well, without incident. He then shouted to us that the ice was good enough. Raddi and I then proceeded to cross. I had a heavy load on my sled, and I could feel the ice giving under its weight. I didn't feel very brave, but I had no choice but to proceed. Raddi was following me so I signalled him to leave my trail and change course a bit. He understood my warning, and ordered his dogs to go to the left. Luckily his leader was good and he avoided the weak spots. Once on the strong ice I felt relieved; it had been a close call. We took a little time to compose ourselves, to discuss our dangerous experience, glad to put it behind us without any casualties. It could have been a tragedy for all concerned, for our lives, our dogs, and our loads. All is well that ends well, it is said. Nevertheless, we decided then to be more careful, and to use more caution in the future.

With these intentions in mind we resumed our journey, aiming at the mainland that remained invisible to us, but to our knowledge and instincts located somewhere to the east. We were more cautious now, as we had been shaken by our recent experience. Before dark a strong westerly wind sprung up. Drifting snow blinded us, and added to this, darkness fell when we were trying to go through a patch of rough ice. Exhausted, we decided to call it a day. We felt that it was too dangerous to sleep in a snow house, so we anchored the dogs, not even unharnessing them, and spent the night on watch, walking round and round, listening to the wind, the violent raging sea somewhere near us but hidden by the dark and the drifting snow. Our vigil was a long one, with apprehension and also a bit of fear whenever we heard the heavy pounding of waves pushing and crushing the ice all around us. We were able to put up some snow blocks, and in this precarious shelter when we felt the cold we lit our kerosene stove, melted some snow and made tea. We had warm winter clothes, so we didn't suffer too much from the cold, only from fatigue and lack of sleep. We awaited for morning with eagerness, and as soon as the light was good enough we were ready and more than willing to proceed eastward again. The weather was not too good, but fair enough. The wind had subsided a little and visibility improved, and we could see land not too far ahead of us. This sight warmed our hearts, and with hope we began another day, a long and weary day.

Where before the storm we had seen open water, now young ice stretched ahead, with only here and there some small patches of older ice. Riding on the sled was out of the question, and we resigned ourselves to walk ahead of the dogs, picking a trail, axe in hand to constantly test the strength of the ice, going around the weak spots. We pushed on with the hope of reaching land before evening, but those hopes were dashed. As we came near land, only a very short distance now... how far? Well, at shooting distance, at a rifle's range... we encountered young ice again, very thin, impossible to walk on. We had stopped on a small piece of old ice, with just enough room for our three teams and a little bit more to spare, but there was snow suitable for a snow house. Disheartened, we camped there, cooked some food for the dogs and ourselves, and after our meal, retired to bed hoping that the weather would remain calm for a few more hours. During the night a westerly wind blew up, but in the morning it settled into a gentle breeze, and the temperature was cold. A break at last. I didn't like the idea of crossing without checking the ice first, so taking only my axe, I carefully stepped onto the young ice and tested it all the way to the land. Then retracing my steps on the same trail I rejoined my companions and told them "Well, I guess we can make it across safely. The ice seems strong enough; the cold temperature last night helped. So let's cross over to the land before this ice begins to move again."

We went across the young ice in a single file, and reached land without any trouble. Pearce Point was on our west side, and we could see the smoke from chimneys. Oh, what a relief! After some ten days on the drifting ice we were now back on solid ground. We discussed our next move. What to do now? We agreed unanimously to leave most of our load there and to proceed to Pearce Point. We needed to dry out our clothes and our blankets, harnesses, and other gear before travelling again. As Pearce Point was only a short distance away, Raddi and Qaatigaaryuk said to me, "Look Jim, what about having some lunch now before leaving?" So we cooked lunch and then continued on.

At Pearce Point Bertram Pokiak greeted us from the RCMP barracks door with a smile on his face and a gesture of his arms, but he didn't come outside. After tending to the dogs, we went inside where Bertram was baking bread. That's why he didn't come out to greet us. He said he was afraid he would burn the loaves already in the oven. We knew we were welcome there, as the table was already set, food on the table and tea steaming on the stove. Our visit there lasted four days. We had plenty of time to dry all our equipment, our clothes and blankets, and to make some minor repairs to harnesses and sleds, and also to buy some more food. The road ahead of us was a long one yet, especially as we determined to travel further east before trying once more to make the crossing. We know this would lengthen our travel, but it would be safer. We said goodbye to the friendly settlement of Pearce Point, which we had now visited twice, and after loading the belongings we had left behind at our landing place set course to the east.

The first night after our departure we spent in a little hut. We remained there the next day, as a storm and drifting snow made it impossible to leave that day, especially since the wind was blowing from the east, the direction we were to travel. Late that afternoon we had visitors who came from the east, but was a fair wind for them, so not too bad for travelling. They were a policeman and his guide, heading for Pearce Point. They took time to warm up, have a cup of tea and a cigarette before continuing, but not before asking us many questions about who we were, and where we were going. So once again I explained the reasons for our trip and all the difficulties we had experienced, including our days drifting on the ice that had brought us here.

The following day the weather was fair, with a westerly breeze, and we set our minds to travel as far as Inman River. We left camp early in the morning, following the coastline. The dogs were eager to go, and travelled at a good speed, now and then lifting their heads as if catching a scent. At first we couldn't see anything, but then something yellow against the whiteness of the snow and ice caught my eye. I pointed it out to Qaatigaaryuk, and he confirmed my opinion that it was a polar bear. It was lying on the snow, but when it heard us it stood up, sniffing and looking around. It must have been hungry, for as soon as we drew near it charged us. I immediately anchored the sled and grabbed my rifle. I have seen polar bears acting this way before. Each time it was a starving animal, unafraid and bold. I waited until he came close to my lead dog, and only then did I shoot – getting him through the head and killing him instantly. Looking around we found that he had snatched a fox from a trap, had eaten it and gone to sleep. For us it was a God sent present, meat for us and for the dogs, not to mention the skin, which we also took.

After this interlude we continued on our journey, and a little later we came upon a tent and a white trapper who was unknown to us. After we introduced ourselves to him he smiled and said that he was Einar Jensen. He had come to this country seeking a livelihood, and maybe a fortune, by trapping foxes. He gave us a friendly welcome, and told me that his camp was ours, and to feel free to eat and to camp there if we wished to. This, he added, would be a token of gratitude and acknowledgement to Fritz Wolki, my father, who years ago had treated him and his partner Carl Patterson so well at Horton River.[8] While eating he told us that close by, maybe only half a day's travelling, he had a little house where we could camp if we wanted to continue our journey that day.[9] He had a cache of food in a tent near the house, and we were welcome to help ourselves. He also told us that we could reach Banks Island by crossing from Inman River to Victoria Island, going up to Walker Bay, and crossing from there to Banks Island. After our meal we continued on our way, as it was only afternoon and there were many hours of daylight were left.

We found his house in the evening and were happy to camp there. We slept there not just one night as we had planned, but four nights, as a strong westerly wind prevented us from continuing our journey. We put a good face on this misfortune. The little house provided us with a safe shelter, food was available and as per instructions we took some canned meat and fruit, so it was not too tough, really. After three days of blowing winds and drifting snow we finally left Inman River, and we began crossing to Victoria Island. The going was fair and we travelled well that day.

When night arrived we stopped and built a snow house. Another storm hit us, a westerly wind, and we spent three days there. When the wind subsided we decided to leave, and were favoured with good weather and good visibility, and a smooth road on the ice. What more can a traveller ask for? By late afternoon land was visible not too far ahead. On the west side of us was open water, but it wasn't so close that we were concerned about it. We continued, happily now, but before we reached land we encountered an open water lead that ran parallel to the shore. We followed it, hoping to find a way to get across, and keeping a lookout for seals in the open water. Finally, we found a way to go ashore, and we once again were very happy travellers, happy to leave behind us the ice pack and the pressure ridges, danger, headaches and anxiety. I think that we had

Trapping camp at Uluksartok (Ulukhaktok), Victoria Island, 1934. (Mrs. Peter Sydney Collection/ Library and Archives Canada/PA-27676)

210

landed somewhere on the south shore of Prince Albert Sound. It was quite a ways to Uluksartok on the other side.[10] We stopped and talked things over, and decided to call it a day. It had begun to get dark, so we built a snow house and spent the night there.

When we left camp the next day we had hopes of making it to Uluksartok that day, and finding some people there, but as it turned out this was not to be. Although we had started early, when night came Uluksartok still wasn't in sight. Many sled tracks were visible, which meant that there was a camp nearby, but unfortunately we weren't there yet so we resigned ourselves to spending another night in a snow house. We were short of dog food, so before departing the next morning we decided to go to the floe edge nearby to hunt seals in the open water. We saw only a few seals, and got just one, but it was enough to feed the dogs for a few days.

The days were longer now and we wanted to benefit from the daylight, and were eager to reach Uluksartok. After lunch we prepared to depart, loading our sleds and hitching the dogs. Just then we saw a dog team, too far away to be identified. At first glance we thought it to be an Eastern team and an Eastern Inuk, a *Qangmaliq*.[11] We kept watching it, observing its moves and watching its direction. They saw us as well, and their dogs caught our scent and began running towards us. As they came closer we made out two men, and when they were near we recognized them. They were my brother Fred Wolki and my brother-in-law Fred Carpenter! The world is small indeed. Of all the people we could have encountered it had to be my two brothers. Shaking hands and welcoming us, they fired question after question at us. They wanted to know everything at once, so great was their surprise and astonishment. "Where are you coming from? How did you get here? Aren't you lost, so far from your home? What is this all about?"

"Well," I replied, "it's too long a story to tell now. Let's say only that we have been travelling for quite a while, all over the ice, trying to get home to Banks Island where we were stranded for the winter without food. After leaving Letty Harbour with a load of supplies we were caught on drifting ice. We went by Pearce Point and finally got to here. So here we are now, and mighty glad to meet with you, believe me. To make it short, that's about it." Fred Carpenter listened intently

Fred (Sitaattaq) Wolki and Fred (Ajgaliaq) Carpenter, hunting geese, spring 1932. (Mrs. Peter Sydney Collection/Library and Archives Canada/PA-027676)

and then shrugging his shoulders and smiling at the same time, he said, "That must have been a tough and rough trip, hey Jim? But why did you go to Letty Harbour? Why not Walker Bay? There are two stores there.[12] It's a lot closer and less hazardous." I answered that Paul Adam and I had attempted to go to Walker Bay last fall, but wasn't successful. I didn't know that country very well, and we ran out of dog food, so we returned empty-handed, even poorer than when we left, so I didn't want to take another chance to go there. The only place that I had thought of was the mainland, and as he could see, we had made it. "Okay," said Fred, "I am glad that you are here now. Look, your brother and I are camped a little ways from here. You are most welcome to stay with us and spend a few days. However, before going home let's try to hunt seals, as it's a long time yet before it gets dark."

We went back to the open water along the floe edge, but the seals didn't show themselves so we gave up hunting for that day and headed out for their camp. My brother Fred drove their team and Fred Carpenter followed on foot, as he wanted to visit some traps he had set along the shore. There were two women at the camp when we arrived, my sister Lucy and my brother's wife Susie.[13] As soon as we entered their tent we had to go through the interrogation again, where had we been, and why had we come there. Anyway, we had a good rest and a good time there, catching up with the news of that part of the world. We spent four days with them, and at the end of those four days my brother Fred offered his services as guide to Walker Bay. He said that it wouldn't be out of his way as he had a trap line in that direction. We appreciated his offer. Besides, it gave us an opportunity to be together a bit longer. Walker Bay wasn't too far away, and we reached our destination in two days without pushing the dogs.

We went to the Canalaska store and bought more supplies, especially food and ammunition. When our bartering was completed our sled loads had increased in weight and in volume. But if our loads were heavier, at least our worries and anxieties became lighter as we left Walker Bay. We headed first for David Piqtuqana's camp, which was nearby, a tent surrounded by snow blocks, but

Left to right: *Fred, Andy (boy) and Lucy Carpenter, Susie Wolki, Naqhaluk, Banks Island, fall 1933. (Mrs. Peter Sydney Collection/Library and Archives Canada/C-038525)*

212

The Canalaska trading post at Walker Bay, Victoria Island, fall, 1933. (Mrs. Peter Sydney Collection/ Library and Archives Canada/C-038541)

very comfortable and well sheltered from wind and storms. We spent a day with David and his family, enjoying their company and friendly welcome.

We were now ready for the last leg of our homebound journey. We were favoured with good weather and good visibility, and soon after departing from Victoria Island some bluffs on Banks Island could be seen on the horizon. I don't need to express my feelings, nor those of my companions; just let it be said that the sight filled us with joy and thoughts of home. Our land at last, and our families beyond those hills. We made good progress that day, but in spite of our efforts we weren't able to reach Banks Island by evening. However, we put a good face to misfortunes and spent the night in another snow house on the ice. Scanning the horizon and taking a good look around, on our left, to the south, we saw black clouds and mist that indicated open water, but we were on good ice and we slept without fear.

The next morning we got up filled with expectations and in good cheer. This was to be the day we would reach familiar country. At first the landscape was not familiar to me, having never travelled there before, but looking at a map I recognized the coastline and many details of the coast. Yes, there was no doubt about it, this was De Salis Bay. I enjoyed travelling that day, a beautiful day with good visibility and good going on smooth ice. My dogs also seemed happy. They pulled well, so I outdistanced my co-travellers and left them behind. With such a good day there was no danger of being separated. Their dogs were in good shape, and they would follow my trail. All day long we went along without incident. In the late afternoon, just before dark, I altered my course, hoping to come across a creek, a good size one where years ago I had a trap line running from Masik River. When I found it I was filled with joy. I no longer needed a map. I was now in well-known country, where each bend, outline and portage brought memories of many other trips. Countless times I had trodden the icy road of that creek, on foot and by dog team. Having set my mind to rest now, I stopped in a sheltered place suitable for camping and began cutting snow blocks and started building a snow house. Before completing the dwelling Qaatigaaryuk and Raddi arrived and helped me to put the finishing touches on the snow house, and we spent the night there.

The following day we followed the course of the creek and then we reached Masik Pass that would take us to the Masik River valley. We spent the night in Masik Pass, and it turned stormy, so we decided to spend the next day there as well. By the following morning the weather had improved. We resumed our journey, travelling all day until we reached the coast where we camped and went to bed early, as we wanted to make a long drive the following day. We felt the urge to end this trip, and reach home as soon as possible.

We left camp early. It was now the middle of March, and we had many hours of daylight in which to travel. Once again I travelled alone, ahead of the others, letting my dogs pick their own pace. I reached Cape Kellett, where I found a snow house on the sand spit, a small one with seal bones scattered all around it. This meant that somebody had come there to hunt seals, although not recently as the tracks were not fresh. I made some tea on my stove, caught up in my own thoughts. When my companions arrived I told them what I had observed, not very encouraging, indeed even disheartening. We had some tea together, respecting each other's privacy. But deep inside, within me, I knew very well that, like myself, they were a bit frightened, bracing themselves for the worst. Maybe our families were in a dire situation, starving, or worse. The only words we said amongst ourselves were words of patience, hope and also resignation to any situation awaiting us at home. After all, we couldn't change the course of events, and in the case of starvation and death we would have to try to accept it.

It was still daylight, and to avoid too much brooding we resumed our journey. We travelled a little ways and found another snow house, standing amongst rough ice. I decided we might as well camp there and tomorrow we would be home. Not much was said that evening. Supper was silent, and for my companions the night probably was like mine, a restless one with sad thoughts creeping into our minds, in spite of nearing home. The next day would be the day we had been thinking of so many times. This would be the last leg of our journey, of the long crossing.

We knew starting off the next morning that we would be home in a few hours, and would learn the fate of our families. Would they still be among the living? Had they survived, one way or another, the ordeal, hardships, cold and hunger? We had to see for ourselves, anyways. Not too far out, a short distance from our last snow house camp, was a place called Blue Fox Harbour, and passing through we saw a polar bear. He was running away, so I set some of my dogs after him to hold him until I got near enough to shoot, and I killed him. We then skinned him, loaded the meat and skin on our sleds as well as some fish I took from a cache there, and on we went again.

Now we were nearing our camp, and we kept our emotions hidden. As soon as we spotted the houses in the distance, we had to stop. The three of us talked together for a while, about our families and about all the possibilities awaiting us. We observed the camp. Was there any movement? Was someone there, visible, moving around? Any dogs? Any sign of life at all, such as smoke? Anything would have satisfied us. For what seemed a very long period, an endless and unbearable time, no sign of life could be detected. Everything stood at a standstill. And then it happened, we saw someone coming out from the house. What a relief, what a sight. I said, "Well, somebody is alive. Let's go and see."

Our dogs seemed to anticipate the eventful meeting ahead of them, and they responded magnificently, galloping all the way right to the camp, home at last. Thank God, all the members of the families were not only alive, but in good health. The only thing that had kept them alive were foxes – they lived on fox meat, and used fox fat for their lamps.

In conclusion of this story of the long crossing, and of the toughest year of my life so far, I wish to say that there was rejoicing, eating, smoking, and drinking tea. After so many months of privation and want, we now had plenty of everything.

What was life like back on Banks Island during the men's three-month absence? Adam Inuałuuyaq and his wife Ellie, their son Paul Adam, Jim Wolki's wife Bessie and their children, and Raddi Kuiksak's wife Ivy Panigak and their children, also faced danger, worries and hardships with courage and tenacity until the happy return of the travellers. Here are stories told by Bessie Wolki, Ivy Panigak and Paul Adam.

~ *Memories of Life Back on Banks Island During the Long Crossing* ~

Bessie Wolki:
That was a hard winter – one that everyone who was there would remember. As the days, weeks and months rolled on, my husband became more and more restless. Our supply of store-bought food was almost gone, and ammunition was running out. In all our misfortune, we had a lucky break. Someone found a tin can of coffee on the shore, one pound only. We used it sparingly, but even so it didn't last long.

Jim toyed with only one thought – crossing to the mainland, to Letty Harbour. I do not know how often he mentioned this plan to me. Each time, I voiced my displeasure, my fears and concerns. I listed all the perils that would lie ahead of him – as if he didn't know – trying desperately to dissuade him from taking such a chance. "You may drown, freeze to death, maybe never come back home alive. What about us here, and our children?" But he didn't heed my arguments. Thoughts of a long separation, of being left at the camp with the children, without food or provisions, brought me grief and heartache. However, before such a determined, strong-minded man, what more could I do? Understanding this, I reluctantly told him, "*Ki*, if you are so decided to go, all right then, go!"

When Jim made his decision known to the other families, Qaatigaaryuk and Raddi said that they were game to follow him in the great adventure. Ivy didn't argue or say anything to her husband, Raddi, but our hearts were heavy with anxiety for our children and ourselves. We were entirely cut off from everything and everyone, and would have to depend on our own resourcefulness. Added to this was our concern for the unknown that our men faced. A trip such as the one they were about to undertake was barely thinkable, even for experienced travellers. But the men had made up their minds. So it was with mixed feelings and emotions hidden inside that we all, children and adults, watched their departure. It was a silent farewell, not many words were said.

For those of us staying behind it was to be a long, long vigil. Our main concern was to stay alive.

This was a time for courage, a time to fight for our survival. This was no time for panic. We made the best of our meager supplies and the resources at our disposal. We tackled our enemies – cold, darkness, wind, storms, hunger – and won, although we suffered greatly through that bitterly cold and windy winter.

Our dwellings were canvas wall tents that were protected by an outside wall of snow, with snow porches for storing provisions. The wind blew so much that, but for the stovepipes that stuck out, no one could have guessed that there were dwellings there. Our porches filled with drifting snow, which made getting into the tent easy – one had only to slide – and getting out difficult – one had to climb. As part of his routine each morning, Adam would come to check on us, especially after each storm when so much snow would piled up inside the porch that we were virtually made prisoners inside our shelter. A window – a piece of fresh ice cut in a nearby lake – provided some light during the day, but the light became dimmer and dimmer as frost built up on the outside and smoke and soot from the stove stained the inside.

Now and then we used a kerosene stove, but fuel was scarce. There was no wood, so we burned seal oil and fat from foxes and owls in home made stoves and lamps. We suffered from the cold, yet no one complained. We would huddle together around the lamps and stoves, desperately trying to steal some warmth.

With the cold tormenting us we had to face an even greater problem: not having enough to eat. How were we to fool our hunger? For breakfast we would melt some snow or fresh ice for a warm drink. Then we would eat a morsel of seal meat or a piece of blubber cooked on the stove, deceiving hunger as we chewed and chewed all day long on one piece. The next and final meal of the day we all ate together in the evening. We called it 'three in one'. The meal consisted of boiled white fox, very lean indeed that winter, or white owl. Sometimes, under even harder circumstances, only a piece of caribou skin provided us with some broth and something substantial to eat. We had little variety, but we were not particular about our meals. While what we did have was not what we would call appetizing, it was still better than just lukewarm water. Boiled meat and broth were divided equally among all, the best part of course going to the children.

Ivy Panigak:
I nursed two babies then, my son James, and Bessie's son Geddes. At feeding time Bessie would come to my tent with the baby, and I took care of both children.

How did we survive such ordeals then? We owe a lot to the determination and persistence of Adam and Paul. They were constantly on the go, on the move, searching for food, hunting inland and on the ice, often going on foot, sometimes by dog team. Only a few dogs survived, and they were weak and thin from living on meager rations.

Paul Adam:
Our ammunition had run out by that time, so we had to rely on traditional hunting techniques. We were thankful to have learned the old ways from the elders. Little by little we mastered these skills, such as catching ptarmigan and white owls.

Whenever I spent the day in camp I would hunt for ptarmigan nearby. I loaded some wooden stakes and an old fish net in my packsack and would set off walking, scanning the white horizon and looking for tracks in the snow. A soon as I saw some signs of ptarmigan I would make a detour to set up my trap, first driving the stakes into the snow and then stretching the net over the pegs. This done, I would walk slowly toward the ptarmigan, driving them toward the net. When they were close to it I would quicken my steps, clapping my hands to frighten the birds. As they ran from me some of the ptarmigan would become enmeshed in the net. My good fortune meant a meal for all. I also caught owls in snares set on high rocks and on knolls. One day I got as many as 70. The meat is delicious, and they also provided us with a source of fat for the lamps and stove. Once when I was travelling away from camp I came across two caribou. They were very lean and in poor condition, but a source of meat nonetheless. We couldn't afford to be particular.

Sometimes Bessie would surprise us with a treat. With her ulu she would scrape hardened pieces of flour from some old flour bags, pound them with a hammer, and then mix these remnants with water, making a dough that she would cook on the stove. Although they had no baking powder, the biscuits were like a dessert, and we savoured them. Those occasions were like feast days, and helped us forget our hunger.

Ivy Panigak:
That is the way we survived, day after day, week after week, hoping and praying for the safe return of our men. As the days lengthened, our fears and anxieties increased. "Will they return?" Doubts sometimes crept into our minds. Even Bessie showed concern, naming her son Jim Kakianaan after her husband. Later, she would change his name and call him 'Geddes'.

Bessie Wolki:
More than once gloom overtook us, and we were on the verge of giving up. In those days of low spirits Adam was, as usual, a tower of strength, a source of optimism and security. Whenever we felt despair and fear, he always found words to console us and to bring back hope, saying "Oh, they'll be back very soon now. Look, the days are longer and spring is almost here." Sometimes Ellie, his wife, when swept by a wave of grief would rebuke him, saying, "How on earth can you talk that way? It has been so long now since they left, how could they have survived?" He made plans for us to move to Masik Pass later in the spring if necessary, where Arctic hare were abundant and living off the country would be easier. He prepared some food – although only a very little – and stored it with some matches in a seal bag as emergency rations for that trip. But how could we have reached Masik Pass with only a few dogs? Many miles separated our winter quarters from the Pass. We would have to do as in the old days, helping to pull small sleds carrying our belongings.

Yes, those were days of physical wants and needs, not to mention mental anguish. We were afraid to even think of the future and what was in store for us. Fortunately, the lonely, fearful days and nights came to an end for both travellers and those living at the camp. When that happened, it was like a dream.

One day, Adam told us through the air vent that three dog teams were in sight on the horizon. That simple statement, so long awaited, was almost too much for our ears and hearts to believe, and we were overcome by deep, strong emotions. So great was our longing for our men, and our desire to know who was approaching our camp, that we could hear our hearts beat fast. Our knees were shaking; our legs folded under us, unable to support our weight.

When I gained control of myself I went out, almost crawling through the porch, unsteady on my feet. On the hill were three men, three teams, too far away for us to identify. They were still, scanning the horizon – looking straight ahead, it seemed, to our camp. Then everything happened. They fired their rifles in greeting, and came towards us hauling their heavy loads.

Ellie, my mother, walked towards the approaching men, and meeting them she fell to her knees, shedding tears of joy and gratitude, and gave thanks to God. I felt tears, burning tears, rolling down my face. The moment was, as I recall it now, as if we were living in a dream world, hallucinating. We felt so lighthearted. Everyone looked – no, not looked, stared – at each other to make sure that it was not our imagination, but reality.

Editor's Note

Later that spring Jim Wolki and Raddi Kuiksak, this time accompanied by Paul Adam, made another trip to the trading posts at Walker Bay, this time going there and back directly from Banks Island, with the round-trip taking about 25 days. By the time they returned game was plentiful around their camp, and in July 1935 the sea ice broke up and they were able to sail back to the Delta in the schooner *Omingmuk*. Other trips to Banks Island for winter trapping of white fox would follow in the coming years.

The schooner 'Omingmuk'. (Mrs. Peter Sydney Collection/Library and Archives Canada/C-038497)

Chapter 18 Notes

1   Jim Wolki's account of 'The Long Crossing', and stories from Bessie Wolki, Ivy Panigak and Paul Adam have been excerpted from an unpublished collection, 'True Experiences – Men of the North' ('Men' referring to 'Inuvialuit'). Although not included in Father Le Meur's original memoir, from his notes, it appears that he intended to include it.

2   Jim Wolki's father, Fritz Wolki, was a Swiss-German trader, whaler and fur trader, which accounts for him being accustomed to *taniktat* – 'white man's food'. His mother was Pisuktoak, an Inupiat woman from Alaska.

3   The type of mirage described is common in the Arctic. Land or other objects in the distance appear to float above the horizon when cold dense air lies on top of the frozen ground or sea ice.

4   Fred Jacobson came north on a whaling ship in the early 1900s. According to family histories he left the ship after it was frozen in near Baillie Island, and many of the ships crew came down with scurvy. He remained in the area and made his living as a trapper.

5   'Dog pot' refers to a pail or other container used to cook food for sled dogs.

6   The Hudson's Bay Company operated a trading post at Pearce Point from 1927-1934. The Royal Canadian Mounted Police maintained a detachment there from 1931 until sometime after the HBC post had closed.

7   The Roman Catholic Church established a mission at Letty Harbour in 1928, and in 1932 the Hudson's Bay Company opened a post at the same location. The HBC post closed in 1935, and the same year the Roman Catholic Church mission was moved to Paulatuk.

8   Fritz Wolki operated a trading post at the mouth of the Horton River from about 1918-1921.

9   The Hudson's Bay Company operated at trading post at the mouth of the Inman River between 1926 and 1932. Einar Jensen's house was probably one of the trading post buildings.

10 Uluksartok is the spelling used by Inuvialuit from the western Arctic of the community later known as Holman, on the north shore of Prince Albert Sound. In 2006 the name Holman was officially changed to Ulukhaktok, the spelling favoured by local people.

11 *Qangmaliq* is a term people in the western Arctic sometimes use for people who live to the east.

12 The Canalaska Trading Company and the Hudson's Bay Company both had trading posts at Walker Bay in the 1930s.

13 Jim Wolki's sister Lucy was married to Fred Carpenter, and Fred Carpenter's sister Susie was married to Fred Wolki.

19

The Trials and Ordeals of a Young Boy

Geddes Wolki hunting seals, date unknown. (Bessie Wolki Collection/Inuvialuit Social Development Program)

The winter of 1942-1943 once again saw Jim and Bessie Wolki on Banks Island with Bessie's family, the Adams. Trapping was good, and the men were often away on the trap lines. The women had plenty of work to do at home – taking care of children, repairing and maintaining all the clothing, as well as skinning foxes and cleaning and stretching their pelts. Bessie's father, Adam Inuałuuyaq – 'Brave true man' in English – worked as best he could. Older people have their pride and don't like to be a burden. He had a short trap line around the camp, and another, longer trap line that he visited from time to time by dog sled, using a few of the old dogs that stayed behind when the able-bodied trappers were away.

One time when Inuałuuyaq went on his trap line, a journey of three or four days to the northeast of the camp, his grandson Geddes, Jim and Bessie's son, went with him. What a pleasure for little nine-year-old Geddes! He was going to learn his trade with a man of experience. He was so excited that he could hardly sleep the night before they left. The next morning, the weather was good, and the two of them headed off on a trip that seemed routine, but would end in tragedy.

The first two days passed without incident. They checked the traps as they went along, removing the foxes that had been caught. In order to avoid overexerting their old dogs they had to take turns riding on the sled, the other walking alongside, so by evening they were quite tired. They spent the nights in small snow houses that Inuałuuyaq had built on a previous trip.

The second night a wind came up, but wasn't too strong and the next morning they decided to continue on one more day to the end of the trap line. Everything started out well, but the weather got worse in the afternoon, and it seemed to Geddes that his grandfather was tiring, and that he had to walk more than on the other days while Inuałuuyaq rode on the sled. But he was young and strong. He ran beside the dogs, calling them by name and giving them orders.

When they reached their final camp that evening Geddes took care of the dogs, unhitching them and attaching them to their chains, while his grandfather took the food, the Primus stove and bedding inside the snow house. Once the stove and some candles were lit there was a bit of warmth and light that was much appreciated by the two travellers, who were chilled through and through by the cold they had endured all day.

As soon as he was finished with the dogs, Geddes filled a pan with snow to be melted for water, and placed a snow block to be used for sealing the door near at hand. For supper they

Left to right: *Adam Inuałuuyaq, John Kuveran, unidentified man, date unknown. (Martha Harry Collection/Inuvialuit Social Development Program)*

had a raw fish. Meanwhile the water was heating, and the tea was soon ready. Usually, once they had warmed up, Inuałuuyaq liked to tell stories, but that evening he wasn't feeling well. He didn't say so, but Geddes knew it. He he had barely touched his fish, drunk only a little tea, and had to lie down, his breathing slow and heavy. It wasn't like his grandfather to stay like that, without saying anything. Geddes observed all that in silence, respecting his grandfather's rest. When Inuałuuyaq awoke from his drowsing, he smiled at the boy, gestured, and asked him how he was doing, apologizing for his weakness and weariness. He added, "It's late, and time to sleep." He covered up his grandson, patted him on the back, wished him goodnight and said, with a note of hope, "Tomorrow will be better. A night's sleep and I'll be back in shape. *Ublaakuptuaq* – see you in the morning." The candles and the stove went out. Once the humming of the pressure stove stopped there was silence in the snow house. The only sounds came from outside – the blowing of the wind, and, from time to time, the clinking of chains when the dogs moved.

When he woke up in the morning... was it morning? Geddes had only a vague concept of the time. He had no watch, but he felt wide-awake and well rested, which meant he'd had a good night's sleep, so it must be morning. Still, he wondered if he was mistaken, because his grandfather, who usually woke up first, wasn't moving yet, and the stove wasn't lit. Doubts came to Geddes' mind, and he tried to go back to sleep, but in vain. He thought about home and the return trip, the foxes, the dogs, and still sleep wouldn't come. He wasn't aware of how long he stayed like that before he realized that something was wrong. Throwing the covers off his head, he listened – silence, only the wind. He wondered what was going on. At the risk of upsetting his grandfather, he decided to light a candle. At first, everything appeared normal. He could see his breath, because of the cold, and it formed a kind of mist that rose and gradually filled the inside of the snow house. Then he realized that he was the only one producing that kind of mist, and that there was no sound of

Martha Kudlak baking bannock on a Primus stove, De Salis Bay, April 22, 1958. (Robert C. Knights/ NWT Archives/ N-1993-002: 0192)

breathing beside him. Inuałuuyaq, his grandfather, wasn't moving at all. Very gently and quietly, Geddes drew his arm out of his sleeping bag and, almost reluctantly, reached over and touched the body beside him, saying *"Ataatak* – Grandfather," No answer. Suddenly he realized that there was something strange, something not right about the way his grandfather felt. He looked at him again and, gathering his courage, touched him and tried to shake him, saying *"Ataatak, suva?* Grandfather, what's the matter?" No answer. With both arms he tried again to shake the form lying beside him but couldn't even budge it, and there was no reaction. How strange it felt, cold and stiff! He stared, himself frozen by his problem, finally realizing that his grandfather was dead. For a moment, all alone, he was lost in thought. Of course, he'd heard that such things happened. Many times he'd listened to people talk about accidents that had occurred on the land, and about people freezing. But here, and to him? He realized that it was a fact, it was happening now, and he was a part of it.

His grandfather was dead. Little by little, he realized he was alone, and the solitude weighed on him. He thought, and tried to remember what he had heard about cases like this, about what Inuvialuit, people of the North – his countrymen, his people – did under those circumstances. What brought him back from his thoughts was the cold. Knowing he had to do something, he got out of his sleeping bag. The first thing to do was to make some heat, to light the stove. He'd watched that being done a number of times, but now he had to do it himself, without help, and felt a bit nervous. He followed the steps to the best of his memory, but no flame took hold. How many times did he start over? But his efforts were in vain. His hands, soaked with kerosene, were really cold by then. From time to time he warmed them by holding them close to the candle flame. When he did that, he realized there was some heat there, above the candle. Giving up on the stove, he concentrated on the candles. Searching his grandfather's pack, he found a few – some just small pieces – and lit some of them. Then he took the pot, put in a little snow, put it over the candles and melted a little water to drink. He didn't have much appetite that first day – too many thoughts were going through his head, and he was feeling anxious. What to do now? There he was, sitting on the covers, his head in his hands. From time to time, he glanced at his grandfather's body, as if to make sure he wasn't dreaming. From time to time, he also bent over the body, which was practically touching him, and clung to it, crying and sobbing out words of affection, "*Ataatak, Ataatak.*" But there was never any response, none of the words he used to hear so often then, especially in the morning, "*Inrutaaluk* – my little grandchild."

Little by little – how long it took he really didn't know – calm returned. He was alone, yes, but alive and able to fend for himself in this vast white desert. After covering his grandfather's body, he put on his parka and boots and ventured outdoors. It was windy and the snow was drifting, but the dogs were there, resting, a light layer of snow covering them like a shroud and insulating them from the wind. From time to time, they shook themselves when it got too thick – the instinct of animals in the North. Geddes tried to see through the snow, which looked like gauze floating and unwinding in the wind. Nothing, nothing, nothing. Whiteness and more whiteness, that was all. There was only one thing to do, although it cost him to do it, with his grandfather's body nearby – that was to go back into the snow house and wait for the weather to improve. So he went back inside and lay down under the covers, without heat. He had to use the candles sparingly and make them last, since the storm could easily last several days. Sleep didn't come easily for the little fellow, all on his own. But despite his pain, his grandfather's presence – even though he was dead – still gave him a kind of reassurance. He was there, and for Geddes that was a kind of encouragement. Grandfather would have said to him, "Go on, my little one. You are already a man, an Inuvialuk, and you have a challenge to overcome. You are a member of a race of people who don't give up."

The whole day went by like that, Geddes alone with his thoughts while outside the wind blew, lifting the snow and making it fly. The time seemed long to Geddes, who was more accustomed to moving and walking than to thinking. Before nightfall, which comes quickly in winter, especially when the weather is very bad, he decided to eat a bit of frozen fish. He drank a little more water, from snow he melted over the heat from the candles, then he lay down again. There was no need to go outside and check the weather, since the noise of the wind left no doubt as to what was happening. Finally he fell asleep again.

The next day – at what time he couldn't know, because he had no watch – it was so quiet, no noise outside. Is that what woke him? He felt a bit depressed. Was it because he felt he would have to make a decision, and do something? Or was it the quietness that was bothering him? Moving quickly he pulled on his parka, and without even doing up his boots he pushed out the block of snow that served as a door and went outside. The weather was fairly good, just a slight breeze and a little snow drifting along the surface of the ground. He looked right, left, ahead and behind, but nothing was visible on the horizon or close by. He felt alone, and it also seemed to him that something wasn't normal, but what? Again he tried to fathom the feeling of unease and anxiety that gripped him. What was it? He had so many things running through his head that it hurt – and it hurt there in his chest, and in his gut. He gazed at the vastness of the land around him, but suddenly he realized that it was close, very close, that something was missing. There was no sound, no barking from the dogs, who were usually moving about and making noise, especially when they hadn't been fed the night before. Yes, that was it, no doubt about it. Where were they? He looked around. Nothing. To make sure, he went closer to the sled, also half-covered in snow.

223

Nothing. Nothing. No sign of them. He called and shouted the dogs' names, "Nikalana, *qain* – 'come here'! Rover, *qain*!" No response. No noise. He started to panic and studied the snow, looking for tracks. But how could they have survived the wind and the snow? Nearby, were some hummocks. He climbed one and looked around. There was nothing in sight. He realized that he was really alone now, with the dead body of his grandfather and not even the presence or help of the dogs. (I have often been completely alone in the Arctic – sometimes for two months at a time – with just the dogs as companions. In cases like that, the only thing they are missing is the ability to talk.)

Since it was now daylight and the weather was good, Geddes – disappointed but still determined, in spite of everything – returned to his snow house. Without eating or drinking anything, he took the snow knife and set off. His plan had been made the night before. He'd been counting on the dogs, but now a new plan had taken shape in his mind. He was going to start walking and, from time to time, he would set up a few snow blocks, spaced quite far apart but visible as a landmark. In the evening, he would come back to the snow house. So off he went, walking south. Here and there he looked around and, when nothing seemed to stand out from the snow, he cut a block of snow with the knife, stood it up on end and added a bit of soil or vegetation that he dug up with the knife. A tiny patch of black, or of colour, can easily be seen from far away. The whole day went by like that for Geddes. When evening approached and daylight began to fade, he retraced his steps, moving quickly, following the markers he'd set up previously. It was already dark when he arrived back at the snow house, but time didn't matter to him, and he didn't have much to do but eat a piece of frozen fish, melt some snow for water to drink, and then sleep. Sleep came quickly that evening. He was tired after walking and running all day without food. Tomorrow would be another day, and another walk, even farther this time.

When he awoke, as soon as he warmed himself from the flame of some candles and had a little water, he set off again. He moved quite quickly at first, but had to slow down well before he reached the last snow marker. He felt both the fatigue and the cold now – the lack of food and warmth had weakened him. He thought about the dogs. If only he had one or two they could have warmed him, his feet at least. He'd heard the elders talk about that, warming their feet against the bellies of dogs that they had brought into the snow house. But he was alone, and he had just his energy and his pure brute will to live and keep fighting. He put up more snow markers, and in the evening, he returned again to the snow house. The way back seemed very long to him, but still he kept going. From time to time, tears escaped from his eyes and flowed onto his parka, freezing there. A thin layer of ice formed without his noticing.

Once again daylight came and found Geddes on his way, but he was walking slowly and his heart was heavy. That third morning, he asked himself how long he could persevere and keep on walking. The snow markers, his landmarks, seemed to be farther apart than before, and he didn't want to look back. It would be so easy to go back and lie down and wait. No. He wouldn't even notice death while he was asleep, because he would never wake up. This thought gave him some energy and the will to continue. He also thought about his parents, his family and the other trappers. They should be back by now at camp now, at least some of them, and since he and his grandfather were overdue, surely one of the trappers would come to look for them. All these thoughts were brewing in his head and kept him going. "Walk, walk", that's what he heard, what buzzed in his ears. Finally, there he was at the end of the markers from the day before. How much longer? How much farther? What did it matter, if he had no answer? He walked, or rather stumbled now, and his eyes were streaming, and saw only through a kind of mist. But, over there... was that a team coming into view? Or was it a mirage? It was moving and very quickly getting bigger. Yes, it was indeed a dog team, and the dogs had seen him, and the driver was pushing them, too. How beautiful a human voice is in that desert! Those final minutes of suffering and waiting were too much for him, and he felt himself falling to the ground, into the snow.

Semi-conscious, he recognized Sam Dick Qaatigaaryuk, who picked him up and immediately put him in a sleeping bag, covered him, and gently comforted him. Warmth returned and, with it, words. He heartily thanked Qaatigaaryuk, who very gently asked for news of his grandfather. The boy answered that he was back there in a snow house, and had been dead for several days. Qaatigaaryuk didn't persist with his questions. There would be time later to get the details. The main thing was that Geddes had been found and was in good health – a little frostbitten perhaps, but only superficially, nothing serious. A few days of rest at the camp, and the whole adventure would be a thing of the past. The return trip wasn't very long, and the boy, warm now, slept and rested. When they arrived at the camp, everyone rushed to greet him and congratulate him. A few cups of tea and some boiled meat revived him and restored his smile and speech. Before going to sleep, he related in detail all that had happened on the trip – the places they visited, the foxes in the traps, his grandfather's fatigue and death, and his own odyssey.

Bessie's Story of Survival

'Naomi Atatahak and Bessie Andreason', no date. (Lennie Family Collection/NWT Archives/ N-1996-007-0042)

Bessie Andreason related the following story to me, a true experience that took place when she was fourteen years old. I recorded it on tape and broadcast it in Inuvialuktun and in English on the community radio station in Tuktoyaktuk. It created quite a sensation, and many of the listeners were inspired by her courage.

~ *Bessie's Story* ~

In late September 1937, my father, Ambrose Agnavigak, my mother, Lena Tammahuin, and I left Coppermine in the schooner *Polar Bear* to go trapping for the winter.[1] The small boat was loaded to the gunwales with all our provisions for the coming winter. Also on the deck were our dogs, tied to the bulwarks and the railings.

My father had decided to spend the winter in the Kent Peninsula area, where he had heard the trapping was good, and there were plenty of seals and caribou. After saying goodbye to friends we wouldn't see again until next summer we were on our way. Our first stop was at Wilmot Island where there was a trading post. It was also a meeting place for the people of that area. The weather wasn't too bad, but a head wind slowed us down and even with our motor running flat out it took us two days to get there. But for my father time didn't matter. Making a detour of several miles and spending several days visiting friends was never considered a waste of time.

As we got closer to the island we noticed a boat was following us. Probably someone hunting seals, we thought, but it kept on following us. Still, we didn't pay too much attention. It was only once we'd reached Wilmot Island and gone ashore that the owner of the boat, the manager of the trading post, told us that he had been trying to catch up to us and warn us not to stop at the island, because, he said, "Everybody's sick here. We've had a measles epidemic for several days and everybody's got them." We'd had the feeling that something wasn't right. Usually, everybody gathered on the shore to greet visitors, but today nobody was there. Since we were already on shore, my parents thought that we might as well stay and visit those who were sick. "We'll see what happens", my father said to me. With that said, he headed for the small house where Patsy Klengenberg, one of my father's friends, lived. My mother and I followed. What a sight! Patsy and the whole family were in bed, all feverish and suffering.

Of course, the inevitable happened. My parents also got sick and had to take to their bed, like the rest. This wasn't likely to have pleased my father, since he wanted to reach his winter camp as soon as possible. He was very concerned about the weather. Anything can happen in late September – strong winds, cold temperatures, and young ice forming in the sea. This made him worry, and didn't improve his condition any. After only a few days he got out of bed often to check on the weather.

I could see that my father was getting impatient. Where usually he was so calm, now he was anxious to be on his way, to reach Kent Peninsula. The store manager pleaded with him, advising him against this early departure. Just a few more days and he would be fully recovered, but Ambrose was impatient, and although still very weak, he began preparing to leave. The dogs had to be brought from shore, where they had been chained, onto the schooner, and some things we had in Patsy's house had to be brought back on board too. Getting everything onto the boat took us quite a while. Only the store manager gave us a hand, since the others were still too weak. I wanted to help too, but my parents wouldn't let me even though I hadn't caught the measles.

We got underway early in the morning. It felt good to be at sea again. The whole day we sailed without stopping, and late in the evening we reached a small bay, protected from the wind and the current. My father decided to camp there, so we unloaded some things from the boat the boat.

First, the dogs were taken ashore and chained. Next came our tent and the skins that served as a mattress, the sleeping bags, then the stove and a wooden box containing utensils, a pot, a small frying pan, some tea and sugar, and a few tins of food. But for supper, my parents just had some tea and a little broth. They didn't feel very well yet, and didn't talk much. They mainly wanted to sleep, to have a good night's rest. "Tomorrow," my father told us, "if all goes well, we should be at the winter camp."

The weather was still good the next morning, with just a light breeze and mild temperature. Our hearts full of hope, we reloaded all our things, and the dogs of course, and got underway. But during the day I noticed that my

'Bessie Andreason in the Tuktoyaktuk Fur Shop, 1981. (Photo credit: Harry Palmer)

227

The schooner 'Polar Bear', Cambridge Bay, 1930. (Charles Rowan/NWT Archives/ N-1991-068-104)

father seemed to be more tired, and he was also having terrible fits of coughing. All I could do to make him feel better was stay close to him, and talk to him. My father told us that there was a small house in the area where he was thinking of settling in for the winter.[2] We watched the shore, but saw no sign of it. Late into the night, and in darkness, we kept going. My father, knowing the waters weren't easy to navigate and the sea wasn't very deep, finally decided to stop. "According to what my friends told me it's somewhere around here," he said. "Tomorrow when it's light I'll go ashore and take a look around." We stayed on board that night. My father dropped the anchor, and we appreciated the calm and the silence after a full day of pitching and rolling, and of constant noise from the engine.

The next morning was one of those beautiful fall Arctic days – clear and cool, a sign that it's very close to freeze-up. After breakfast, my father went ashore in the dory. As soon as he landed, he headed for a small hill where he would have a clear view of the whole region. I watched him from the boat, and noticed that he wasn't going very fast, and even had to stop quite often, probably out of breath. He climbed the hill slowly, having frequent fits of coughing, but he made it to the top. Sitting down, he looked around, scanning the area, and made a sign as if to tell us that this was the place we were going to spend the winter. Once back on the schooner he told us: "Yes, this is the place. I saw the house."

It was still early in the day, and after a short rest and a cup of tea my parents began unloading the boat. Again, I mainly watched, handling only small, light things. "Don't you worry about us, Bessie," my father said to me, "once we are on land there will be more for you to do." It was hard for me to watch them, my father especially, tired and out of breath, transferring the dogs, tent, food, cooking equipment, and an oil-burning lamp made of soapstone, to shore. We had a good stove and coal on the boat, but – probably being too tired that day – he left it there. Maybe tomorrow or the next day we would bring it ashore, or maybe my father intended to get it when our winter quarters were finished. But that won't be very soon, I thought, because no sooner had a tent been put up and the bedding been spread out and made ready than my father lay down on it and tried to get some rest. There was no more doubt about it, he was still sick. I was there beside my father, not saying anything, looking at him and not knowing what to do, while my mother prepared the oil lamp. I wasn't even aware of the time, and maybe I was dreaming, lost in my thoughts, when my father spoke to me and asked me to go to look for some water.

So off I went towards a lake, following my father's directions, and inspecting the surrounding area as I walked. The ground I was walking on was stony, with little vegetation, and my hope of finding some berries vanished. I reached the small lake, and it was frozen too, though I didn't have any problem breaking the ice with my *ulu*, a gift from my father who had spent hours crafting it, making the handle from caribou bone, and the blade from a piece of an old saw. I filled a pot with water and a bucket with ice. This trip to haul water would be followed by many others in the days to come.

My mother didn't seem too bad yet and she watched over and took care of her husband. I helped by looking after the oil lamp, cooking meals, and melting ice for water. My father's condition was getting worse; it was obvious, it could be seen on his face. He was suffering a lot, but he never complained. Each day he asked about the weather, the boat, the dogs, but unlike his usual self – happy, good-natured and full of life – he hardly spoke otherwise. The provisions we had brought to shore ran low, and that worried my father. Since the wind was favourable he asked me if I was able to row the small boat out to the schooner. "But," he added, "be very careful not to miss the schooner, or you'll be blown off course and driven ashore on the other side of the bay, and it will be a long walk back for you." He told me what he wanted from our provisions, including fish for the dogs, who gone without food the day before.

Just as I was leaving he called me back to the tent and told me to also bring back a bottle of spirits. I was glad to please him. The trip to the anchored schooner didn't take me too long. The wind was behind me, and all I had to do was keep the rowboat heading towards the *Polar Bear*. Once the provisions were loaded on the rowboat, I headed back to shore, but this time it took me all my effort to get there. The wind was strong and the current very fast. I felt exhausted and worn out when I landed, but happy. Without even taking time to rest, I started putting things away.

Then my father asked me if I'd brought the bottle too. I didn't say anything. Rooted to the spot, I reproached myself for being so absent-minded. How could I have forgotten the one thing that could have done him a little good? I told him I was going to go back and get it, but he strongly objected, telling me that he had watched me and observed my progress, and had seen that I'd had trouble getting back. In spite of my protests, and my wish to make the trip again, I had to give in. I realized he was thinking more about me than himself.

My father was failing quickly now, and my mother stayed with him constantly, always at his side. The last two days and nights that my father spent with us were very, very difficult for me, morally and physically. Alone out there, so far from any medical help, without any medicine to ease his suffering, I racked my brains trying to think what to do for him. Day and night I looked after the lamp now, and I sang. I sang because my father had said my singing calmed and soothed him. Unfortunately, I didn't have a very big repertoire, so I sang all the hymns and choruses I knew. Day and night I remained awake, just a short nap now and then, tending to the lamp, and singing softly. The morning of the third day my father seemed to be past recovery. He was at the end of his life, and my mother told me to sing and pray. My mother herself didn't seem to be doing very well. She wasn't herself, and seemed to be suffering. I tried hard to stay awake, but nature was stronger than me. Sleep covered me, as we say. My mother noticed, and she woke me, saying "Bessie, how can you sleep when your father is so sick? Come on, sing and say some prayers." I nodded and started up again, but not for very long. Sleep was too strong, and I fell asleep again. I don't know how many times my mother woke me like that, but, no matter how hard I tried, I couldn't stay awake. The last time she shook me, my mother said very gently, "Bessie, don't sleep any more now, it's just you and me, your father has just died." These words brought me awake and I started to cry, to sob, while Lena, my mother, gently covered my father's head with a cloth. My mother didn't say anything, but I had the feeling she didn't want me to see my father's face in death. With this gesture, she was trying to tell me to remember him alive, always smiling, in good humour, and always true to himself under any circumstances, strong in adversity, generous in times of plenty. I didn't say anything either, but respected the silence and my mother's grief, retreating into my own thoughts – thoughts that were far from happy and reassuring, because I could see that my mother was also very sick.

What was I going to do? She was coughing frequently and her breathing was very loud, so loud in the oppressive silence surrounding us that it startled me. There was a kind of fear, hard to define, an uneasy feeling that grips your insides and paralyzes you. She had lain down beside my father's body, almost touching it, and I stayed at her side, wiping the beads of sweat that formed on her forehead, to soothe her and cool her down a little. Now all of my time was taken up with tending the lamp – the only source of light and heat – and caring for my mother. She was feverish and sometimes a bit delirious. In one fit of delirium and dreams she told me she was finding it very hard to breathe, and that she was burning up. "Give me a little fresh air. Open the tent flap, or at least pull it back a little." I was strongly opposed to that idea, but after a moment's silence she begged me again, "Please Bessie, just for a minute that's all, or even better, help me get to the door." I refused again, telling her it would kill her. But it was in vain. She had set her mind on cooling off. Too weak to stand or even to drag herself along, she rolled from her blankets onto the ground, and started crawling towards the opening. I cried to her to stop, but it was in vain. Inch by inch she was getting closer, so, seized with compassion, and at the same time telling her she was going to kill herself, I helped her as much as I could. After lifting the flap that closed the tent my mother sighed, struggled to her knees, and sat on her heels, with me at her side, trying to hold her up. She gave two or three sighs, then was seized with convulsions and began vomiting blood. She wasn't showing any signs of life, so I called to her. No answer. I touched her on the neck and on the back – there was still a little warmth, but no movement. She lay there at the door, lifeless. To make sure, in spite of my reluctance and my fear, I touched her again, on the back, on the neck. I found no sign of life. I was afraid to look her in the face, realizing, without believing it, without wanting to believe it, that my mother, Lena Tammahuin, had also left me forever.

Little by little, the idea of being in an unknown land, in the presence of two dead people, my father and mother, sank in. I stayed there beside my mother, rooted to the spot, not knowing what to do, afraid and unable to move. My whole being told me to go outside, but I didn't dare step over my mother's body at the door. I tried in vain to move her body back into the tent, but it was a wasted effort. I cried with vexation and sorrow.

230

When I was finally able to get control of myself I went outside. It was morning, very early. I remember seeing a few stars shining in the sky, and I looked around me, at the sea, which was beginning to freeze, at the clear sky, where day was beginning to break, at the land, with its contours vague and rugged in the half-light, at anything at all to escape my gloomy thoughts, and to make me forget that I was a little orphan now and, what's more, alone. This reminded me of the stories about those orphans we call *iliappaaluit*, who always, after some suffering and hardship, ended up becoming worthy people. This restored my courage, and I swore not to let myself sink into despair, but to persevere and fight and live. And then, looking closer around me, I noticed the dogs. I wasn't alone. They were there too – companions, or even friends, that would get me out of this bad situation if necessary. I felt better and was comforted by these thoughts.

Another idea struck me, and gave me back some of my courage. When my father was very low, he had told me that my songs and my prayers helped him. Why wouldn't they help me? Without fear now, I went back into the tent. Passing beside my mother, I picked up my prayer book and started turning the pages. We value that book and we like to have it close to us, especially when we're sick. It, too, seemed like a friend to me. Holding it tightly, I looked at the words, the letters, the paragraphs, unsure, not knowing where to begin. I hadn't read it for a long time, and my reading skills were weak. I gave it a try here and there, and made out one or two words. I kept trying, going slowly, underlining the words with my index finger, spelling out loud, and finally my efforts were rewarded. I could read again. I had found the key to the letters, and I started reading – awkwardly, yes, but still I understood, and those words made sense to me.

That discovery, that success, filled me with joy, and my feelings of fear and terror also began to fade. I read and read, anywhere in my book, and everything made sense. I also felt much lighter and started singing again, those hymns and prayers that my father had liked and that had given him some comfort. It seemed to me that those songs were now having the same effect on me. And – was it a dream? A product of my overworked, overexcited imagination? – I heard around me, there in the tent, a sound like the beating wings of birds in flight, but right inside my dwelling. Outside, it would have been strange enough – at that time of year, only the willow ptarmigan could still be in the area – but inside? Each time I stopped singing, the same thing happened, and in the silence, the rustling of wings – which also seemed to be coming from outside, against the tent – put my nerves on edge and made me shiver with superstitious fear. The only solution I had was to sing and hum to fill the silence and to hear myself.

How long did I remain under that spell? I have no idea. I remember that, from time to time, I drank a cup of coffee or tea, dozed a little, and thought about the two dead people, lying so close to me. I heard the dogs howling, as well as other dog noises – moaning sounds – and it seemed to me that something outside was beating against the tent. Fear gripped me again, and I would have cried out, but my throat was too tight to make the slightest sound. I threw myself on my bed and covered my head, holding the blanket around me with both hands so I couldn't see or hear anything. Immediately after that, I fell asleep, my book over my head as protection. When I woke up, it was still dark, but clear. Still half-asleep, I tried to think clearly, because I'd had a beautiful dream, and I was trying to remember it. My father and my mother were both there with me, and were speaking to me. I was listening carefully to my father's words: "Bessie, don't be afraid of our dead bodies lying near you. They are only our remains. The best part of us, our being, *anirnik* –

spirit – isn't inside those remains, but somewhere else, and we're thinking about you and want you to be happy and content. It's important to both of us. Your state of mind will also be ours. If you're happy, we'll also share your happiness, and if you're sad, we'll be sad too."

Still with those thoughts, I became wide-awake and alert, because it seemed to me that there was an unusual noise outside, very close to the tent. But what was it? I tried to identify it and I didn't feel at all at ease. Regaining my calm, I recognized some of the noises as the rustling of chains and the moaning of dogs. Pulling on my parka, I went outside and discovered the reason the dogs were barking and moaning. What a sight! All the dogs were crowded together, with their chains tangled. The end anchor of the main dog chain had given way. The dogs could move around, and had taken advantage of this opportunity to play. I knew what I had to do. The first step was to let them all loose – fortunately they weren't aggressive – and then I began untangling the chains. What a job! Every so often the tips of my fingers would go numb from my bare hands being in contact with the metal, so I'd stop and put them in my mouth and breathe on them to thaw them, and then go back to work.

While I was warming my hands I'd look toward the horizon. Once, turning my eyes towards the lake that I got my water and ice from I thought I saw something white behind a rock. I didn't pay any attention to it the first time, but the second time, it intrigued me, and I looked a little longer. The white speck seemed to be about the height of a man. Was it moving? Maybe a little. I kept at my work and wanted to finish it as soon as I could, because my hands were very cold and the cold hurt, but my thoughts kept turning towards that white speck. From time to time I glanced towards the lake, and always I saw that white form, and I wondered what on earth it could be. I wanted to find out for sure. Going back into the tent, I grabbed the binoculars and took a look. Yes, the white whatever-it-was was still there. I rubbed my eyes and trained the binoculars on the apparition again. Now I could make out the details – as tall as a person, the form even seemed to have arms, and seemed to be signaling to me to come. No matter how hard I tried to see the face, I couldn't make it out, because it was held a bit to one side. I looked again, but couldn't see it. Another problem to solve, a mystery. What is it? What does it want with me? Should I go to the lake and find out? Or is it a trick? All these questions went around in my head as I went back to work untangling the dogs' chains. At last I succeeded, and after stretching the main chain out on the ground I put the anchor into the ground. I went to call the dogs by their names, but no sound came out of my mouth. I was probably too shocked by that white vision. Fortunately that didn't last for more than a moment, and I was able to attach all the dogs without difficulty. While I was working my thoughts became clearer, and I decided I would go and meet that form, if it appeared again.

For another few days – hard to say how many – I continued to rest and think and pray. It was the only thing I could do, given my circumstances. I was waiting for the sea to freeze hard enough that I could walk on the ice and go back to the schooner. Every day, I ventured out onto the ice. Just at the very edge of the shore to begin with, and later a little farther out, always carrying a hatchet to test the strength and thickness of the ice. When I thought it was strong enough, I set out for the schooner. I had decided to go live there. On board was everything I needed, and I didn't have to bring anything from the tent. I didn't go alone. As a companion, I took one of the young dogs, my favourite, and he skipped playfully along beside me. Having that company would help me bear the solitude and would give me the illusion of not being alone.

232

Once on board the schooner I settled in and got myself organized. For reasons that are hard to explain, I didn't light the coal stove, but simply made use of a small kerosene stove, which at that time of year – it was now October – wasn't enough to take away the chill or give enough warmth to say it was comfortable. I spent the first days on board simply going out on deck and surveying the horizon. Every day, I ventured ashore to take care of the dogs and get a little water from the lake, then came back to my retreat.

My father had said that somewhere, not very far from here, there should be some people. That was what Patsy Klengenberg had told him. I waited for them. The sea ice grew stronger, and they might come this way soon. The days went by, and still nothing. Finding courage and hope again, one morning I went exploring, taking just a walking stick and bringing my dog along for company. First I visited a nearby island. I could still see the schooner, and could even catch a glimpse of the shore back there. I walked almost all day and didn't get back to the boat until very late in the evening, tired, with a stomach ache and cramps – I hadn't eaten anything since morning – and very low in spirits. My thoughts were dark, and as I got into bed I decided not to go on any more expeditions. Why bother? There's no one around me. I'm just as well off here in the schooner. I have food and I have fuel. We'll see what happens.

I spent the following days preoccupied with such thoughts, unaware of the time or the day, or anything in fact, hoping against hope to be rescued, for an end to this nightmare. One morning I was pulled from these thoughts by the dogs on the shore. They were barking, and seemed to be very excited. Maybe a bear, or caribou or another animal had ventured into the area. Or perhaps a dog team, and people? My feelings were mixed: I felt joy at the thought of seeing someone again, but also fear – what if it was a bear? I was rooted to the stool I was sitting on, without the strength to move. The young dog also felt that there was something unusual and he lay at my feet, chewing on the hem of my long parka. Then I heard the rustling of footsteps on the ice and snow around the boat, and footsteps on the deck. Someone was walking, and there was a sound, the sound of talking, words: "Is anyone there?" I clung to my seat, trembling. Who was it? I couldn't say a word. The footsteps came closer to the front of the boat, and hands pushed the sliding door slowly, oh so slowly, and eyes looked inside, and those eyes saw me and stared at me, trying to work out who I was. Since neither of us could identify the other, he asked, "Who are you?" I answered, "Bessie." He recognized me instantly, and immediately asked me where my parents, Ambrose and Lena, were. At first, I didn't answer, but finally, gaining my courage, I said that they were both dead, that their bodies were on shore, at the tent.

While I was talking other people came in and gathered around me, holding my hands and trying to comfort me. The presence of other human beings quickly brought me back into action and I made them some tea. I didn't forget our law of hospitality – to treat all visitors well. They suggested taking me with them to a nearby camp where I could stay while they continued their journey to Wilmot Island, which was where they were headed. There they would notify Patsy Klengenberg. I gladly accepted their suggestion.

When we arrived at their camp I had a few bad moments because I had to relate again, in detail, the tragedy that had struck me. But after that everything went well. What generosity and what kindness! A few days later, Patsy Klengenberg arrived and took charge of me. He had sent a message to the Royal Canadian Mounted Police in Cambridge Bay. They came right away, by dog sled, and looked after funeral arrangements for the two bodies, and they took charge of sorting all my parents' possessions. As for me, Patsy suggested that I live with him and his family. He said that, to him, I would be just like one of his daughters, no difference. I didn't need to think twice about that proposal, and I agreed right away. So I went to Wilmot Island with my adoptive father and spent my last years as a young girl in Patsy's home, sharing their life in every way until the day of my marriage.[3]

Chapter 20 Notes

1   The official name of Coppermine is 'Kugluktuk'.

2   This may have been an abandoned building from a trading post on Kent Peninsula that was operated by the Hudson's Bay Company from 1920-1927.

Charlie and Persis Gruben's
Last Crossing from Banks Island

Persis and Charlie Gruben, 1938. (Inuvialuit Social Development Program/Eddie Gruben Collection Number 14)

Persis Lennie, daughter of Sarah and Lennie Inglangasuk, whose story of her first year on Banks Island during the winter of 1928-1929 has already been told, married Charlie Gruben and together they spent many winters trapping on Banks Island. Here is what Charlie and Persis told me about their adventures in the summer of 1955.[1]

Persis:
We spent the winter of 1954-1955 at De Salis Bay – us and our children, Willie and Helen Gruben and their three children, and my brother Sam Lennie. We'd crossed from Tuktoyaktuk to De Salis Bay on board the *Reindeer*, the Lennie family's schooner, and we'd hauled it ashore for the winter. Charlie, our son John, Willie and Sam trapped all winter. Since spring we'd been short of quite a few things that maybe weren't necessary, but were still nice to have. There was no tea left, no sugar, just a little flour, almost no tobacco. It wasn't the first time we'd run short of provisions, but still we felt a bit deprived without them. I don't need to tell you how impatiently we were waiting for the snow to melt and for the ice to disappear so that we could return to Tuk.

But first we had a problem to deal with. Sam had taken the schooner's engine apart, intending to reassemble it that summer after giving it a good inspection and cleaning. But before finishing the job he left to go overland to work for a group of anthropologists. So we found ourselves in an awkward situation. We weren't very familiar with the motor, and there were a lot of parts! The *Reindeer* had a sail, but to cross from Banks Island to Tuktoyaktuk we absolutely had to have the motor. And we wanted to cross as soon as possible.

First, we changed location. The place where we had spent the winter wasn't very well protected from the winds, and there was no fresh water nearby. So, in July we packed up all our stuff – at least 1,000 fox skins, and 17 polar bear skins, the tent and the little food we had left, which was mainly seal, and we were ready. A simple trip across the bay, although it seemed to take us forever, and we settled in on the other side, next to a small creek. Our first concern was food. Charlie and John went inland to hunt caribou, and when they brought back some meat it was a real feast. At that time of the year the caribou head off to the north, so they had to walk for a long time to reach them – a few 100 kilometres there and back. After having eaten seal and more seal, and even good fish like char, a change – especially caribou – was much appreciated.

Charlie:
All we took with us was our rifles and a few pots, plus a little seal meat and a few dried fish, no sleeping bags. We slept in the open, under the stars, wherever we were. It was July, but the weather wasn't kind to us. We had wind, and rain and snow, but we walked all the same.

Persis:
All of us, including the children, would gather whatever we could find on the land – berries from the past year, and sweet roots, *masu*. I made an effort to prepare appetizing dishes, although they were inevitably seasoned with seal oil. From time to we caught *kanatdjut*, bullhead fish that we didn't usually eat and even the dogs didn't care for. But in our situation we couldn't be fussy. Still, nothing could beat caribou meat, cooked or dried, and each time the hunters returned with a load on their backs it was a great delight for us. Drinking water also was a problem. The creek was practically dry, and we were only able get about two pails of water a day by patiently scooping it with a cup from the mud in the creek bed. For laundry and bathing seawater was fine, but for drinking we relied on this water, even though it was a bit salty. We also collected rainwater by spreading out sheets of canvas.

We worked every day on the *Reindeer* when Charlie wasn't away hunting. Fortunately, we had the manual. My husband doesn't know how to read, so I read the manual, and translated it to Inuvialuktun for him. Together, the two of us tried to identify the many parts scattered here and there. After a while I got tired of reading numbers and words that didn't make much sense to me. I asked my sister Helen to take my place, but she wasn't a mechanic either and she got tired even faster than me. Charlie also stopped once in a while to hunt and to do other chores, then got back to work on the engine. July went by that way, and the beginning of August. My husband was fed up with mechanics, and with our deprivation. The season was advancing, and he wanted to leave Banks Island and go back to Tuktoyaktuk.

*The two men in this photograph are Fred Carpenter (**left**) and Charlie Gruben (**right**). Next to Charlie Gruben is his son John. Sachs Harbour, June 21, 1951. (Photo credit: T.H. Manning)*

Charlie:

Finally, I couldn't stand it anymore. The weather was deteriorating, so I told Persis that my mind was made up, I was going to walk to Sachs Harbour.[2] This was to be a 150 kilometres trip by land, a long, long walk indeed, especially since my leg was giving me trouble. I had wounded it a few days before when I was repairing an axe. A splinter of steel went into my leg, and in trying to remove it, I made it worse. As far as I know it's still there. It was only with great difficulty and great pain that I could lift my leg at all. I tried to ease the pain and help the wounded leg by tying a piece of string to the sole of my boot, holding the other end in my hand and lifting the leg.

So early in the morning, my boy John accompanying me, we left camp and set off in a northwesterly direction. We didn't rest much along the way, only now and then taking a short break to eat some dried meat and drink some water. We went at a good pace, and after one-and-a-half days reached Sachs Harbour. My visit there was short, only a few hours, just time to get some sugar, tea, coffee, lard, flour and other items, and I was able to obtain a fuel pump from the Department of Transportation, which had just begun their operations there. Leaving John at Sachs Harbour, I and got a ride back to camp on an airplane.

Everyone at De Salis Bay was glad to see me so soon, and with a good supply of food. Most of all Persis was glad that I had found a part for the motor. However, our joy was cut short the next day. I didn't feel well and had to lie down. For twelve long days I was bedridden with a high temperature and unable to undertake any work. As soon as I felt a bit better, back I went to work on the schooner, trying desperately to start the engine. After several unsuccessful trials, our efforts were rewarded, and how sweet to our ears the engine sounded. It sounded good enough, although perhaps running slower than usual, but this would have to do.

Persis:

We prepared for our departure. Food came first. We had no meat left, so I gathered up all the bones that I'd piled next to the tent, broke them open and boiled them in some water that was half sea water, half fresh water, and made a broth. Helen and I made a sail from our canvas tent, and Charlie and Willie got busy making ropes from sealskins. The weather was fine when, with no regrets, we left De Salis Bay for Sachs Harbour with our heavily loaded boat. There were the fox and polar bear furs taken during the winter, as well as caribou skins, barrels of seal oil, sleds and toboggans and all dogs, as well, leaving hardly any room left for us.

We didn't have very much fuel, so since the wind was in our favour we raised the sail to help the engine move us forward. Before we reached Nelson Head the wind came up and got stronger and more violent. It was a strong headwind, and we tacked as best we could. Charlie started to think that we should change direction and go with the wind, crossing over to the mainland. This didn't appeal to me at all – not that there was doubt about Charlie's abilities as a sailor, but I was afraid of ending up somewhere on the other shore far away from everyone else. Besides, John was at Sachs Harbour, and I was also thinking about the children we had on the boat who weren't feeling very comfortable in that storm. Many times I went back and forth between the cabin and the pilothouse at the back of the boat to ask Charlie how it was going, and to ask him where we were headed. Charlie didn't say much and didn't want to commit himself, but finally, while I was lying down in the galley, he came to see me and told me that he'd made his decision and that we were going to make the crossing and head for Tuktoyaktuk. Since I sat there without answering and without saying anything, he said, "What do you think? What should we do? Where should we go?" I simply told him again, "Let's go to Sachs Harbour first." "But why? And what will we do there?" I answered, "The Department of Transportation and the police are at Sachs Harbour, and they'll help us. Maybe they'll be able to give us enough fuel for the crossing. John is there, and we'll also be able to get some food for the children. Right now they are sick, and unhappy."

Charlie went back to the rear of the boat to keep an eye on the engine and to help Willie. A few minutes later, I went there myself and asked him what he was going to do. Shrugging his shoulders and shaking his head, he answered, "We're going to Sachs Harbour." I don't need to tell you how happy I was and how relieved I felt. The storm was raging now, and the sea was really rough. In that downpour and those constantly moving mountains and hills, Charlie spotted three polar bears swimming in more or less the same direction as us. He shot them with the rifle, and while the boat was turning to pick them up a part of the rudder gave way, and there we were adrift, and being pushed toward the land.

Charlie:
I quickly went below deck and attached the rudder cables as fast as I could, asking Persis how close we were to land. I was afraid that if we were driven against the rocks we wouldn't have a chance of getting out safe and sound.

Persis:
Charlie managed to make a temporary repair, and then he took the wheel and moved in close to the bears and hoisted them onto the deck of the schooner, using pulleys that were attached to the mast. I cut off a piece of meat right away and put it into the pot. The broth I had prepared from bones was already long gone. The children were seasick, and with empty stomachs they suffered even more. With the rolling and pitching of the schooner I had to remain near the stove and hold

onto the pot, but still I managed to cook the meat. Once the children had eaten their fill they felt much better, although the storm was raging outside, and through the portholes we could see water cascading over the schooner's sides and the roof of the cabin, and some was finding its way inside. Besides the wind, we saw snow whirling and flying around and mixing with the seawater. We were going up and down as if we were travelling across snow banks in winter. From time to time I went up to the pilothouse and took some tea to Willie and Charlie. Those short visits also allowed me to check on the weather and find out where we were. Charlie, pointed out the places I knew, and satisfied that we were making progress and heading in the direction of Sachs Harbour, I went back to the cabin to keep the children company. They were able to sleep, but I couldn't stay lying down for very long with the continual noise of the wind, the heavy sea breaking over the deck, and the constant movement of the dogs, who were sliding back and forth along the deck to the full length of their chains. There was nothing we could do for the poor animals.

We weren't moving very fast travelling against the wind and the tide and the waves, but we were slowly making headway. At the helm Charlie was being soaked with water, and more. The barrels of seal oil that were on the rear deck were thrown about, and their contents spilled out and splashed all over the deck and on Charlie. I felt sick at the sight and smell of it. Below deck, inside the cabin and in the engine room, the damage was also increasing. Engine oil and some fuel ran out and spread all over the beautiful white fox and bear furs. So many hours had been spent cleaning those furs, and in next to no time they were green and brown and sticky. To add insult to injury, a large box full of clothes and other items became wedged against the door between the forward galley and the back of the boat. I couldn't get to the pilothouse that way any more, and going up onto the deck was too dangerous. I was a prisoner in the galley. That was probably better for my husband. He must have been fed up with me, and especially my questions. A little peace could only do him good.

*The schooners Reindeer (**left**) and North Star of Herschel Island at Sachs Harbour, 1951. (Photo credit: Thomas H. Manning)*

Finally, we reached Sachs Harbour. Charlie had seen lights and had gone in, passing round the rocks at the entrance to the harbour. Just as we were entering the harbour our engine began coughing, then stopped. But that didn't bother us now. We had found shelter.

We dropped anchor, and after and making sure everything was safely secured we went to bed. We didn't sleep for long, though. Around four o'clock in the morning, the noise of footsteps on the deck woke us and voices said, "Hey in there, are you sleeping?" A few people were already on board and were examining the skins of the bears we'd killed the day before. They were Department of Transportation workers. They bought the skins just as they were, green and dirty. They then left, only to return a few minutes later in a truck. They brought us cans of food, and offered us fuel for the engine. Department of Transportation mechanic repaired our engine, and everything seemed to be in order again. We took advantage of the few days we spent there to get some rest.

Charlie:

The manager of the Department of Transportation station offered me a job, but as attractive as the offer was, it didn't appeal to me. I thought about the fortune that I had on board the boat – nearly 1,000 white fox and 17 polar bear skins – but they weren't worth anything until I could get across to Tuktoyaktuk or Aklavik. When I decided to set off again and continue on my way to Tuk, my brother-in-law Timothy Lennie joined us. Not long after we had headed out, the wind came up again, an east wind this time. But since the engine was running well, we had no problem getting to Baillie Island, where we took refuge in the harbour behind the island. But we got an unpleasant surprise when we were about to leave. No matter what we did or how hard we tried, the engine refused to start.

Persis:

I watched the men work on the engine, dismantling parts and reassembling them to no avail. The batteries seemed to be dead, and the men weren't able to charge them enough for the engine to turn over. I got an idea that made the men laugh. "Maybe you could use the small motor from the washing machine to start the engine," I said. They made fun of me, and asked me if I was planning to do the wash once the engine was running. I let them laugh, and I went about connecting the washing machine's motor to the engine's dynamo using a belt, while the sailors looked on smiling. And the impossible happened. The schooner's engine coughed a bit, and then turned over. I had won the challenge. Then came the fastest action I'd ever seen on the *Reindeer*. The anchor was raised, and even before it was properly secured on the forward deck, the boat had turned about, left land behind and was sailing on the open sea.

Off Atkinson Point, 100 kilometres from Tuk, we met two schooners that were well known to us, the *North Star* and the *Fox*. They were on the way to Banks Island, where they were going to spend the winter. We stopped for no more than a few minutes, just time enough for us to exchange some news and for Timothy to change boats. He'd decided to go back to Sachs Harbour and parted company with us, climbing onto the *Fox*. As for us, we got to Tuktoyaktuk late that the evening.

~◆◆◆~

The winter of 1954-1955 was the last that Charlie and Persis Gruben spent trapping on Banks Island. On their return to Tuktoyaktuk in the fall of 1955 they decided that they would stay there permanently.

Charlie and Persis Gruben at their camp at Nalluq, near Tuktoyaktuk, 1985. (Inuvialuit Communications Society)

Chapter 21 Notes

1   This story, as it originally appeared in Father Le Meur's memoir, has been supplemented with additional information from a longer version contained in an unpublished collection of stories, "True Experiences – Men [People] of the North" compiled by Father Le Meur.

2   By the early 1950s Sachs Harbour had become a year-round community, with several families staying there year round. Fred Carpenter, who is generally acknowledged to be the founder of the community, ran an informal store. The Department of Transportation set up a weather station, and the Royal Canadian Mounted Police established a detachment there.

22

Reflections

Father Le Meur holding a seal skin tapestry presented to him in 1981. The message reads: "To Our Beloved Father – Thank You For Your 35 Years Of Service Along The Coast". (Le Meur Family Collection)

I was fortunate to have been given the opportunity to be a missionary to the Inuvialuit. I devoted myself entirely to them, and I tried to become like them, one of them. For me, it was and still is a question of being there, and of sharing everything they have and everything I have. If I think I have something good and beautiful, and it all comes from God, I have the right and the duty to share it.

On a number of occasions I have been asked: "Why did you go up there to the North, in the cold, to preach the Gospel and carry out your priestly mission? Did you, do you have the right to change a people's ideas by preaching about Christ?" Before I answer, may I tell you how the people I live with look at this question? I don't think they have ever seen me as an intruder in their homes, or their culture, or the context of their lives. An elder once told me, "You are like one of us, like a relative, and we'll be sorry to see you go. You'll be talked about for a long time." I could add many other examples of words and deeds that are proof that the presence of the church and the actions of missionaries weren't resented. Even people who weren't my parishioners looked to me for help in times of difficulty, when there were accidents or tragedies. As a result, there was more than an atmosphere of trust – they knew that I knew and understood them.

At times I may have been a puzzle to the Inuvialuit. I presented myself as what I am, a minister of God and Christ, and as such, I can't help but be different. Did Christ not do the same, and wasn't he the first to do it, in his life, his words and his teachings? He came to put an end to an old religion, one as old as the world itself, and replace it with his own very different one. And

Father Le Meur standing with children in front of Our Lady of Grace church, Tuktoyaktuk, circa 1960s. (Le Meur Family Collection)

to do that, he presented his Gospel, and proclaimed that he had come to change and overturn everything that had come before. There was a choice to be made, a position to be taken. That's the way I went about it too, presenting the truth as it is written in the Gospel. And it was up to the people to make their own choices. How can anyone today judge those who left their faith and their religion in the past to follow Christ, or judge the church for its actions? According to Inuvialuit elder Felix Nuyaviak, Christianity brought liberation and freedom that people wanted, and sought, and were waiting for.

As for judging my life in terms of results, positive or negative, I leave that to He Who Judges. I can only say that my life has been full up to now, that I wouldn't change a thing, and that I love every part of it. This is my home, my family, my country, and I hope to live here for quite a while yet if my health continues. The cold is a great preservative, and I must admit I've been blessed in that regard. No problems yet. When I look at this life, and think about it, I see a life full of many experiences and many different jobs, a little bit of everything – fisher, hunter, traveller, sailor, to some extent builder, translator, lawyer, doctor, counselor, radio operator, announcer and producer, social and political advocate, point man, grave digger (and how!), and always, in everything, a priest. I don't know if I would have had the courage to do all that without the training and the deep faith instilled in us by the Oblates of Mary Immaculate. It's not what's written down, or recorded, or said that counts, but life itself, and the gift of self, with nothing in return. For me, that's a positive balance.

Father Le Meur in a quiet moment while visiting family in Saint Jean du Doigt, France, 1972. (Le Meur Family Collection).

At times when I went back to France, or when I was visiting in the south, some people said I should stay there, where there were more people that needed me. But all the priests who devote themselves to the North are needed, and there aren't many of us. In any case, here we are and here we stay, waiting for people to replace us, if not from the south, then from among the people themselves. That is what we're working hard on right now, asking them to find amongst themselves, with God's help, priests and others to lead their church. The first time I raised this idea in church the people looked at me strangely, and then later I had a lot of questions to answer. "So tell us, are you going?" "Are you thinking of leaving?" My response was, "No, no, but you have to plan for the future, and start thinking about it now."

I can't judge whether I've made much of a difference to the Inuvialuit, but I can say that I'm taking away a lot. I've learned a lot from them, maybe more than I had to offer. I have a better understanding of true human values, patience, a certain philosophy of accepting whatever life brings, sharing whatever a person has, hospitality, and joy and smiles. As I wrote in 1966 when I was preparing a short history of Tuktoyaktuk after spending a quarter of a century among the Inuvialuit, "I don't have enough words to express my feelings of gratitude and joy to all of you who I've tried to serve to the best of my abilities and within my limitations, and for a place where I've encountered so much friendship among all of you, young and old. The only hope I have and dare express is that I can continue devoting myself to you, among you, for the rest of my life, and that my final resting place will be in Tuktoyaktuk."

Editor's Note

Father Robert Le Meur died on July 15, 1985. He lies buried beside the schooner '*Our Lady of Lourdes*', in Tuktoyaktuk.

Father Robert Le Meur's longtime friend and fellow priest, Father Max Ruyant, standing in front of the Roman Catholic Church mission schooner, 'Our Lady of Lourdes'. Father Le Meur's grave is surrounded by the picket fence behind Father Ruyant. Tuktoyaktuk, circa 1980s. (Bern Will Brown/NWT Archives/N-2001-002: 6298)

Made in the USA
San Bernardino, CA
09 April 2017